STRICT LIABILITY

Recent Titles from Quorum Books

U.S. Protectionism and the World Debt Crisis
Edward John Ray

The Social and Economic Consequences of Deregulation: The Transportation Industry in Transition
Paul Stephen Dempsey

The Accountant's Guide to Corporation, Partnership, and Agency Law
Sidney M. Wolf

Human Information Processing in Accounting
Ahmed Belkaoui

Alternative Transportation Fuels
Daniel Sperling

The Design and Implementation of Administrative Controls: A Guide for Financial Executives
John P. Fertakis

Financial Futures and Options: A Guide to Markets, Applications, and Strategies
Todd E. Petzel

Problem Employees and Their Personalities: A Guide to Behaviors, Dynamics, and Intervention Strategies for Personnel Specialists
William T. Martin

The Banking System in Troubled Times: New Issues of Stability and Continuity
Jeremy F. Taylor

Real Interest Rates and Investment Borrowing Strategy
Peter S. Spiro

The Political Limits of Environmental Regulation: Tracking the Unicorn
Bruce Yandle

Summary Judgment and Other Preclusive Devices
Warren Freedman

Distinction Between Measurement and Interpretation in Accounting: A Living Systems Theory Approach
G. A. Swanson and James Grier Miller

STRICT LIABILITY

LEGAL AND ECONOMIC ANALYSIS

Frank J. Vandall

Q
QUORUM BOOKS
New York • Westport, Connecticut • London

Library of Congress Cataloging-in-Publication Data

Vandall, Frank J.
Strict liability : legal and economic analysis / Frank J. Vandall.
p. cm.
Includes index.
ISBN 0-89930-396-X (lib. bdg. : alk. paper)
1. Strict liability—United States. 2. Strict liability—Economic aspects—United States. I. Title.
KF1292.V36 1989
346.7303′8—dc19
[347.30638] 89-3868

British Library Cataloguing in Publication Data is available.

Library of Congress Catalog Card Number: 89-3868
ISBN: 0-89930-396-X

First published in 1989 by Quorum Books

Greenwood Press, Inc.
88 Post Road West, Westport, Connecticut 06881

Printed in the United States of America

The paper used in this book complies with the Permanent Paper Standard issued by the National Information Standards Organization (Z39.48-1984).

10 9 8 7 6 5 4 3 2 1

Copyright Acknowledgments

The author and publisher are grateful to the following for granting the use of material:

Vandall, *Applying Strict Liability to Pharmacists*, 18 *Toledo Law Review* 1 (1986). Reprinted by permission of The University of Toledo Law Review, Volume 18 (1986).

Vandall, *Design Defect in Products Liability: Rethinking Negligence and Strict Liability*, 43 *Ohio State Law Journal* 61-87 (1982). Copyright ©1982 The Ohio State University.

To Shiela, Megan and Josh
for their continuing support
and inspiration

Contents

Preface

> What has happened and is continuing to happen is that a new theory has taken hold—that victims should be compensated. . . . More and more we are trying to run a compensation system in a fault liability framework.[1]

Recently we have seen an expansion in strict liability and a decrease in the importance of proving fault. This shift to a compensation system is most obvious in products liability, but can also be seen in the expansion of the institution of insurance, a narrowing of defenses such as assumption of risk and contributory negligence, the adoption of comparative fault and the continuing decline of charitable, family and governmental immunities. Most of this has been chronicled elsewhere.[2] The goal of this book is to illuminate the role of strict liability in the unheralded development of an American compensation system. The task is to examine and explain the expansion of strict liability during the last 121 years and, more particularly, within the last 29 years.

Our personal injury system has its foundation in strict liability, not in negligence as is commonly assumed. The historical development of strict liability is presented in chapter 1. A theme of the book is that the policies that have supported the growth of strict liability within products liability also support its application in other areas. These policies are examined in chapter 2.

Of substantial interest is why state court judges, predominantly conservative, have been the architects of strict liability. The answer is presented in chapter 3. The United States has been drawn toward the adoption of strict liability because it lacks socialized medicine. The compensation system of the United States is contrasted with that of Great Britain in chapter 3 in order to clarify the role of strict liability as a substitute for socialized medicine in our system.

The purpose of chapter 4 is to define and set forth various tests for strict liability. Problems with several tests are examined. The chapter makes clear that strict liability is neither absolute liability nor negligence, but contains elements of both.

Chapter 5 uses economic and legal analysis to critique the negligence-efficiency theory that one merely calculates the costs and benefits of an activity to decide whether an injurer was negligent. It is an examination both of efficiency theory and of traditional negligence. The chapter concludes with a rejection of the overlap between traditional negligence and efficiency theory.

Chapter 6 sets out the present scope of strict liability. It outlines cases to which strict liability has been applied. The chapter includes a discussion of the frontier cases: those involving handguns, cigarettes, alcohol and blood.

The thesis of chapter 7 is that if a strong case can be made for the application of strict liability to professionals, such as medical doctors, then a case can be made for the extension of strict liability far beyond the area of products liability. The chapter argues that the policies underlying strict liability support its application to doctors, lawyers and beyond.

The pharmacist is different from the doctor and the lawyer in that he or she exercises little discretion. Chapter 8 explores the application of strict liability to the pharmacist. It concludes that strict liability is appropriate even when the pharmacist has "done nothing wrong."

As a backlash, numerous reforms have been aimed at strict liability over the last ten years. Chapter 9 evaluates and critiques several of these reforms. It concludes that the facts underlying the alleged crisis are not clear and the suggested return to negligence is therefore premature.

NOTES

1. M. A. FRANKLIN & R. L. RABIN, CASES AND MATERIALS ON TORT LAW AND ALTERNATIVES, 483 (3d ed. 1983).

2. *See* W. P. KEETON, D. B. DOBBS, R. E. KEETON & D. G. OWEN, PROSSER AND KEETON ON THE LAW OF TORTS, 451-98, 534-96, 677-724, 1032-76 (5th ed. 1984).

Acknowledgments

I thank Harold J. Berman, Nathaniel E. Gozansky, David Haddock, Harriet M. King, Jonathan R. Macey, Fred S. McChesney and Gary R. Smith for their valuable comments on portions of the manuscript. I also appreciate the research assistance of the following: Marianne Bradley, Joice Elam, James L. Hickey, Deborah Mann Keene, Paul F. Novak, Briggs Tobin, Jane Tuttle and Linda Whitt. Mistakes, however, are mine.

I am also indebted to the following secretaries for typing the manuscript: Jean Gerwig, Radine Robinson and LaVonne Schoffner.

1

Strict Liability: A Historical Perspective

Little attention has been devoted to the role of strict liability in early society. It is therefore important to examine the roots of personal injury law to discover the origins of strict liability. An additional goal is to discover whether there are reasons that have not been articulated for expanding or limiting the development of strict liability. The first lesson to be learned is that there is enormous disagreement concerning the reliability of the available evidence and the conclusions that can be drawn from that evidence. The nucleus of the debate surrounds the period from 1850 to 1900. This chapter will make clear that there is substantial agreement on two points, however. First, the foundation of tort law is absolute liability, not negligence. Second, strict liability has been expanding since approximately 1900.

THE PERIOD BEFORE 1850

The key element of "primordial law" was that if the plaintiff was able to show causation in fact, the defendant was absolutely liable. Negligence or fault was not an issue:

> At your request I accompany you when you are about your own affairs; my enemies fall upon and kill me, you must pay for my death. You take me to see a

wild beast show or that interesting spectacle, a mad man; beast or mad man kills me; you must pay. You hang up your sword; someone else knocks it down so that it cuts me; you must pay. In none of these cases can you honestly swear that you did nothing that helped to bring about death or wound.[1]

This short statement constitutes a summary of tort law up to the year 1300.[2]

Although court reports begin to become available during the period 1300 through 1850, there is substantial disagreement over their legal import. Little can be said about personal injury law before 1800 because there are few reported cases: "The meager quality of the English and American evidence counsels caution in making any dramatic assertions about pre-nineteenth century tort doctrine."[3] In discussing research into personal injury laws of this period, Professor Fifoot states: "To ransack the Year Books for large statements of doctrine made in irrelevant circumstances by judges barely conscious of their significance is neither a pleasing nor a profitable task."[4]

An argument can be made that prior to 1850 there was no liability. Professor Rabin states: "[T]he focus on a dominant tension between strict liability and fault seems misplaced. To the contrary, I will argue that fault liability emerged out of a world-view dominated largely by no-liability thinking."[5] There are several reasons for the suggestion that before 1850 there was no liability:

Throughout the "heyday of negligence," the common law courts wrestled with issues that forced a choice between powerful no-liability principles and a fledgling doctrine of fault liability. Gradually the no-liability principles–immunities, privileges, and no-duty considerations imported from other conceptual systems (property, contract and such)–retreated, like a melting glacier in a hostile environment, before the successive onslaughts of fault and, later, strict liability rules.[6]

Professor Rabin's theme is that industrialization forced an expansion of liability:

[I]n this period of rapid modernization, industrial growth and the fault principle typically worked in combination to *expand* liability rather than to limit it.

. . . .

Viewed against a parsimonious early common law, then, it is the steadily growing compensatory influence of the fault principle, rather than its insulating effect, that emerges as the notable characteristic of industrialization.[7]

Prosser's view is that strict liability reigned before 1850. In this period the remedies for wrongs were dependent upon the issuance of writs. There were two principal writs: trespass, and trespass on the case.

> Writs in trespass were confined to forceable acts in breach of the King's peace. The writ of trespass on the case developed out of a practice of applying to the Chancellor, in cases where no writ could be found in the Register to cover the plaintiff's claim, for a special write, in the nature of trespass, drawn to fit the particular case.
>
> . . . .
>
> [I] n its earlier stages trespass was identified with the view that liability might be imposed without regard to the defendant's fault.[8]

Professor Malone's theory is that liability up to about 1800 was absolute: "The imposition of virtual no-fault liability in both Trespass and Trespass on the Case in England continuously throughout the Middle Ages and, in fact, up until the nineteenth century . . . reflected the ethical, social and economic needs of the times. . . ."[9] The absolute liability theory was first recorded in the 1466 case of *Anonymous.*[10] The judge concluded, "In my opinion if a man does a thing he is bound to do it in such a manner that by his deed no injury or damage is inflicted upon others."[11]

It was the mid-1800s before the modern concept of negligence emerged. Before that time it meant merely breach of duty or custom: "It is conceded everywhere that negligence, meaning a failure to use the care of a reasonable prudent man, is a much later development. This mythical creature did not make its appearance in English tort law until the nineteenth century was well underway."[12]

Fault was not mentioned until the case of *Weaver v. Ward* in 1617.[13] While the plaintiff and the defendant were skirmishing in a military exercise, the defendant fired his rifle and injured the plaintiff. The defendant was held liable in trespass, but the court stated: "[N] o man shall be excused of a trespass . . . except it may be judged utterly without his fault."[14] It must be noted, however, that "for nearly three hundred years after the case was decided we do not find a single English decision in which a defendant charged with accidental shooting manages to escape liability through the loopholes of *Weaver v. Ward*—'utterly without his fault'. . . ."[15]

THE YEARS 1850 THROUGH 1900

During the period 1850 through 1900 there was an emergence of negligence as well as a continued growth in strict liability. These important legal developments were spawned by the industrial revolution.

Brown v. Kendall[16] is the foundational case in the development of negligence theory. Decided in 1850, it involved a man separating dogs that were fighting. While backing up, he beat the dogs with a stick. While doing so, he hit the plaintiff in the eye. The court rejected the trespass action and made new law by holding that in order to win, the plaintiff must show either negligence or intent. The plaintiff's trespass argument resting on strict liability failed. *Brown v. Kendall* is a unique case for several reasons. The facts are too weak to support a theory that was ostensibly developed to protect industry. Plain and simple, it was a dog-fight case involving injury to a third party, not a suit against an industry such as a railroad or a manufacturer. *Brown v. Kendall* was also wrong in regard to the law. Judge Shaw rejected the plaintiff's contention that he could win in trespass because the essence of an action in trespass was strict liability:

> In these discussions, it is frequently stated by judges, that when one receives injury from the direct act of another, trespass will lie. But we think this is said in reference to the question, whether trespass and not case will lie, assuming that the facts are such, that some action will lie. These *dicta* are no authority, we think, for holding that damage received by a direct act of force from another will be sufficient to maintain an action of trespass, whether the action was lawful or unlawful, and neither wilful, intentional, or careless.[17]

The law before 1850 was the opposite of what Judge Shaw stated it to be. Shaw's cavalier statement of the law has been criticized:

> To be sure, Shaw was correct in pointing out that many of the cases decided during the preceding century involved merely the question of whether or not the plaintiff had properly sued in trespass or in case as a purely procedural matter. But he did not mention the older precedents which indicated that an unintended but harmful contact . . . was actionable trespass in itself.[18]

The *Brown v. Kendall* decision is often explained on the basis that it was decided in order to subsidize the newly developing industries in the United States. That rationalization is never mentioned in the case, however. The subsidy theory is explained as follows: "[A] consistent theory of liability based on fault was developed to confer on industrial enterprise an immunity from liability for accidental harm to others. Apparently, the idea was to tax enterprise with the cost of only those damages avoidably caused."[19] Professor Horwitz is more forceful in explaining a subsidy basis of negligence:

> [Common] law doctrines appeared to present a major cost barrier to social change. . . . In an undeveloped nation with little surplus capital, elimination or reduction of damage judgments created a new source of forced investment, as landowners whose property values were impaired without compensation in effect were compelled to underwrite a portion of economic development.
>
> . . . .
>
> Under the pressure of damage judgments, American courts before the Civil War began to change legal rules in order to subsidize the activities of great works of public improvement [such as] . . . "factories, machinery, dams, canals and railroads."[20]

The subsidy theory has not been accepted by everyone. Professor Gary Schwartz read every nineteenth-century personal injury case in two states and concluded: "[T]he New Hampshire and California case law resists the claim that the nineteenth century negligence system can properly be characterized or disparaged as an industrial subsidy."[21] He found that "the New Hampshire Supreme Court held railroads liable to passengers for 'even the smallest neglect.' If a railroad car derailed, the California Supreme Court declared a presumption of negligence on the railroad's part. . . ."[22] In New Hampshire the subsidy theory lacked any basis in fact: "There were no suits brought by any injured employees against their employers, and no tort claims of any sort brought against the textile factories. . . . With respect to the textile industry, therefore, the tort law subsidy thesis is not so much false as irrelevant."[23]

In apparent disregard of the subsidy theory, both strict liability and negligence expanded after 1850. The two grew together. *Hay v. Cohoes Co.*[24] was an influential early American decision. This New York case was decided in 1849. While involved in construction on his own land, the defendant set off a substantial explosion. The plaintiff's house was damaged by flying fragments of stone and debris. Clearly the physical invasion of the plaintiff's property was not intentional, and there was no evidence of negligence in setting off the blast. However, the highest court in New York held that the palintiff should recover. Professor Gregory, in evaluating *Hay v. Cohoes*, concluded: "A fair reading of the opinion shows that the defendant was held liable on some . . . notion of absolute liability. . . ."[25] New York recently reaffirmed the decision in *Hay v. Cohoes*: "[C]ases in our own court . . . had held . . . that a party was absolutely liable for damages to neighboring property caused by explosions."[26]

In 1868 the keystone strict liability case of *Rylands v. Fletcher*[27] was decided. The defendants, owners of a mill, had a reservoir constructed on nearby land. When the reservoir was being filled, the water leaked into connecting passageways and flowed into the nearby coal mines of the plaintiff. The defendant was not at fault because he had hired an independent contractor to build the reservoir. Therefore, the plaintiff brought an action in strict liability. The court held:

> We think that the true rule of law is, that the person who for his own purposes brings on his lands and collects and keeps there anything likely to do mischief if it escapes, must keep it in at his peril, and, if he does not do so, is prima facie answerable for all the damage which is the natural consequence of its escape.[28]

Although this decision was at first rejected in the United States, it has been gradually accepted.[29] Over more than one hundred years it has been applied to a diverse set of facts, including drilling for natural gas and overflowing sludge ponds.[30]

During the period 1850–1900 the United States saw a growth of negligence along with the continued expansion of strict liability. It also witnessed the deciding of the famous case of *Rylands v. Fletcher* and the twisting and molding of negligence to accomplish strict liability. The railroads played an important role in the development of tort law. They provided two essential ingredients: injuries and a party with enough assets to be worth suing. During this period the railroads crisscrossed the country, breaking, burning and killing as they went. Industries, towns, injuries and recoveries all grew together: "The railway injury rate doubled between 1889 and 1906. At the turn of the century, industrial accidents were claiming about 35,000 lives a year, and inflicting close to 2,000,000 injuries."[31]

SINCE 1900

There is agreement that after 1900 liability expanded in favor of the injured party. This section will examine that development. Products liability is the subject of the most complete and persuasive expansion. Growth also occurred in the areas of abnormally dangerous activities, res ipsa loquitur, and negligence per se. The continued deterioration of immunity defenses has also worked to expand the liability of persons who had formerly been protected from suit. This section will end with an exploration of the decline of the industrial era and a parallel decline in the need for protecting subsidies.

The early products liability cases refused to permit recovery by the consumer because of the doctrine of privity: only parties to the contract could recover. In *Winterbottom v. Wright*, the foundational case, an injured mail coach driver was unable to recover because he was outside the scope of privity.[32] The court reasoned:

> We ought not to permit a doubt to rest upon this subject, for our doing so might be the means of letting in upon us an infinity of actions. . . . There is no privity of contract between these parties; and if the plaintiff can sue, every passenger, or even any person passing along the road, who was injured by the upsetting of the coach, might bring a similar action. Unless we confine the operation of such contracts as this to the parties who entered into them, the most absurd and outrageous consequences, to which I can see no limit, would ensue.[33]

The *Winterbottom* case was followed by over seventy-four years of conceptual growth. The courts endeavored to move products liability closer to the general torts theory, which by this time had grown to include negligence. The courts expanded the scope of products liability by means of various legal fictions, which concealed their examination of relevant social policies. The function of these fictions was to skirt privity and make it easier for the consumer to recover. For example, fraud was the fiction used by the courts to find liability in a case involving a lamp that exploded.[34] The court used the fiction of an invitation in order to skirt privity and permit a new trial in a case involving a defective scaffold.[35] Finally, several cases developed the theory of an "imminently dangerous" article that would permit recovery by one who was not in privity.[36]

The erosion of the rule of no liability based on the absence of privity reached a turning point with the 1916 case of *MacPherson v. Buick Motor Co.*[37] The court held that the purchaser could recover in negligence and need not show privity. The point of *MacPherson* was that the exceptions had finally consumed the privity rule. Strict liability emerged as a basis for recovery in cases involving food three years before the *MacPherson* decision. In *Mazetti v. Armour & Co.*[38] recovery was in a form of strict liability known as implied warranty. The court reasoned:

> Remedies of injured consumers ought not to be made to depend upon the intricacies of the law of sales. The obligation of the manufacturer should not be based alone on privity of contract. It should rest, . . . upon "the demands of social justice."
>
> . . . .
>
> Our holding is that, in the absence of an express warranty of quality, a manufacturer of food products under modern conditions impliedly warrants his goods when dispensed in original packages, and that such warranty is available to all who may be damaged by reason of their use in the legitimate channels of trade.[39]

In the period from 1913 through 1944, the courts struggled with various theories such as negligence, fraud, express warranty and implied warranty in products liability cases. The results were unsatisfactory because the consumers continually lost cases that they should have won. The judicial frustration with these adverse results was articulated by Justice Traynor in his concurring opinion in *Escola v. Coca-Cola.*[40] He said that recovery in products liability cases should rest upon absolute liability.[41] His reasons for departing from negligence theory were founded upon social policy: "[T]he risk of injury can be insured by the manufacturer and distributed among the public as a cost of doing business. It is to the public interest to discourage the marketing of products having defects that are a menace to the public."[42]

In the early 1960s a woman purchased a Shopsmith for her husband. While her husband was using the lathe attachment to this product, a block of wood came loose and hit him in the head. This led to the foundational case of *Greenman v. Yuba Power Products.*[43] In that case the California Supreme Court adopted the strict liability that had been suggested in *Escola.* The court held: "The purpose of such liability is to insure that the costs of injuries resulting from defective products are borne by the manufacturers that put such products on the market rather than by the injured persons who are powerless to protect themselves."[44] The trend in the reasoning and holding of the courts since *Greenman* has been to rely upon strict liability and to remove barriers to recovery. The courts have emphasized the social policy reasons for their decisions with one distinction. The policy reasons emphasized have been those that favor consumer recoveries, such as loss shifting, availability of insurance and ease of prevention.[45] The courts have engaged in an inquiry weighted at the beginning in favor of the consumer. This has not been a neutral balancing of interests. In a 1978 California case,[46] for example, the court held that once the plaintiff proves that the product's design proximately caused his injury, he has established a prima facie case, and the burden of proof shifts to the manufacturer to show that the benefits of the design exceed the costs of avoiding the defect.

The growth in strict liability represented in *Greenman* and *Escola* as well as the emphasis on policies that favored the consumer permitted Dean Guido Calabresi to conclude: "Today, in product liability, the risk is initially placed on the producer and remains there unless complex circumstances, more powerful than user fault, justify a shift in riskbearing from producer to user."[47]

From 1944 to 1972, two different products liability theories developed. One was negligence, based essentially on the reasonable-man concept. The other was strict liability, resting firmly on loss shifting. At some point these two conceptual frameworks had to meet. This occurred in the 1972 California case of *Cronin v. J. B. E. Olson Corp.*,[48] in which the California Supreme Court rejected the negligence line of authority and set the stage for defining defect. The plaintiff in this case was the driver of a bread truck who was involved in a crash while passing another vehicle. As a result of the impact, the bread trays broke loose, came forward and seriously injured the driver of the bread truck. The plaintiff argued that the hasp holding the trays of bread was defective. The defendant argued that the Restatement (Second) of Torts Section 402A test for strict liability required the consumer to show that the defect was "unreasonably dangerous."[49] The court held that the plaintiff must prove that the product is defective, but need not prove an "unreasonably dangerous defect."[50] In the court's view the "unreasonably dangerous" test sounded of negligence and would require the plaintiff to prove absence of reasonable care, which had been disavowed in *Greenman*. The *Cronin* court emphasized that the plaintiff need only prove a "defect" and that strict liability is not negligence.[51]

Since *Cronin* the growth of strict liability has been dramatic. In recent years the action has been applied, for example, to airplanes, automobiles, leased trucks, buses, steam vaporizers, drugs and perfume. The class of plaintiffs has expanded to include donees, third parties and bystanders. The class of defendants has also expanded enormously to include retailers, wholesalers, manufacturers and component-part suppliers. In short, there is neither a product nor a seller who is clearly beyond the reach of a strict liability action.

ABNORMALLY DANGEROUS ACTIVITIES

Strict liability for abnormally dangerous activities has been expanding for over eighty years. It has grown from cases involving fire and trespassing animals to cockroach extermination, blasting, pile driving, crop dusting and aviation ground damage. In a suit against the Cities Service Company, strict liability was also applied to the escape of phosphate slime from a sludge pond.[52]

The theory underlying strict liability has been refined. Now it is clear that the reason for strict liability is to shift the loss to the injurer: "The question, in other words, was not *whether* it was lawful or proper to engage in blasting but *who* should bear the cost of any resulting damage—the person who engaged in the dangerous activity or the innocent neighbor injured thereby."[53]

Recently the theory of abnormally dangerous activity had been applied to the manufacturer of a Saturday night special firearm. In the case of *Richman v. Charter Arms Corp.*[54] a person used a handgun to rob, rape and murder a third-year medical student. The trial court held that the manufacturer could be liable to the parents of the decedent on the basis that the manufacture and sale of Saturday night specials was an ultrahazardous activity.[55] The case was reversed on appeal, however.[56] The reasoning of the appellate court was that the theory of abnormally dangerous activities must be limited to torts involving the use of land. Blasting is the classic example of an abnormally dangerous activity.

RES IPSA LOQUITUR

Elements of strict liability are contained within the doctrine of res ipsa loquitur. The theory of res ipsa is that the event itself speaks of the defendant's negligence. The plaintiff can take his case to the jury if he presents circumstantial evidence from which the jury may infer that the defendant was negligent. Res ipsa is applied when the court feels that the plaintiff should recover, but the court is not ready to embrace the doctrine of strict liability. Res ipsa, then, is strict liability in negligence clothing.[57] From the time a barrel of flour fell from a window above a shop in 1863, res ipsa has been applied to a missing airplane (1967),[58] a car that left the road and struck a culvert (1967)[59] and most dramatically to a team of doctors and nurses who insisted that they knew nothing about the injury to an anesthetized patient (1944).[60]

IMMUNITIES

A number of defenses or immunities developed that protected entire categories of defendants from suit. These emerged during the 1800s. The most important immunity, of course, was governmental. It protected the federal, state and local governments from liability.[61] Government is the largest industry and has succeeded in committing its proportionate share of injuries. Therefore, governmental immunity was important.

Tort liability has expanded during the last few decades through the overthrow of several key immunities:

> Thus, almost everywhere, the tort immunity of charitable institutions has been done away with. Intrafamilial immunities increasingly have been discarded, rendering spouses liable to each other, parents liable to their children, and vice versa. In addition, a broad, insensitive doctrine of governmental immunity generally has been replaced by a carefully selected set of particular immunity rules.[62]

The conventional wisdom is that negligence has been accepted by American and English courts because of the need to subsidize developing industries.[63] Within the last thirty years, however, we have seen a substantial decrease in industrial production. Major steel plants that were once household words have closed. Large numbers of automobile manufacturers, such as Studebaker, Packard, Hudson and AMC, have closed. Radio and television manufacturers have moved abroad, as have textile, clothing and shoe manufacturers. Raw materials such as steel and products such as automobiles, ships, shoes and shirts are now produced in Japan and other Asian countries. With the decline of the American industrial era has come a corresponding reduction in the need for subsidization.[64]

A historical analysis makes it clear that personal injury law rests upon a foundation of absolute liability and that since 1900 the development of legal theory has been toward strict liability and away from negligence. If there is a debate, it is narrow and extends to the reliability of fragmentary case law before 1850 and whether negligence has developed as a form of industrial subsidization since 1850. This debate does not affect the conclusion that feudal law rested upon absolute liability and that since the beginning of the twentieth century doctrinal growth has been in the area of strict liability. Historically, then, the importance of negligence has been overstated, and the foundational role of strict liability is clear.

NOTES

1. Malone, *Ruminations on the Role of Fault in the History of the Common Law of Torts*, 31 LA. L. REV. 1, 3 (1970).

2. *Id.* at 9.

3. Schwartz, *Tort Law and the Economy in Nineteenth-Century America: A Reinterpretation*, 90 YALE L. J. 1717, 1722 (1981).

4. C. FIFOOT, HISTORY AND SOURCES OF THE COMMON LAW: TORT AND CONTRACT 189 (1949).

5. R. RABIN, PERSPECTIVES ON TORT LAW 44 (2d ed. 1983).

6. *Id.* at 68.

7. *Id.* at 69.

8. W. PROSSER, J. WADE & V. SCHWARTZ, CASES AND MATERIALS ON TORTS 2-3 (6th ed. 1976).

9. Malone, *supra* note 1, at 24.

10. Anonymous, Y. B. 5 Edw. 4, f. 7, pl. 18 (K.B. 1466).

11. *Id.*

12. Malone, *supra* note 1, at 18.

13. Weaver v. Ward, Hobart 134, 80 Eng. Rep. 284 (K.B. 1617).

14. *Id.*

15. Malone, *supra* note 1, at 18–19.

16. 60 Mass. (6 Cush.) 292 (1850).

17. *Id.* at 295.

18. Gregory, *Trespass to Negligence to Absolute Liability*, 37 VA. L. REV. 359, 366 (1951).

19. *Id.* at 382.

20. M. HORWITZ, THE TRANSFORMATION OF AMERICAN LAW, 1780-1860, at 70–71 (1977), *quoting* Losee v. Buchanan, 51 N.Y. 476, 484 (1873).

21. Schwartz, *supra* note 3, at 1773.

22. *Id.* at 1743.

23. *Id.* at 1737.

24. 2 N.Y. 159 (1849).

25. Gregory, *supra* note 18, at 371.

26. Spano v. Perini Corp., 25 N.Y. 2d 11, 15, 250 N.E. 2d 31, 33, 302 N.Y.S. 2d 527, 530 (1969).

27. 3 H. & C. 774 (Ex. 1865), *rev'd*, [1866] L.R. 1 Ex. 265, *aff'd*, [1868] L.R. 3 H.L. 330.

28. *Id.* at 279.

29. *See* W. P. KEETON, D. B. DOBBS, R. E. KEETON & D. G. OWEN, PROSSER AND KEETON ON THE LAW OF TORTS 549 (5th ed. 1984).

30. *Id.* at 549–50.

31. L. FRIEDMAN, A HISTORY OF AMERICAN LAW 422 (1973).

32. 10 M. & W. 109, 11 L.J. Ex. 415, 152 Eng. Rep. 402 (Exch. P. 1842).

33. *Id.* at 113–14, 11 L.J. Ex. at 417, 152 Eng. Rep. at 404–05.

34. Longmeid v. Holliday, 6 Ex. 761, 155 Eng. Rep. 752 (1851). "There are other cases, no doubt, besides those of fraud, in which a third person, though not a party to the contract, may sue for the damage sustained, if it be broken." *Id.* at 767, 155 Eng. Rep. at 755.

35. Devlin v. Smith, 89 N.Y. 470 (1882).

36. *See* Huset v. J. L. Case Threshing Mach. Co., 120 F. 863 (8th Cir. 1903); Loop v. Litchfield, 42 N.Y. 351 (1870); Thomas v. Winchester, 6 N.Y. 397 (1852).

37. 217 N.Y. 382, 111 N.E. 1050 (1916):

> We hold . . . that . . . [i] f the nature of a thing is such that it is reasonably certain to place life and limb in peril when negligently made, it is then a thing of danger. Its nature gives warning of the consequences to be expected. If . . . there is added knowledge that the thing will be used by persons other than the purchaser . . . then, irrespective of contract, the manufacturer of this thing of danger is under a duty to make it carefully.

Id. at 389, 111 N.E. at 1053.

38. 75 Wash. 622, 135 P. 633 (1913).

39. *Id.* at 627–30, 135 P. at 635–36.

40. Escola v. Coca-Cola Bottling Co. of Fresno, 24 Cal. 2d 453, 461, 150 P. 2d 436, 440 (1944) (Traynor, J., concurring).

41. *Id.* at 461-68, 150 P. 2d at 440–44.

42. *Id.* at 462, 150 P. 2d at 441.

43. Greenman v. Yuba Power Prods. Inc., 59 Cal. 2d 57, 377 P. 2d 897, 27 Cal. Rptr. 697 (1963).

44. *Id.* at 63, 377 P. 2d at 901, 27 Cal. Rptr. at 701.

45. *See* Greenman v. Yuba Power Prods. Inc., 59 Cal. 2d 57, 377 P. 2d 897, 27 Cal. Rptr. 697 (1963); Henningsen v. Bloomfield Motors, 32 N.J. 358, 161 A. 2d 69 (1960); Phillips v. Kimwood Mach. Co., 269 Or. 485, 492 n.6, 525 P. 2d 1033, 1036 n.6 (1974).

46. Barker v. Lull Eng'g Co., 20 Cal. 3d 413, 573 P. 2d 443, 143 Cal. Rptr. 225 (1978): "[O] nce the plaintiff makes a prima facie showing that the injury

was proximately caused by the product's design, the burden should appropriately shift to the defendant to prove, in light of the relevant factors, that the product is not defective." *Id.* at 431, 573 P. 2d at 455, 143 Cal. Rptr. at 237.

47. Calabresi, *Product Liability: Curse or Bulwark of Free Enterprise*, 27 CLEV. ST. L. REV. 313, 319 (1978).

48. 8 Cal. 3d 121, 501 P. 2d 1153, 104 Cal. Rptr. 433 (1972).

49. Restatement (Second) of Torts § 402A (1965).

50. The *Cronin* court stated:

> Yet the very purpose of our pioneering efforts in this field [strict liability] was to relieve the plaintiff from problems of proof inherent in pursuing negligence. . . . We think that a requirement that a plaintiff also prove that the defect made the product "unreasonably dangerous" places upon him a significantly increased burden and represents a step backward in the area pioneered by this court.

Cronin, 8 Cal. 3d at 133, 501 P. 2d at 1162, 104 Cal. Rptr. at 442.

51. *Id.* at 133-34, 501 P. 2d at 1162, 104 Cal. Rptr. at 442.

52. Cities Serv. Co. v. State, 312 So. 2d 799 (Fla. Dist. Ct. App. 1975).

53. Spano v. Perini Corp., 25 N.Y. 2d 11, 17, 250 N.E. 2d 31, 34, 250 N.Y.S. 2d 527, 530 (1969).

54. 571 F. Supp. 192 (E. D. La. 1983).

55. *Id.* at 209.

56. Perkins v. F. I. E. Corp., 762 F. 2d 1250 (5th Cir. 1985).

57. Gregory, *supra* note 18, at 383. But compare res ipsa with *Helling v. Carey*. In *Helling* a woman under the age of forty had substantial problems with her eyes. Over a number of years she continued to return to her ophthalmologist for assistance. Finally the ophthalmologist diagnosed her as having glaucoma, but it was too late for treatment. During the trial of the case the standard of care was that of the reasonable ophthalmologist: tests for glaucoma were not administered to patients under the age of forty because it was very rare for such patients to develop glaucoma. On appeal, the Supreme Court of Washington threw out the standard of the ophthalmologists and held that it was evidence of negligence for the ophthalmologist not to give the glaucoma test to those under the age of forty. The key to the decision is that the test for glaucoma is extremely cheap and has no side effects. *Helling v. Carey* is a cautionary reminder that if the conduct of a profession, as a whole, is found to be unacceptable, the court reserves the power to reject it. Helling v. Carey, 83 Wash. 2d 514, 519 P. 2d 981 (1974).

58. Cox v. Northwest Airlines, Inc., 379 F. 2d 893 (7th Cir. 1967), *cert. denied*, 389 U.S. 1044 (1968).

59. Johnson v. Foster, 202 So. 2d 520 (Miss. 1967).

60. Ybarra v. Spangard, 25 Cal. 2d 488, 154 P. 2d 687 (1944).

61. K. DAVIS, ADMINISTRATIVE LAW TEXT 466 (3d ed. 1972).

62. Schwartz, *The Vitality of Negligence and the Ethics of Strict Liability*, 15 GA. L. REV. 963, 964-65 (1981).

63. *See* M. HORWITZ, *supra* note 20, at 70, 100; Malone, *supra* note 1, at 33-34.

64. Gregory, *supra* note 18, at 382.

BIBLIOGRAPHY

Calabresi, "Product Liability: Curse or Bulwark of Free Enterprise." 27 *Clev. St. L. Rev.* 313 (1978).

Davis, K., *Administrative Law Text* (3d ed. 1972).

Fifoot, C., *History and Sources of the Common Law: Tort and Contract* (1949).

Friedman, L., *A History of American Law* (1973).

Gregory, "Trespass to Negligence to Absolute Liability." 37 *Va. L. Rev.* 359 (1951).

Horwitz, M., *The Transformation of American Law, 1780–1860* (1977).

Malone, "Ruminations on the Role of Fault in the History of the Common Law of Torts." 31 *La. L. Rev.* 1 (1970).

Prosser, W., W. Keeton, D. Dobbs, R. Keeton & D. Owen. *The Law of Torts* (5th ed. 1984).

Prosser, W., J. Wade & V. Schwartz, *Cases and Materials on Torts* (6th ed. 1976).

Rabin, R., *Perspectives on Tort Law* (2d ed. 1983).

Restatement (Second) of Torts, § 402A (1965).

Schwartz, "Tort Law and the Economy in Nineteenth-Century America: A Reinterpretation." 90 *Yale L. J.* 1717 (1981).

Schwartz, "The Vitality of Negligence and the Ethics of Strict Liability." 15 *Ga. L. Rev.* 963 (1981).

2

The Reasons for Strict Liability

The reasons that the courts have adopted strict liability fall under four headings. First, the judges were dissatisfied with liability under commercial law. Second, the courts concluded, over time, that the results under negligence were unjust. Third, at the same time the courts were developing specific policy reasons for favoring strict liability. Fourth, although this was not a conscious goal, the courts developed strict liability to provide medical assistance in the absence of socialized medicine. The first three reasons will be discussed in this chapter. The socialized medicine rationale will be considered in the following chapter. The economic rationale for strict liability will conclude this chapter.

DISSATISFACTION WITH COMMERCIAL LAW

The commercial law's express and implied warranties, disclaimers, limitations and notice requirements[1] were found to leave the consumer without a recovery in a very large number of cases. Professor James stated, for example: "Warranty is a case in point. This was fashioned to serve commercial needs in a commercial context, and however well or ill adapted it is to that end today, its technicalities and limitations reflect those needs. If it occasionally happens to fit the needs of accident law, that is pure coincidence."[2]

One of the main issues in *Greenman v. Yuba Power Products* was whether the notice provision of the Uniform Commercial Code was controlling. That is, must the plaintiff give notice to the defendant of his intent to sue within a set period of time?[3] In rejecting the notice requirement, the California Supreme Court stated:

> The notice requirement of Section 1769 . . . is not an appropriate one for the court to adopt in actions by injured consumers against manufacturers with whom they have dealt. . . . "As between the immediate parties to the sale [the notice requirement] is a sound commercial rule, designed to protect the seller against unduly delayed claims for damages. As applied to personal injuries, and notice to a remote seller, it becomes a booby-trap for the unwary. The injured consumer is seldom 'steeped in the business practice which justifies the rule. . . .' [I]t will not occur to him to give notice to one with whom he has no dealings." . . . We conclude, therefore, that even if plaintiff did not give timely notice of breach of warranty to the manufacturer, his cause of action based on the representations contained in the brochure was not barred.[4]

In a much-quoted statement the *Greenman* court held: "The remedies of injured consumers ought not to be made to depend upon the intricacies of the law of sales."[5]

The American Law Institute stated, in comment m to section 402A of the Restatement (Second) of Torts, that strict liability is separate and apart from the provisions of the Uniform Commercial Code and the Sales Act:

> The rule stated in this Section is not governed by the provisions of the Uniform Sales Act, or those of the Uniform Commercial Code as to warranty; and it is not affected by limitations on the scope and content of warranties, or by limitation to "buyer" and "seller" in those statutes. Nor is the consumer required to give notice to the seller of his injury within a reasonable time after it occurs, as is provided by the Uniform Act. The consumer's cause of action does not depend upon the validity of his contract with the person from whom he acquires the product, and it is not affected by any disclaimer or other agreement, whether it be between the seller and his immediate buyer, or attached to and accompanying the product into the consumer's hands.[6]

In an article Prosser stated that reliance upon the term "warranty" was the root of the problem with the Uniform Commercial Code:

> Although the writer was perhaps the first to voice it, the suggestion was sufficiently obvious that all of the trouble lay with the one word "warranty". . . . Why

not, then, talk of the strict liability in tort, a thing familiar enough in the law of animals, abnormally dangerous activities, nuisance, workman's compensation, libel, misrepresentation, and respondeat superior, and discard the word "warranty" with all its contract implications?[7]

NEGLIGENCE LEADS TO UNJUST RESULTS

Judge Traynor argued for the adoption of absolute liability against manufacturers in his concurring opinion in the 1944 case of *Escola v. Coca-Cola.*[8] This call to arms was not to be met with action in California until *Greenman v. Yuba Power Products.*[9] In that case California adopted strict liability against the manufacturer of products, but rejected Traynor's phrase "absolute liability." After *Greenman* the American Law Institute adopted section 402(a) of the Restatement. This is perhaps the most widely adopted statement of strict liability and provides: "One who sells any product in a defective condition unreasonably dangerous to the user or consumer or to his property is subject to liability for physical harm thereby caused to the ultimate user or consumer. . . ."[10] This language created the threshold problem of whether a product must be defective, whether it must be unreasonably dangerous or whether it must be both defective and unreasonably dangerous. What, for example, is the difference between defect and unreasonably dangerous?

This semantic battle raises the question of how the phrase "unreasonably dangerous" happened to appear in the Restatement (Section) 402A provision of strict liability. The explanation is that Professor Prosser drafted section 402A of the Restatement and suggested the words "unreasonably dangerous" as the test for strict liability.[11] The word "defect" was added later to the Restatement draft in order to show that something must be wrong with the product.[12] The drafters of the Restatement never intended for liability to apply to manufacturers of whiskey, cigarettes or butter.[13] These are dangerous products, but it can be argued that there is nothing "wrong" with them.

Cronin v. J. B. E. Olson Corp. faced squarely the question of whether a product must be both defective and unreasonably dangerous.[14] The California Supreme Court held that the plaintiff must only prove that the product is defective and need not prove that the product is also unreasonably dangerous. The court reasoned:

> The result of the [unreasonably dangerous] limitation . . . has burdened the injured plaintiff with proof of an element which rings of negligence. . . . [I]t has

been observed that the Restatement formulation of strict liability in practice rarely leads to a different conclusion than would have been reached under laws of negligence. . . .[15]

The court went on to firmly reject the unreasonably dangerous requirement of the Restatement (Section) 402A:

Of particular concern is the susceptibility of Restatement section 402A to a literal reading which will require the finder of fact to conclude that the product is, first, defective and, second, unreasonably dangerous. . . . A bifurcated standard is of necessity more difficult to prove than a unitary one. . . . We think that a requirement that a plaintiff also prove that the defect made the product "unreasonably dangerous" places upon him a significant increased burden and represents a step backward in the area pioneered by this court.[16]

In short, the *Cronin* court felt that the "unreasonably dangerous" phrase smacked of negligence and that this would create a burden that was inappropriate for the plaintiff to carry. The *Cronin* case makes it clear that with strict liability the courts are trying to distance themselves from negligence and to favor the consumer while at the same time reducing his burden of proof. The scales are being tilted in the consumer's favor.

SPECIFIC POLICY REASONS FOR STRICT LIABILITY

The policies that have been adopted by the courts in holding manufacturers and sellers of products strictly liable to consumers are fundamental and support the application of strict liability to cases outside the area involving products. This section will examine these specific policies. Later chapters will examine the wider application of strict liability.

Loss Shifting

The theory behind loss shifting is that the seller is in a better position than the consumer to bear the damages.[17] The seller can raise the price of his goods in order to cover the damages, and the costs of the damages will therefore be spread among the various consumers. One response on the part of sellers to the loss-shifting argument is that it will put them out of business. If strict liability is adopted widely, then after a period of time all sellers will be subject to it, and no seller will have an advantage over another. That is, in the short run, it may be true that the first seller who is subject to a large judgment based on strict liability will be at a competitive disadvantage. However, after his competitors are subject to damage suits based on strict liability, their advantage will be eliminated. The point of loss shifting, then, is that the seller is better able to bear the loss than the innocent consumer and, after a period of time, will be able to pass the loss on to the consumers in the form of higher prices.

It is also true, however, that if a seller is unable to bear the damages and must go out of business, other sellers who exercise more care will absorb the market abandoned by the defendant. In this way, loss shifting will encourage sellers to study and implement safety.

The concept of elasticity of the demand curve should be considered at this point. Elasticity manifests how responsive the amount demanded is to a change in price.[18] If the demand for a product is very elastic, a small increase in price will lead to a substantial loss of total revenue. On the other hand, if the demand schedule for a product is inelastic, then a small increase in price will lead to a parallel small loss in total revenue. The point is that the impact of an increase in the price of a product brought on by the adoption of strict liability will depend upon the elasticity of the demand curve facing the manufacturer or seller.

Safety

The second reason for subjecting sellers to strict liability is to protect human life and health.[19] The theory is that if the seller is held strictly liable, he or she will exercise a high degree of care in order to avoid injury and damage suits. If he is subject to a large number of damage suits, the price of his products will soon rise and he will no longer be able to compete. Another way of saying this is that sellers who exercise care will not likely be subject to suit and, therefore, will be able to charge lower prices and obtain more business. In this way, strict liability encourages safety and protects the health of the consumer.

Superior Knowledge

One of the key reasons for holding a seller strictly liable is that he is treated by the law as an expert. The courts have suggested that because of superior knowledge on the part of the product manufacturer, it makes sense to hold the manufacturer liable as compared to the uninformed consumer.[20]

In a market where both the seller and the consumer had perfect knowldge, this argument would have little weight. But in the real world consumers often know very little about the safety of their purchases. Superior knowledge, then, is a strong argument for holding sellers strictly liable. For example, the young man who was severely burned in the Pinto crash had no idea that he was riding in a car that would explode if hit from behind.[21] The same can be said of the teenage woman burned to death in the Indiana Pinto crash.[22] Also, the parents who placed a steam vaporizer on a chair had no knowledge that the water inside the vaporizer would become superheated and, therefore, scald their young child.[23] The child apparently tripped and fell into the chair holding the vaporizer while walking to the bathroom in the middle of the night. Few automobile purchasers realize that some car roofs are likely to collapse in a roll-over crash.[24]

Insurance

The courts, because of the availability of insurance, have held that it makes more sense to place the loss on the manufacturer or seller rather than the innocent consumer.[25] Judge Traynor stated in *Escola v. Coca-Cola*: "The cost of an injury and the loss of time or health may be an overwhelming misfortune to the person injured, and a needless one, for the risk of injury can be insured by the manufacturer and distributed among the public as a cost of doing business."[26]

ECONOMIC ANALYSIS

If it is accurate to suggest that economics relies on the functioning of the market, then it is valid to argue that the prices upon which the market depends must reflect all of the costs.[27] One of the costs that must be reflected in the product's price is damages. That is, if the damages caused by a product are not reflected in the price, then the product will be underpriced and too much of it will be consumed.

From an economic point of view, negligence results in the product being underpriced and leads to overconsumption.[28] For example, if a ten-speed bicycle costs $150.00, then a certain number of ten-speed bicycles will be purchased. However, if that price were to reflect all of the injuries caused by ten-speed bicycles, then the price would be higher, perhaps $175.00 or $200.00. The theory is that if the bicycle were priced to reflect the actual damages caused, the socially correct number of bicycles would be purchased and the market would function efficiently.[29] Another way to say this is that with bicycles priced at $150.00, too many are consumed, and strict liability adjusts the price upward so that the correct number of bicycles will be purchased.

Professor Polinsky summarizes the economic argument in favor of strict liability and against negligence as follows: "In essence, the rule of strict liability induces efficient behavior because it forces the injurer . . . to take into account all of the adverse effects of his behavior on the victim. . . ."[30] He concludes that strict liability is especially appropriate when a third party is injured:

> When the victim is a third party, the argument for using a strict liability rule is strengthened relative to the argument for using a negligence rule. . . . Under strict liability, the price of the product will equal its full cost, including the expected accident losses *to third parties.* Consumers will therefore purchase the correct amount. . . . [T]he problem with the negligence rule, that it encourages too much output, is generally worse when the victim is a third party.[31]

Perhaps the chief opponent of strict liability is Judge Posner. His theory is that as compared with negligence, strict liability is inefficient:

> A negligence standard differs from strict liability in that under negligence the injurer is liable only for those accidents that he could have avoided at a lower cost than the expected accident cost. . . . The difference between strict and negligence liability is that under the former system injurers must pay the losses of victims of accidents that are not worth preventing, whereas under the latter system injurers have no duty to pay victims of such accidents.[32]

Posner's reasoning has not been accepted by the courts, apparently because strict liability, in functional terms, is like insurance. That is, strict liability means that the manufacturer or seller, rather than the consumer, must purchase insurance. Professor Polinsky argues: "Under strict liability, producers will be fully insured by liability insurance, and under negligence, consumers will be fully insured by first-party accident insurance."[33] This makes sense, because insurance is not readily available to consumers to cover products liability losses.[34] Often the consumer is unaware of the defect in the product and does not sense the need for insurance.

A novel theory of strict liability has been suggested by Judge Posner. It is a challenge to traditional notions of strict liability and, therefore, must be examined closely. Posner's concept of strict liability is: "If the expected loss . . . cannot be reasonably averted by taking greater care but can be by an adjustment in the activity level, an economic case for strict liability is made out."[35] Several points should be noted. First, his definition of strict liability is contrary to the cases. In a common strict liability case, blasting, the goal of the courts is not to alter the level of activity, but just the opposite. Blasting is highly valuable to society and to be encouraged.[36] The goal of strict liability is not to reduce the level of activity; it is to spread the inevitable losses.[37] Second, there is no reason for concluding that strict liability will lead to a change in the level of activity. Indeed, all that flows from a strict liability action is damages. This is also what results from a negligence action. The defendant in a negligence action may decide to reduce his level of activity, as may the defendant who is held strictly liable. The calculation of damages is based on the losses the plaintiff has suffered,[38] not whether the defendant was sued in strict liability or negligence.

Judge Posner challenges the traditional rationale for strict liability, loss shifting, on two grounds. First, "there is an element of conjecture involved in supposing that taking a concentrated loss off the back of the victim of some accident and dividing it up into many small losses to customers or shareholders will increase total utility."[39] Professor Calabresi takes the contrary position and states that the party "in the best position to make the cost-benefit analysis between accident costs and accident avoidance costs"[40] should bear the loss. In this way the defendant will soon adjust his conduct.[41] Also, Calabresi notes that placing the entire loss on one person is not economically beneficial.[42]

Second, Posner argues that "there is an alternative . . . method of loss spreading available to potential victims besides strict liability; they can buy insurance."[43] Professor Calabresi suggests that this is invalid to the extent that there is little deterrence value in placing the loss on the victims.[44] They rarely have the ability to make changes in the conduct that is causing the injury. In order to purchase insurance, the consumer must be aware of the risk. But in strict liability situations the consumer is often uninformed in regard to the dangerous nature of the product. He does not know of the need for insurance.

In a recent series of articles Professor Priest has mounted a direct attack on strict liability.[45] He blames it for the general high prices of insurance and its unavailability.[46] Priest suggests that strict liability essentially performs an insurance function and has led to the unraveling of the insurance market.[47] He concludes with the suggestion that we return to the negligence standard and expand the use of first-party insurance.[48] My critique of Priest's theory may be found in chapter 9.

NOTES

1. *See, e.g.*, Greenman v. Yuba Power Prods., Inc., 59 Cal. 2d 57, 377 P. 2d 897, 27 Cal. Rptr. 697 (S. Ct. 1963).

2. James, *Products Liability* (pt. 2), 34 TEX. L. REV. 192, 227-28 (1955).

3. Greenman v. Yuba Power Prods., Inc., 59 Cal. 2d 57, 377 P. 2d 897, 27 Cal. Rptr. 697 (S. Ct. 1963).

4. *Id.* at 900.

5. *Id.* at 901.

6. RESTATEMENT (SECOND) OF TORTS § 402A (1965).

7. Prosser, *The Fall of the Citadel (Strict Liability to the Consumer)*, 50 MINN. L. REV. 802 (1966).

8. Escola v. Coca-Cola Bottling Co. of Fresno, 24 Cal. 2d 453, 150 P. 2d 436 (S. Ct. 1944).

9. Greenman v. Yuba Power Prods., Inc., 59 Cal. 2d 57, 377 P. 2d 897, 27 Cal. Rptr. 697 (S. Ct. 1963).

10. RESTATEMENT, *supra* note 6.

11. 38 ALI PROCEEDINGS 87-88 (1961).

12. *Id.*

13. *Id.*

14. 8 Cal. 3d 121, 501 P. 2d 1153, 104 Cal. Rptr. 433 (1972).

15. *Id.*

16. *Id.*

17. Escola, *supra* note 8.

18. P. A. SAMUELSON, ECONOMICS 358 (11th ed. 1980).

19. *See* Escola, *supra* note 8.

20. *See* Borel v. Fiberboard Paper Prods., 493 F. 2d 1076 (5th Cir. 1973), *cert. denied*, 419 U.S. 869 (1974).

21. *See* Grimshaw v. Ford Motor Co., 119 Cal. App. 3d 757, 174 Cal. Rptr. 348 (1981).

22. *See* L. P. STROBEL, RECKLESS HOMICIDE 27 (1980).

23. *See* McCormack v. Hankscraft Co., 278 Minn. 322, 154 N.W. 2d 488 (S. Ct. 1967).

24. *See* Turner v. General Motors Corp., 514 S.W. 2d 497 (Ct. App. Tex. 1974).

25. Escola v. Coca-Cola Bottling Co. of Fresno, 24 Cal. 2d 453, 150 P. 2d 436 (S. Ct. 1944).

26. *Id.*

27. *See* Shavell, *Strict Liability Versus Negligence*, 9 J. LEGAL STUD. 1 (1980); A. M. POLINSKY, AN INTRODUCTION TO LAW AND ECONOMICS 98 (1983).

28. A. M. Polinsky, *supra* note 27, at 98.

29. *Id.*

30. *Id.* at 39.

31. *Id.* at 103.

32. R. A. POSNER, TORT LAW (CASES AND ECONOMIC ANALYSIS) 4, 5 (1982).

33. A. M. POLINSKY, *supra* note 27, at 100.

34. *See id.*

35. R. A. POSNER, *supra* note 32, at 477, 511.

36. *See* Spano v. Perini Corp., 25 N.Y. 2d 11, 250 N.E. 2d 31, 302 N.Y.S. 2d 527 (1969).

37. *Id.*

38. *See* W. P. KEETON, D. B. DOBBS, R. E. KEETON & D. G. OWEN, PROSSER AND KEETON ON THE LAW OF TORTS 165 (5th ed. 1984).

39. R. A. POSNER, *supra* note 32, at 517.

40. Calabresi & Hirschoff, *Toward a Test for Strict Liability in Torts*, 81 YALE L. J. 1060 (1970).

41. G. CALABRESI, THE COSTS OF ACCIDENTS: A LEGAL AND ECONOMIC ANALYSIS 68-94 (1970).

42. *Id.* at 39-45.

43. R. A. POSNER, *supra* note 32, at 517-18.

44. G. CALABRESI, *supra* note 41, at 55.

45. *See* Priest, *The Monsanto Lectures: Modern Tort Law and Its Reform*, 22 VAL. L. REV. 1 (1987); Priest, *Satisfying the Multiple Goals of Tort Law*, 22 VAL. L. REV. 643 (1988).

46. *See* Priest, *id* at 22 VAL. L. REV. 1.

47. *Id.*

48. *Id.*

BIBLIOGRAPHY

Calabresi, G., *The Costs of Accidents: A Legal and Economic Analysis* (1970).

Calabresi & Hirschoff, "Toward A Test For Strict Liability in Torts." 81 *Yale L. J.* 1060 (1972).

James, "Products Liability" (pt. 2). 34 *Tex. L. Rev.* 227 (1955).

Keeton, W. P., D. B. Dobbs, R. E. Keeton & D. G. Owen, *Prosser and Keeton on the Law of Torts* (5th ed. 1984).

Polinsky, A. M. *An Introduction to Law and Economics* (1983).
Posner, R. A., *Tort Law (Cases and Economic Analysis)* (1982).
Priest, "The Monsanto Lectures: Modern Tort Law and Its Reform." 22 *Val. L. Rev.* 1 (1987).
Priest, "Satisfying the Multiple Goals of Tort Law." 22 *Val. L. Rev.* 643 (1988).
Prosser, "The Fall of the Citadel (Strict Liability to the Consumer)." 50 *Minn. L. Rev.* 802 (1966).
Restatement (Second) of Torts, § 402A (1965).
Samuelson, P. A., *Economics* (11th ed. 1980).
Shavell, "Strict Liability Versus Negligence." 9 *J. Legal Stud.* 1 (1980).
Strobel, L. P. *Reckless Homicide* (1980).

3

Strict Liability: A Substitute for Socialized Medicine

The growth in strict liability is part of the more general growth in population. More people have generated more activity, more injury and more suits. A general growth in prosperity has also contributed to the expansion in litigation. As people have acquired more goods of increasing value, they have felt it appropriate to hold liable those who damage their property or cause personal injury and death.

There has been a corresponding expansion of liability in numerous areas of the law: persons who can sue (elimination of the defense of privity), softening of defenses such as assumption of risk, the application of comparative fault to civil actions, the discovery rule, the development of informed consent, res ipsa loquitur and the gradual elimination of immunities. These developments have made it easier to sue and to recover.

Professor Franklin argues that insurance has played a key role in the general expansion of liability:

Although judicial opinions rarely spoke of liability insurance, its impact was unmistakable. Courts are now becoming somewhat more explicit, as in *Rowland*, . . . for example, which refers to the prevalence of liability insurance—but not to whether the particular defendant was insured. The overruling of various immunities was undoubtedly facilitated by the opportunity for families and charities to insure themselves. In intra-family cases, what might have been a bitter internal feud over allocation of family assets instead becomes a way to obtain outside assistance when one member has caused injury to another. . . . Judge Friendly has been particularly explicit about the role of liability insurance in affecting attitudes toward the boundaries of tort liability. Recall that in *Kinsman*, . . . he observed that "Where the line will be drawn will vary from age to age; as society has come to rely increasingly on insurance and other methods of loss sharing, the point may lie further off than a century ago." Also, in a footnote in Steinhauser, . . . after observing the broad acceptance of the "thin-skull" doctrine, he stated, "The seeming severity of this doctrine is mitigated by the prevalence of liability insurance which spreads the risks." . . .

Judge Friendly's observations undoubtedly find support in the greater frequency with which juries are permitted to find negligence and to find no contributory negligence in the great mass of unspectacular cases. They undoubtedly also go far to explain such judicial developments as the family purpose doctrine making the owner of a car liable for the negligence of members of his family using his car with his permission. Automobile liability insurance also helps explain such recent cases as *Maloney* v. *Rath*, . . . in which the car owner was held liable for the negligence of her service station mechanic.[1]

The contingent fee system in the United States permits anyone to obtain a qualified attorney. In countries without this system, such as England, it is likely that many suits are not brought because of the absence of an attorney. In addition, it may be true—although this has not been examined empirically—that more plaintiffs' verdicts are obtained before juries than before judges.

Professor James suggested in 1955 that strict liability was born from the crush of numerous accidents:

As the accident toll of modern life has increased, the urge towards strict liability has grown. Many older forms of liability were vehicles for such a principle but none of them is well adapted to solving our present accident problem. . . . Why should not the courts of today—entirely within the tradition of a dynamic common law—develop a . . . theory in products liability cases which is tailored to meet modern needs in that field. . . ?[2]

Justice Traynor put forth the following rationale for strict liability:

[P]ublic policy demands that responsibility be fixed wherever it will most effectively reduce the hazards to life and health inherent in defective products that reach the market. It is evident that the manufacturer can anticipate some hazards and guard against the recurrence of others, as the public cannot. . . . The cost of an injury . . . can be insured by the manufacturer and distributed among the public as a cost of doing business. It is to the public interest to discourage the marketing of products having defects that are a menace to the public.[3]

Over the last 150 years, society has become more complicated and impersonal. The wagon maker no longer lives next door. A Chevrolet product may have its origin in Japan. Other products are manufactured around the world: in Germany, Japan, Korea, China and Yugoslavia, for example. Justice Traynor reasons that this social and marketing metamorphosis is, in part, responsible for the growth in strict liability:

As handicrafts have been replaced by mass production with its great markets and transportation facilities, the close relationship between the producer and consumer of a product has been altered. Manufacturing processes, frequently valuable secrets, are . . . inaccessible to or beyond the ken of the general public. The consumer no longer has means or skill enough to investigate for himself the soundness of a product . . . and his . . . vigilance has been lulled by the steady efforts of manufacturers to build up confidence by advertising and marketing devices such as trademarks. . . . The manufacturer's obligation to the consumer must keep pace with the changing relationship between them. . . .[4]

These reasons for the development of strict liability have been noted elsewhere and do not require further consideration. However, there is one important policy that has received little attention and is in need of careful examination. In order to appreciate this policy, we must undertake a comparative law approach. In the United States, strict liability functions in part as a substitute for socialized medicine. The purpose of the remainder of this chapter is to compare and contrast two legal systems, tort liability in the United States and socialized medicine in Great Britain, in order to make clear the functional role of strict liability in providing compensation for medical and other expenses. By examining the law of a jurisdiction with the same language and origin as the United States, I intend to shed light on the reasons for the growth of strict liability in the United States and to show that strict liability in the United States has developed to allow injured consumers to purchase medical treatment that might otherwise be unavailable.

BRITISH LAW

A person suffering injury from a product in England has traditionally been limited to two courses of action: negligence or contract. Until 1988 there was no strict liability.

Negligence

The law of negligence in England begins in 1932 with the famous case of *Donoghue v. Stevenson.*[5] A woman apparently said to her friend, "This one is on me," and purchased an opaque bottle of ginger beer for her friend. The bottle contained a decomposed snail, and the friend became ill after consuming the ginger beer. She was not able to recover in contract because of the absence of privity. The issue on appeal to the House of Lords was whether a duty extended to one not in privity. They answered in the affirmative. The case follows the keystone American case, *MacPherson v. Buick Motor Company.*[6] The noteworthy point is that while *MacPherson* was merely the first paragraph in the development of American products liability law, *Donoghue* is the final chapter for the British.

Negligence law in the United Kingdom is clear: third parties can sue since privity is not required and manufacturers as well as sellers are liable. The hurdle for the plaintiff is proving negligence, however.[7]

Negligence has expanded only slightly since 1932: "The manufacturer's duty of care in England has been extended to repairers, assemblers, retailers, and distributors, and a limited duty to inspect has been placed on dealers and suppliers. In an early case, protection was afforded to the bystander. . . ."[8] Extensive protection is afforded the manufacturer through the defense of intermediate examination: "[W]here there has been a reasonable opportunity to inspect the article, the manufacturer or repairer will not be liable, whether or not such an inspection has been made."[9]

Although cases had previously gone both ways, since 1955 it appears that a strict liability result will not be available by means of res ipsa loquitur.[10] The American theory of negligence per se is not followed in England, and therefore there is no civil damage action available for failure of the manufacturer to comply with a statutory duty.[11]

Contract

Privity must be shown in order to recover in contract.[12] The Uniform Commercial Code theory extending the right to sue to members of the purchaser's household or family is unknown in English law.[13] The buyer can recover from the seller if there is injury and the product was not "fit" or "merchantable."[14] This is a form of strict liability because no negligence need be shown. The plaintiff must merely show that the product was not fit or not merchantable. This is a very limited recovery because injured third parties are not protected and the manufacturer is not liable.[15] R. M. S. Gibson summarized the English contract cause of action as follows:

> The manufacturer's citadel of privity remains alive and well . . . in England. . . . Section 3 of the Supply of Goods Act 1973, in England replaced Section 14 of the Sale of Goods Act, 1893, which dealt with implied terms of quality and fitness, but the law remains virtually the same. Although minor damage was inflicted by the 1973 Act[,] . . . its arrows of implied conditions of fitness and merchantable quality may still only be shot from the bow of the purchaser and only at the seller. While such arrows are sharpened by the fact that fault does not need to be proved, they fall far short of the manufacturer, except by means of a long and cumbersome process of third- or fourth-party proceedings based on the same implied warranties.[16]

TORT REFORM IN ENGLAND

Because of problems with the law made obvious by the Thalidomide disaster, two commissions were appointed to examine civil liability.[17] The first, "a Royal Commission under the leadership of Lord Pearson, was formed on March 19, 1973 . . . to study the remedies available for death and personal injury in England."[18] The Pearson Commission report came out in 1978. Strict liability for injuries caused by products was embraced by the report, but the report received little debate in Parliament. The argument in Parliament was that strict liability might be considered, but only if the manufacturer could defend on the basis of the "state of the art." Parliament did not adopt strict liability in 1978.[19] At the time of the Pearson report, England was in the throes of a serious recession, and nothing would be adopted by Parliament that might adversely affect the anticipated economic recovery.[20]

A combination of the Law Commission and the Scottish Law Commission constituted the second commission. It was developed specifically to evaluate the British products liability laws. This joint report, published in 1977, also proposed strict liability for products: "We have concluded that the main considerations of policy . . . and the criticism of existing law . . . justify the imposition of strict liability for injuries resulting from defects in products . . . and that liability should rest primarily on the producer."[21] The most important policies that led the commission to embrace strict liability were that the loss should be borne by the person who created the risk, and liability should be imposed on the producres in the chain of manufacture "who are in the best position to exercise control over the quality and safety of the product."[22] Presented to Parliament in 1977, the report was never debated or adopted.

THE EUROPEAN ECONOMIC COMMUNITY AND STRICT LIABILITY

The Common Market Council of Ministers has the power to enact legislation that changes the laws of Europe. The representatives of the twelve member states (including Great Britain) enact legislation that is binding on the member states.

France has strict liability and believes that the cost of insurance to cover this liability puts her at an economic disadvantage when trading with other countries. France has therefore lobbied to persuade the Common Market to enact strict liability for injuries resulting from products.[23] As a result, the European Economic Community (EEC) proposed the following directive in 1976:

> The producer of an article shall be liable for damage caused by a defect in the article, whether or not he knew or could have known of the defect. The producer shall be liable even if the article could not have been regarded as defective in the light of the scientific and technological development of the time when he put the product into circulation.[24]

A product is defective "when it does not provide for persons or property the safety which a person is entitled to expect."[25] The policies underlying this proposed EEC directive are the same as the policies presented in American cases.[26]

On March 1, 1988, the Consumer Protection Act 1987 went into effect in England.[27] It builds upon the previous proposals and provides for strict liability against "producers":

> The general effect of Part I of the Act is to establish a system of strict, rather than fault-based, liability in respect of loss caused by defective products. Existing tort and contract remedies remain available, but are now supplemented by a new conceptual structure which focuses primarily on the condition of a product rather than the conduct of its producer.[28]

Importantly, England has elected to adopt the "state-of-the-art" defense:

> Under section 4(1)(e) it will be a defense to show that the state of scientific and technical knowledge at the relevant time (when the product was put into circulation) was not such that a producer "might be expected" to have discovered the defect.[29]

The recent adoption of strict liability in England raises the question whether there is anything in Britain's long delay that provides insight for the United States.

BRITAIN PREFERS NEGLIGENCE

The United Kingdom continued to embrace negligence because of the nature of British society and British legal institutions. The British experience is different from the American experience, and there is nothing in their long adherence to negligence that constitutes a critique of the American expansion of strict liability. We will see that (1) Britain avoided strict liability because of its extensive National Health Service; (2) the British judges do not make law; and (3) access to the courts is severely restricted.

Socialized Medicine

The National Health Service pays for a citizen's every medical necessity.[30] If an Englishman breaks his leg playing football, walking down steps in his home or as the result of a car crash because of a defective part, his medical treatment is provided, in each case, without charge by the National Health Service.[31] There is a slight charge for prescription drugs, however.[32] There are delays for elective surgery, to be sure. If it is not an emergency, a person who wants to have a hip socket replaced may have to wait as long as eighteen months, for example.

If, because of the broken leg, the driver loses two months' work, a portion of the lost wages will be covered by British Social Security. These payments are scaled in relation to the wages earned. They are substantial and may continue for the rest of the injured person's life. Indeed, the Social Security payments to an injured person over the remainder of his life could be greater than the recovery at trial.[33] Prosthetic devices and rehabilitative services are also covered by the National Health Service.

Within such a system, the solicitor, contacted by the injured driver, faces a weak lawsuit: special damages, zero (covered by National Health Service); future medical expenses, zero (covered); lost wages, small amount (covered to a large extent by Social Security); pain and suffering, substantial (not covered). The prospect of suing the car manufacturer for a small amount of lost wages (the portion not covered by Social Security) and pain and suffering will often lead the solicitor to decline the case. In addition, the solicitor realizes that the case will be tried before a judge without a jury, and the judge is aware that most damages have been compensated.

The personal injury case in Britain is unique. In England the medical expenses and a substantial portion of the wages are covered. Often the only issue left to be litigated is pain and suffering. The United States has embraced strict liability to make certain that the injured citizen is compensated. Until 1988 Britain accomplished the same thing by means of a welfare state.

English Judges Do Not Make Law

English judges follow the mandate that making law is for Parliament; judges merely apply the law:

> In large part the difference in products liability law between England and the United States lies in the fact that English Judges have been far less willing to assert a role of law and policy-making than their American brethren. The reasons for this are several; in the first place, there is no written constitution in England for the courts to interpret. Sovereignty and the final judgment in all matters rest not in the courts, but in Parliament. As a result, they have no power to question the validity of Acts of Parliament or to declare them unconstitutional.[34]

Law commissions are appointed to make recommendations to Parliament for changes in the law. Since the courts do not make law, the law commissions as evaluators and spokesmen of social policy take on unique importance.[35]

The English courts have also avoided an activist role because they lack the stimulation and criticism provided by diverse jurisdictions in the American system:

> [T]he sheer quantity of judgments which pour forth from the federal judiciary and the courts of 50 states provides a much greater choice for the Judge in the United States and thus makes it much easier to avoid strict adherence to precedent. With support for almost any proposition, there is much greater freedom to make judicial law.[36]

The Gates to Justice Are Heavy

A key reason for the traditional adherence of the English courts to negligence theory is the difficulty involved in bringing a personal injury suit. With few torts suits being brought, the system appeared to function well. When entrance to the courts involves numerous hurdles, fewer cases will be brought. This will result in correspondingly less pressure for reform and will support an acceptance of the status quo. Access to English courts is restricted in two ways. First, there is no contingent fee system.[37] Therefore, many suits are not brought because the injured persons lack the finances to support the case. Legal aid is sometimes available,[38] but it is oversubscribed and underfunded as in the United States. Second, in English suits the loser pays. The party losing a personal injury suit in Britain is obligated to pay the attorney fees, the court costs, and related costs such as the expenses of the experts on the winning side. This is in addition to his attorney's fees and the costs of his experts.[39] If personal injury litigation is a game of chance under the best of circumstances, then the requirement that the loser must pay likely discourages a large number of close cases.

When novel and high-risk tort cases were not brought, it was possible to infer that there were few problems with the legal system. Negligence, on the surface, appeared to work well, and there was little pressure within the British litigation system to adopt strict liability. With medical expenses and a substantial portion of lost wages being covered through the welfare state, the system, in fact, functioned smoothly for most cases.[40] Pressure for change came from the Common Market.

In short, England adhered to negligence until 1988, while the United States adopted strict liability much earlier because the social and legal systems are completely different. In Britain the National Health Service and Social Security cover most of the expenses that constitute damages. The British judges have a long tradition of applying, rather than making, law. All of this suggests that negligence may well have been appropriate for the British and highlights the important compensation role of strict liability in the United States. The impact of strict liability in Britain remains to be seen.

One of the important conclusions reached from comparing the British and American legal systems is that the American preference for strict liability much earlier grows out of the nature of the American society. Britain provides for injured persons through the National Health Care System. Personal injury litigation constitutes a backup. Despite the Judeo-Christian ethic in America, which supports the notion that injured persons should not be left to bear losses caused by others, there is no American national health care system. Even so, the American Medical Association has consistently supported a private health care system and opposed socialized medicine. In the United States the courts have recognized that under a negligence cause of action, parties who should win often lose.[41]

These factors have led the American courts to endorse an expansion of strict liability because it leads to compensation of injured persons who would otherwise receive "free" medical treatment under a system comparable to the British system. Strict liability enables injured parties to purchase expensive medical care in the market. An important side effect is that strict liability permits lower taxes and reduces the pressure in the United States for socialized medicine. In short, our system, with strict liability as an essential element, is cheap, efficient and surgically precise.

NOTES

1. M. A. FRANKLIN & R. L. RABIN, CASES AND MATERIALS ON TORT LAW AND ALTERNATIVES, 489 (3d ed. 1983).

2. James, *Products Liability* (pt. 2), 34 TEX. L. REV. 192, 227-28 (1955).

3. Escola v. Coca-Cola Bottling Co. of Fresno, 24 Cal. 2d 453, 462, 150 P. 2d 436, 440-41 (1944) (Traynor, J., concurring).

4. *Id.* at 467, 150 P. 2d at 443 (citations omitted).

5. Donoghue v. Stevenson, [1932] A.C. 562.

6. *MacPherson*, 217 N.Y. 382, 111 N.E. 1050 (1916).

7. Gibson, *Products Liability in the United States and England: The Difference and Why,* 3 ANGLO-AM. L. REV. 493, 504 (1974).

8. *Id.* at 505 (footnote omitted).

9. *Id.* at 512.

10. *See id.* at 508 n. 90; Samuel, *Strict Liability: Advance, Retreat–or Advancing Backwards?*, 6 ANGLO-AM. L. REV. 99 (1977); Tobin, *Products Liability: A United States Commonwealth Survey*, 3 N.Z.U. L. REV. 377 (1969).

11. *See* Plummer, *Products Liability in Britain*, 9 ANGLO-AM. L. REV. 65, 74-77 (1980).

12. *See* Kasler & Cohen v. Slavouaki, [1928] 1 K.B. 78 (1927).

13. Interview with Professor A. L. Diamond, Director of the Institute for Advanced Legal Studies, London, England (Mar. 17, 1984).

14. *Id.*

15. *Id.*

16. Gibson, *supra* note 7, at 504.

17. Movement toward reform in England was ignited by the Thalidomide disaster. Because of the use of the drug by the mother, children were born with only rudimentary hands or fingers: "Since [1961] over 400 children in England alone have been affected by the drug. . . . In British terms, it was one of the worst of all peacetime accidents." Gibson, *supra* note 7, at 509. Because the children were not in privity, the suit against the manufacturers had to be brought in negligence. But in negligence the manufacturer could defend on the basis of "state of the art." He could argue that at the time the drug was produced, no one was testing fetuses before marketing drugs. After a prolonged and sensational battle, the Thalidomide case was finally settled out of court. Diamond, *supra* note 13; Plummer, *supra* note 11, at 78.

18. Gibson, *supra* note 7, at 511.

19. Diamond, *supra* note 13.

20. *Id.*

21. Law Commission and Scottish Law Commission, CMD No. 6831 at 11 (1977).

22. *Id.* at 6.

23. Diamond, *supra* note 13; interview with Dr. Peter North, Law Commissioner (Apr. 10, 1984).

24. Law Commission, *supra* note 21, at 79. The European Economic Community, on July 25, 1985, adopted a directive on products liability that companies will be liable for damage caused by goods they have manufactured or imported, without the victim having to prove negligence. The EEC's member states had until 1988 to implement the provisions of the directive. PROD. SAFETY & LIAB. REP. (BNA) 547 (Aug. 8, 1986). England adopted strict liability under

the EEC directive in March, 1988. Clark, *The Consumer Protection Act of 1987*, MODERN L. REV. 614 (1987).

25. Law Commission, *supra* note 21, at 79.

26. The Law Commission stated the policies as follows:

> Whereas an equal and adequate protection of the consumer can be achieved only through the introduction of liability irrespective of fault on the part of the producer of the article which was defective and caused the damage; whereas any other type of liability imposes on the injured party almost insurmountable difficulties of proof. . . . Whereas liability on the part of the producer irrespective of fault ensures an appropriate solution . . . because he can include the expenditure which he incurs to cover this liability in his production costs when calculating the price and therefore divide it among all consumers of products which are of the same type. . . .

Law Commission, *supra* note 21, at 76.

27. 1988 Management Today 93 (Jan.).

28. Clark, *The Consumer Protection Act of 1987*, MODERN L. REV. 614 (1987).

29. *Id.* at 619.

30. Diamond, *supra* note 13.

31. Diamond, *supra* note 13; 1 ROYAL COMMISSION ON CIVIL LIABILITY AND COMPENSATION FOR PERSONAL INJURY 48 (1978).

32. *E.g.*, $2.30 in Britain versus $15 in the United States.

33. ROYAL COMMISSION, *supra* note 31.

34. Gibson, *supra* note 7, at 516.

35. *Id.* at 518.

36. *Id.*

37. Diamond, *supra* note 13.

38. *Id.*

39. *Id.*

40. Plummer, *supra* note 11, at 77-80.

41. Barker v. Lull Eng'g Co., 20 Cal. 3d 413, 432, 573 P.2d 443. 455-56, 143 Cal. Rptr. 225, 237-38 (1978).

BIBLIOGRAPHY

Clark, "The Consumer Protection Act of 1987." *Modern L. Rev.* 614 (1987).

Franklin, A., & R. L. Rabin, *Cases and Materials on Tort Law and Alternatives.* 3d ed., 1983.

Gibson, "Products Liability in the United States and England: The Difference and Why." 3 *Anglo-Am. L. Rev.* 493 (1974).

James, "Products Liability." 34 *Tex. L. Rev.* 192 (1955).

Plummer, "Products Liability in Britain." 9 *Anglo-Am. L. Rev.* 65 (1980).

Samuel, "Strict Liability: Advance, Retreat—or Advancing Backwards?" 6 *Anglo-Am. L. Rev.* 99 (1977).

Tobin, "Products Liability: A United States Commonwealth Survey." 3 *N.Z. U. L. Rev.* 377 (1969).

4

Strict Liability Defined: Nine Tests

A study of products liability cases beginning in 1842 manifests two competing doctrines: negligence and strict liability. Historically, negligence rested upon the policy of holding persons to the standard of the reasonable person,[1] while strict liability rested upon the policy of loss shifting.[2] The American Law Institute misstated the meaning of strict liability in 1965 by announcing in Restatement (Second) of Torts section 402A that the key to strict liability was the finding of an "unreasonably dangerous defect."[3] Section 402A generated conflicting cases and articles.[4] Because of this confusion, there is a need to evaluate the concepts of negligence and strict liability and to examine the origins of the Restatement's definition of defect. There is also a need to discover why the existing theories have been rejected by the courts or have created new problems when followed by the courts. This chapter considers the impact of negligence, strict liability and warranty on the concept of defect and evaluates nine tests for defect. Defect is the key concept in the meaning of strict liability. Throughout this chapter, "defect" will refer to design defect and not manufacturing defect.[5]

Judges and authors have had difficulty defining defect. This stems from a failure to examine the causes of action that form the conceptual boundaries of strict liability. Before defining defect, it will be helpful to explore these keystone tort actions: negligence, strict liability (abnormally dangerous activities) and warranty.

NEGLIGENCE

Two authors have stated that strict liability is a form of negligence.[6] This contradicts what the courts have held. The courts have stated that negligence is not strict liability and should not be considered in defining defect.[7] To discover whether the commentators or the courts are correct, it will be necessary to examine the elements of negligence.

Negligence is composed of five factors: duty, breach, cause in fact, proximate cause and damages.[8] Judge Learned Hand in *United States v. Carroll Towing*[9] stated, in a negligence action involving a ship that broke away from its moorings, that duty was a matter of balancing three variables: "(1) The probability that she will break away; (2) the gravity of the resulting injury, if she does; (3) the burden of adequate precautions."[10] The well-known *Palsgraf* case,[11] in contrast, states that duty is a question of whether the defendant could foresee that the plaintiff could be harmed. The courts cite these duty cases only to ignore them when deciding the case.[12]

Breach of duty involves the question of whether the defendant conducted himself as a reasonable person would have conducted himself under the same or similar circumstances.[13] Cause in fact is primarily a question of whether the defendant's act was a substantial factor in bringing about the damages.[14] Dean Leon Green states that cause in fact is a scientific question of whether the defendant's act had anything to do with the injury to the plaintiff.[15] The most challenging aspect of negligence is proximate cause. It limits the scope of liability and is often defined by the court asking whether the damages were foreseeable by the defendant.[16] Damages are fundamental and must be proved as part of the negligence cause of action.[17]

Judge Richard Posner argues that negligence is a matter of economics–in determining liability, the courts must balance costs against benefits.[18] Judge Posner's article does not support his position, however. The only cited proponent of the test is Judge Learned Hand, who, Judge Posner admits, may have stumbled upon it rather than intended it as the rationale of the *Carroll Towing* case.[19] It should be noted that Hand rejected the test within two years of deciding the case.[20] None of the 1,528 appellate decisions studied by Judge Posner expresses a cost-benefit test.[21] Posner's work has been helpful in suggesting the role of economic analysis in tort law. His thesis is only partly accurate, however. The courts weigh many factors in deciding a question of negligence, of which the cost, probability of injury and burden of preventing injury are only a few.[22]

The argument that negligence is primarily a question of cost compared with benefit is more a statement of how economists would like negligence to be treated by the courts than a description of the existing analytical process. In a negligence case the social policy questions are neither candidly nor clearly examined. A determination of duty would often be dispositive of the case, but instead of deciding the duty issue, the courts rest the decision upon another element, such as proximate cause.[23] The issue of whether the defendant's duty has been breached is commonly given to the jury, and the policy questions are not faced by appellate or trial courts.[24]

The most troubling concept in negligence theory is proximate cause. The purpose of proximate cause is to enable the courts to control the scope of the jury's deliberations.[25] In answering the scope of liability question, the courts should look at important social policies such as prevention, loss shifting and availability of insurance.[26] Instead of using a policy-balancing approach, however, the courts usually resolve the proximate cause issue by asking whether the damages were foreseeable by the defendant, the injury was remote, the occurrence was natural, or the defendant's act was the sole proximate cause.[27] In short, instead of using social policy to define the scope of liability in negligence cases, the courts generally rely upon the misleading term "foreseeability."[28] The result is that policy questions are not examined.[29] To be sure, Dean Green's thesis that proximate cause be eliminated from the negligence formula and that the courts focus on the duty concept has been largely ignored.[30]

The courts decide negligence cases on the basis of feelings or hunches rather than by weighing important policies. None of the following cases, for example, expressly weighs policies such as administrative difficulty, prevention of injury, ability to carry the loss, insurance or impact upon society.[31] In the famous *Wagon Mound I* case[32] the court found that the defendant shipowner was not liable for discharging oil into the water, because it was not "foreseeable" that oil floating on water would ignite. In *Polemis*,[33] another well-known case, a plank slipped and caused a spark, and an entire ship was consumed in the resulting flames. The court found in favor of the plaintiff because the fire was a "direct" result of the plank's falling.[34] In *Whetham v. Bismarck Hospital*[35] a nurse dropped the plaintiff-mother's newly born infant in front of her. The court refused to permit the mother to recover for the mental distress that followed because the mother was not within the "zone of danger."[36] In *Schwinn Sales South v. Waters*[37] the court found no negligence on the part of a manufacturer who produced a child's bicycle without reflectors. The child was hit by a car at night. The decision rests on the fact that absence of reflectors was patent. In none of these cases were the costs and benefits evaluated.

Authors have suggested that an important difference between negligence and strict liability is that in negligence the key consideration for the courts is the major policies involved, that is, whether the cost exceeds the benefit of the activity.[38] In practice, the courts avoid discussing the policy questions. Therefore, a distinction between negligence and strict liability is that in strict liability the court is asked to face directly the question of whether the cost of the activity exceeds the benefit.[39] This express weighing of critical policies in products liability cases is the central theme of *Escola*, *Greenman*, and *Cronin*. The proposed similarity between negligence and strict liability has existed only because of the commentators' molding of negligence into something it has never been: a frontal consideration of important social policies.

Several theories may be suggested to explain why the courts have clearly articulated the operative policies in strict liability. The defendant in a strict liability case is often a major manufacturer, such as Ford or General Motors—a signal to the court that the case is important and careful analysis is necessary. In addition, the results in strict liability cases will, in part, dictate whether the products will continue to be marketed and at what price. Finally, the manufacturers have learned that "squid function" words, such as "foreseeable," will result in their being held liable in most cases.[40]

STRICT LIABILITY

The theory of strict liability in dangerous activities and in products liability is similar.[41] The question of strict liability in dangerous activities, such as blasting, is primarily an issue of policy: who should bear the loss.[42] A conceptual roadblock, namely, the Restatement (Second) of Torts section 520, has obscured this point. It provides:

> In determining whether an activity is abnormally dangerous, the following factors are to be considered:
>
> (a) existence of a high degree of risk of some harm to the person, land or chattels of others;
> (b) likelihood that the harm that results from it will be great;
> (c) inability to eliminate risk by the exercise of reasonable care;
> (d) extent to which the activity is not a matter of common usage;
> (e) inappropriateness of the activity to the place where it is carried on; and
> (f) extent to which its value to the community is outweighed by its dangerous attributes.

Section 520 presents several misleading factors. First, requiring the court to consider whether the risk cannot be eliminated by the exercise of reasonable care suggests an issue that is not supported by the cases.[43] There is no requirement in the foundational case, *Rylands v. Fletcher*,[44] that there be a finding that the risk cannot be eliminated by reasonable care. The reporter, in drafting section 520, apparently intended to limit the scope of strict liability to blasting cases.[45]

A second misleading factor is that the activity must not be a "matter of common usage."[46] This test is not supported by the cases.[47] It takes the focus away from the important question of whether the activity is "natural."[48] Under *Rylands* and later cases, the term "natural" has been used to evaluate whether an activity is one that should be subject to strict liability.[49] The Restatement's "common usage" test can lead to bad results. In *Wood v. United Airlines*[50] the court held that since airplanes were "common," strict liability would not apply to a crash of an airliner into an apartment house in New York City. Because airplanes are not "natural," United should have been held strictly liable.

The key question in strict liability is who should bear the loss.[51] The courts state that "the justification for strict liability . . . is that useful but dangerous activities must pay their own way."[52] There is a close analogy between strict liability in the blasting cases and in products liability. The question of strict liability from dangerous activities is for the court. It is essentially a question of policy involving whether the defendant is in the best position to bear the loss.[53] The cases have been firm in stating the fundamental policy issue. Therefore, the Restatement stands out as having introduced red herrings.

WARRANTY

Three forms of warranty need to be considered in examining the boundaries of strict liability: express warranty, implied warranty in tort and implied warranty under the Uniform Commercial Code. Express warranty is based on the fact that the defendant has said something about his product, such as "shatter-proof glass windshield."[54] The state of the law in this area accounts for the vacuous nature of contemporary automobile ads, which uniformly say nothing of substance about the product.

Fearing liability under theories of express warranty, manufacturers soon learned to avoid making express statements about their products. In response, courts developed implied warranty in tort in order to shift the loss resulting from defective products to the manufacturer.[55] Under implied warranty the seller is held liable by law even though he made no express statement about the product.[56] The foundation for the implied warranty doctrine is: "[T]he burden of losses consequent upon use of defective articles is borne by those who are in a position to either control the danger or make an equitable distribution of the losses when they do occur."[57] In essence, implied warranty is a form of strict liability.

Implied warranty created problems, however. In some cases the courts asked, "Where is the warranty?"[58] They reasoned that if there is no statement by the manufacturer, there can be no implied warranty.[59]

The Uniform Commercial Code may still provide an avenue of recovery in a few products liability cases. Section 2-318 (alternative A) of the Uniform Commercial Code provides that

> [a] seller's warranty whether express or implied extends to any natural person who is in the family or household of his buyer or who is a guest in his home if it is reasonable to expect that such person may use, consume or be affected by the goods and who is injured in person by breach of the warranty.

Therefore, a member of the purchaser's family is in privity and may sue, but a third party is out of privity and out of luck.

In summary, express warranty is not generally available because manufacturers no longer make express statements about their products. Implied warranty was the precursor of pure strict liability and has been absorbed within it. Both the former implied warranty and the present strict liability rest upon the policy that losses should be borne by the producer rather than by the innocent consumer. At this point, having examined the three tort theories that surround strict liability (negligence, strict liability [abnormally dangerous activities], and warranty), we will consider the foundational concept in strict liability (products): defect.

NINE TESTS FOR DEFECT

Numerous tests have been suggested to define the critical element in strict liability: defect. It is the critical element because it distinguishes strict liability from both absolute liability and negligence. Strict liability is communicated to the court and the jury through the various tests for defect. In evaluating the tests, it will be helpful to ask whether they are responsive to the foundational policy as stated by the New Jersey Supreme Court in *Henningsen v. Bloomfield Motors* (1960): "[T]he burden of losses consequent upon use of defective articles is borne by those who are in a position to either control the danger or make an equitable distribution of the losses when they do occur."[60]

Section 402A "Unreasonably Dangerous"

The Restatement's foundationless test for strict products liability provides that "[o]ne who sells any product in a defective condition unreasonably dangerous to the user or consumer or to his property is subject to liability for physical harm thereby caused to the ultimate user or consumer."[61] The term "unreasonably dangerous" has caused a great deal of confusion.[62] The drafters' reasons for using the term "unreasonably dangerous" were to make it clear that the product must be defective and that the manufacturer of an ordinary product that contains some danger, but is not defective, will not be held liable.[63]

The Restatement test has been heavily criticized. It is misleading because the term "unreasonably dangerous" suggests that the product must be more than dangerous.[64] Additionally, it requires the plaintiff to prove that the defendant has been negligent.[65] Attempts have been made to neutralize these criticisms by suggesting that "unreasonably dangerous" and "defective" mean the same thing and should not be interpreted to imply either that the plaintiff must prove negligence or that something more than mere danger of the product must be shown.[66]

Most disturbing, however, is the fact that the term "unreasonably dangerous" is not supported by precedent.[67] Why did Dean Prosser, the Restatement reporter, use the phrase "unreasonably dangerous" in section 402A rather than the word "defect," which would have reflected the developing case law? Insight comes from the *American Law Institute (ALI) Proceedings* in 1961. The following is a discussion between Professor Reed Dickerson and the reporter, Dean Prosser, on a draft of section 402A (Food):

> *Professor Dickerson*: . . I would think that if he [the purchaser] showed that it [the product] was unreasonably dangerous, it would per se be legally defective, and it is only gilding the lily to add the word "defective." . . .
>
> *Dean Prosser*: Mr. Dickerson has stated an original point of view which I first brought in to the Council of the American Law Institute in connection with this section. ". . . food in a condition unreasonably dangerous to the consumer" was my language. The Council then proceeded to raise the question of a number of products which, even though not defective, are in fact dangerous to the consumer–whiskey, for example [laughter]; cigarettes . . . and they raised the question whether "unreasonably dangerous" was sufficient to protect the defendant against possible liability in such cases.
>
> Therefore, they suggested that there something must be [*sic*] wrong with the product itself, and hence the word "defective" was put in; but the fact that the product itself is dangerous, or even unreasonably dangerous, to people who consume it is not enough. There has to be something wrong with the product. . . . "Defective" was put in to head off liability on the part of the seller of whiskey, on the part of the man who consumes it and gets delirium tremens, even though the jury might find that all whiskey is unreasonably dangerous to the consumer.[68]

This discussion makes it clear that Prosser originally drafted section 402A using the "unreasonably dangerous" test. He added the word "defect" at the urging of the ALI Council. Why, however, did he initially ignore the developing strict liability language of the cases for the negligence phrase "unreasonably dangerous"? One may suggest that since Dean Prosser was such a central figure in the analysis and synthesis of negligence law, he used the "unreasonably dangerous" test because he was familiar with it.[69] The "unreasonably dangerous" test was never considered by the ALI in terms of products in general. Dean Wade recalls that the term "unreasonably dangerous" was never discussed by the Torts Section of the ALI as it might be applied to inedible products.[70] It was only discussed in its application to food.[71]

Risk-Benefit

The reason for the risk-benefit test is that any evaluation of a design hazard must necessarily involve the weighing of danger against utility.[72] Strict liability is not insurance. Dean Keeton is the author of the risk-benefit test:

> A product is defective if it is unreasonably dangerous as marketed. It is unreasonably dangerous if a reasonable person would conclude that the magnitude of the scientifically perceivable danger *as it is proved to be at the time of trial* outweighed the benefits of the way the product was so designed and marketed.[73]

Each term must be defined. Risk is determined by the likelihood of harm, the seriousness of the harm and the nature of the danger.[74] Benefit is determined by the need for the product, the feasibility of a safer design, and the availability of substitute products.[75] The risk-benefit test is flawed in using the term "unreasonably dangerous." This implies negligence and requires the plaintiff to prove more than defectiveness. It suffers the same shortcomings as the Restatement test.[76] The emphasis on magnitude of the risk and benefit of the product is valid, but continuation of the "unreasonably dangerous" language is misleading.[77] Dean Keeton agrees that the test closely parallels negligence, but explains that it "differs from negligence primarily because . . . the danger in fact as proven at trial determines whether a product is good or bad. This difference would seem to be obvious."[78]

The California Test

The California Supreme Court has developed a bifurcated test for defect:

> [A] product may be found defective in design, so as to subject a manufacturer to strict liability for resulting injuries, under either of two alternative tests. First,

a product may be found defective in design if the plaintiff establishes that the product failed to perform as safely as an ordinary consumer would expect when used in an intended or reasonably foreseeable manner. Second, a product may alternatively be found defective in design if the plaintiff demonstrates that the product's design proximately caused his injury and the defendant fails to establish, in light of the relevant factors, that on balance, the benefits of the challenged design outweigh the risk of danger inherent in such design.[79]

A key reason for this definition is to continue the California theory that the term "unreasonably dangerous" unfairly burdens the injured plaintiff with proof of negligence.[80] A second reason is an acknowledgment that "it is simply impossible to eliminate the balancing or weighing of competing considerations in determining whether a product is defectively designed or not."[81]

The California test contains several traps. First, the expectations of the ordinary consumer cannot be viewed as the yardstick for evaluating design defect: "[I]n many situations . . . the consumer would not know what to expect, because he would have no idea how safe the product could be made."[82] For example, how much safety would a purchaser expect in an automobile's rotor, a boom vang, a backstay or a differential? Second, a substantial flaw is the use of the words "proximate cause" in the second prong of the test. The term "proximate cause" is unclear and superfluous.[83] Findings of proximate cause and defect involve the same policy inquiries. It is repetitious and misleading to ask whether the defect was the proximate cause of the damage. The policy question is asked once when the court weighs the various factors to see whether the product is defective.[84] It is confusing to the court, the jury and the attorneys to ask the same policy question again, but under a different label, proximate cause.

On the plus side, however, the second part of the California test is quite good. It dramatically reduces the burden on the plaintiff and shifts the locus of proof to the manufacturer or seller. The defendant must prove that the product is free from defects. This is fair because the defendant will usually possess superior knowledge and expertise. The second test would be even better if "cause in fact" were substituted for "proximate cause." That is, the plaintiff's burden would be merely to show that the defendant was the cause in fact of his injury. The defendant would then have the burden to establish that the benefits of the design outweigh the risk of danger.

Negligence with Imputed Knowledge

The Oregon Supreme Court has developed a test based upon a modification of the traditional negligence approach:

> A dangerously defective article would be one which a reasonable person would not put into the stream of commerce *if he had knowledge of its harmful character.* The test, therefore, is whether the seller would be negligent if he sold the article *knowing of the risk involved.* Strict liability imposes what amounts to constructive knowledge of the condition of the product.[85]

This test is embraced by both Dean Wade and Dean Keeton.[86] The professors disagree on whether it is a test of negligence, however. Dean Wade says, "It may be argued that this is simply a test of negligence. Exactly."[87] Dean Keeton, in contrast, states, "Since the test is not one of negligence, it is not based upon the risks and dangers that the maker should have, in the exercise of ordinary care, known about."[88] The Oregon court adds that "[t]he Wade and Keeton formulations of the standard appear to be identical except that Keeton would impute the knowledge of dangers to the manufacturer at time of trial, while Wade would impute only the knowledge existing at the time the product was sold."[89]

The most serious drawback to the test is the use of the term "negligent." The courts consistently have held that strict liability is not negligence.[90] It must be noted that the imposition of constructive knowledge by the Oregon court is not new. This is often done when circumstantial evidence is strong enough to permit an inference that the manufacturer had knowledge of the defect, even though he insists that he had no knowledge.[91] The manufacturer is routinely treated as an expert. In summary, the "negligence with imputed knowledge" test for defect would require the plaintiffs to prove negligence. This is contrary to the cases.[92]

Nevertheless, Dean Keeton's point will be crucial in a small number of important cases. In those cases where the manufacturer states that he lacked knowledge of the defect when the product was manufactured, or where he in fact lacked knowledge at the time of manufacture, the Keeton interpretation of the imputed knowledge test will be critical. Three examples come to mind. The first example is diethylstilbestrol (DES).[93] The manufacturers of DES contend that they lacked knowledge that the drug caused vaginal cancer in the children of mothers who consumed DES.[94] The second example is asbestos.[95] The manufacturers contend that they lacked knowledge that it caused cancer. A third example is cigarettes.[96] These manufacturers also argue that they did not know at the time of manufacture that their product caused cancer. Under Keeton's approach the knowledge will be imputed at the time of trial in each of the three cases.

The Communicative Tort

Dean Leon Green has suggested a solution to the strict liability morass. He proposed "a communicative tort action based on the duty to inform or to give reliable information, set off distinctly from the . . . negligence action based on the duty of care."[97] Dean Green suggests that sellers should be informed that if their defective product injures a consumer because of the absence of a warning or adequate instructions, they will be held liable.[98] In short, sellers will be taken at their word.[99] If the product is not safe, the obligation rests upon the seller to so warn the public. The reason for the new tort is the "corporate seller's command of all the media of communications to support his aggressive campaigns."[100]

The late Dean Green has performed an invaluable service by pointing the courts toward one of the most critical elements of products liability: information, or lack of information, communicated by the seller. It is unlikely, however, that the communicative tort will be fully adopted by the courts because the amount of information communicated by the seller has little impact on a case brought by a bystander or donee.[101] Even if the seller had provided a warning, the third party or donee would not have received it in most cases. In some cases, however, the nature of the warning is determinative.[102]

Cheapest Cost Avoider

Dean Guido Calabresi has done much to clarify fundamental concepts in strict liability through the application of economic analysis.[103] In applying these economic principles, he has found that the cost-benefit test, as put forward by Judge Learned Hand, delivers predictably skewed results: "The present Learned Hand test tends to make injurers richer at the expense of victims."[104] He argues that the reason for strict liability is not merely to accomplish distributional goals.[105] The reason for the trend toward strict liability, as in products liability, respondeat superior, ultrahazardous activity liability and worker's compensation, is based "at least in part on a desire to accomplish better primary accident cost reduction."[106]

In order to achieve these savings, Dean Calabresi suggests a unique test:

> The strict liability test we suggest does not require that a government institution make such a cost-benefit analysis. It requires of such an institution only a decision as to which of the parties to the accident *is in the best position to make the cost-benefit analysis between accident costs and accident avoidance costs and to act on that decision once it is made.* The question for the court reduces to a search for the cheapest cost avoider.[107]

For example, "a violinist is the best evaluator of the relative advantages and costs of working in a steel mill, with regard to the suffering he will feel if he loses his hand."[108]

By presenting an economic test for strict liability, Dean Calabresi has made a substantial contribution to the development of tort theory. However, the cheapest cost-avoider test is framed in nonjudicial terminology and is, therefore, unlikely to be adopted by the courts. In addition, products liability suits usually pit a relatively unsophisticated consumer or user against a knowledgeable seller.[109] In these cases, the cheapest cost avoider is always going to be the seller. To this extent, the Calabresi test reflects absolute liability.

One other qualification needs to be mentioned. Calabresi's theme is that we need to adopt the cheapest cost avoider theory in order to accomplish "primary accident cost reduction." By this he means that we need to save court time and to reduce the number and complexity of the cases that go before the courts. At first blush, that sounds like a laudable goal. We should save the courts for important cases and work to reduce the amount spent on the judicial process. But this flies in the face of realty. The trend has been to dramatically expand the number of actions that are brought before the courts. This growth has been accomplished by means of statute, common law and silly cases. Statutory examples are the Clean Air Act, the Federal Water Pollution Control Act, and the Civil Rights Act. In terms of common law, the leading example is the explosion of asbestos litigation.

The award for the silliest case has to go to the recent America's Cup litigation in the New York courts.[110] Over the past several months, the New York Supreme Court has been trying to decide whether New Zealand's challenge to the San Diego Yacht Club is valid. They are also examining whether Dennis Conner can respond to the challenge with a two-hulled (catamaran) boat rather than a single-hulled boat.[111] The point is that if the courts can be used to answer trivial yacht-racing questions, the limits to jurisdiction are very broad indeed. Further, it suggests that few, other than Dean Calabresi, are concerned with reducing the number of cases that go before the courts.

Absolute Liability

One approach to products liability is absolute liability: hold the seller liable for all injuries caused by the product, with no defenses other than cause in fact. Absolute liability was first suggested as a basis for products liability by Justice Traynor in *Escola v. Coca-Cola.*[112] "In my opinion it should now be recognized that a manufacturer incurs an absolute liability when an article that he has placed on the market, knowing that it is to be used without inspection, proves to have a defect that causes injury to human beings."[113] He reasoned that "the risk of injury can be insured by the manufacturer and distributed among the public as a cost of doing business."[114]

The far-reaching scope of absolute liability has led the courts and the commentators to reject it. Professor Calabresi, for example, concluded: "Strict liability has never meant that the party held strictly liable is to be a general insurer of the victim no matter how or where the victim comes to grief."[115] Dean Keeton reported, "[T]he product must be defective as marketed in order to subject the manufacturer to liability."[116] No court has followed Traynor's position on absolute liability.[117]

Strict liability is not absolute liability. The seller is not an insurer and is not liable for all injuries caused by the product. The scope of liability is the central question in strict liability cases, and the answer to the question is determined by the concept of defect.[118] Although the only issue in absolute liability is cause in fact, there are several defenses available to a strict liability action. These may include: assumption of the risk, misuse, comparative fault and proximate cause.

Causation

Professor Richard Epstein redefines the common tort theories in developing a doctrine of strict liability resting upon causation: "[T] he concept of causation, as it applies to cases of physical injury, can be analyzed in a matter [*sic*] that both renders it internally coherent and relevant to the ultimate question who shall bear the loss."[119] He rejects the traditional two-step, cause in fact and proximate cause analysis of causation.[120] Epstein transforms many of the basic tort concepts to such an extent that it is unlikely that his theory will gain much of a judicial following.[121] For example, he states, "Negligence and intent should be immaterial to the prima facie case of assault, and for the same reasons as with trespass,"[122] and "There will be no attempt to give a single semantic equivalent to the concept of causation."[123]

Epstein's theory is a throwback to the absolute liability of the 1400s: "Briefly put, the argument is that proof of the proposition *A* hit *B* should be sufficient to establish a prima facie case of liability. . . . The choice is plaintiff or defendant, and the analysis of causation is the tool which, prima facie, fastens responsibility upon the defendant."[124] Just as the term "foreseeability" has failed by becoming overloaded, Epstein's attempt to make causation solve all of torts' problems has proven unsuccessful.[125]

Defect: A Functional Test

The history of strict liability in the products area reflects a movement away from the restrictive concepts of privity and toward a clear statement of the operative policies to be considered in deciding whether a manufacturer should be held liable for the damages caused by his product.[126] These policies define the defect concept. One reason for confusion is the failure to analyze the function of the defect concept in products liability litigation. There is a need, therefore, to examine the defect test in terms of the allocation of authority between the court and the jury.

The keystone concept in strict liability is defect. It is a matter of social policy for the court to decide as part of its responsibility in controlling the jury. Through the concept of defect, the courts implement the values of the American society. The question before the court is the appropriate amount of safety in the product. The answer depends upon an examination of various factors. For example, the effectiveness of a Jeep's roll bar,[127] the placement of a Pinto's gas tank,[128] the front end of a Volkswagen bus[129] and the top speed of a Chevrolet[130] are all matters of social policy. Of course, there may be questions of fact involved in the case, such as whether the explosion resulted from the gas tank hitting the differential or from a bystander lighting a match. Such cause in fact questions are left to the jury.[131] If the defect question is such that "reasonable minds could not differ," then the court should direct a verdict. For example, if the court found that a driver's inability to see a child's bike at night could be cured by a fifty-cent reflector, the court could direct a verdict for the plaintiff on the question of defect.[132] If the court has doubts about whether the product is defective, then the question of defect should be given to the jury.

The court's test for whether the product is defective involves a balancing of operative factors. First, the court must consider that the primary reasons for strict liability are to shift the loss from the consumer to the seller and that the loss should be borne by the person who created it.[133] This is given substantial consideration. Second, the court should weigh (1) the product's utility, including style or aesthetic appeal;[134] (2) the alternative designs;[135] (3) the substitute products;[136] (4) the likelihood of injury;[137] (5) the nature of the injury;[138] (6) the cost of making the product safer;[139] (7) the availability and effectiveness of warnings;[140] (8) the ability of the seller to obtain insurance or otherwise carry the loss;[141] (9) the impact upon society of finding the product defective;[142] and (10) the experimental nature of the product.[143] This is not an exclusive list, and the court may consider other factors that it deems relevant.

Primary weight is given to shifting the loss to the seller because that is the foundational reason for strict liability. The list of ten factors is examined only to discover if there is some reason why the loss should not be placed on the seller. No priority is given among the ten secondary factors because the weight allocated to each factor will vary with the facts of the case. For example, cost is the key factor in deciding whether a child's bicycle should have factory-installed reflectors.[144] Prevention and cost are both involved in deciding whether a forage wagon should have protective covers on the conveyor belt,[145] and the utility (the cargo-carrying ability) of the Volkswagen bus is the most important policy in deciding whether the engine should be placed in the front or the rear.[146]

The functional test clearly informs the court of the primary precedential reason for strict liability: loss shifting.[147] Placing the loss on the seller is important because the consumer usually lacks insurance and expertise, and the seller is best able to change the product or engage in safety research. In addition, the functional test states the policies that are relevant to holding a manufacturer liable. It avoids "squid function" words such as proximate cause and foreseeability.[148] The test excises negligence from strict liability, except to the extent that the "likelihood of injury" is retained. This is a relevant consideration, but not necessarily determinative. The test is not whether the seller was negligent, but whether, after balancing all of the operative factors–including the foundational concept of loss shifting–the seller of the product should be held liable. The test assumes that strict liability is not absolute liability and that the seller is not in all cases an insurer of plaintiff's loss.[149]

In strict liability the scales of justice are tipped in favor of the consumer. This is accomplished by telling the court and the jury to consider the policy of loss shifting. Under negligence, on the other hand, the scales are tipped in favor of the seller. With absolute liability, if the seller caused the injury, he or she will be liable. There is still balancing to be done in strict liability, but only after the scales are preweighted to favor the consumer.

Little agreement on the formulation of jury instructions covering defect exists.[150] Several approaches to the problem have been suggested. First, Dean Wade's factors[151] might be submitted to the jury to weigh in deciding whether the product was defective. This approach has been criticized on the basis that the jury is not sophisticated enough to handle the subtle issues involved in weighing complex factors.[152] Second, the jury might simply be asked: "Was the product defective?"[153] A third approach emerged in *Barker v. Lull Engineering*,[154] in which the California Supreme Court was faced with an important issue: whether the trial court could define defect, or whether it must ask the jury to determine, "[W]as the product defective?"[155] The court responded that the charge to the jury in a strict liability case has two elements:

> [I]n design defect cases, a court may properly instruct the jury that a product is defective in design if (1) the plaintiff proves that the product failed to perform as safely as an ordinary consumer would expect when used in an intended or reasonably foreseeable manner, or (2) the plaintiff proves that the product's

design proximately caused injury and that defendant fails to prove, in light of the relevant factors, that on balance the benefits of the challenged design outweigh the risk of danger inherent in such design.[156]

I have critiqued *Barker v. Lull Engineering* earlier in this chapter.

A better approach is to charge the jury with the same test for defect that I have suggested should be used by the court in deciding whether there is sufficient evidence of defect to give the jury. That is, the jury should be charged to first consider the primary policy of shifting the loss to the seller. They should be told that they can find the defendant not liable if one or more of the ten factors proves to outweigh the threshold policy.[157] In reply to those who argue that the jury is too unsophisticated to evaluate such complex issues as loss shifting, substitution of other products and prevention of injury, it must be remembered that the products liability jury likely has gone through weeks or months of expert testimony on such complex questions as modification costs, alternatives, utility of the product, metal stress, attractiveness of the product and sales problems.[158] The jury should be charged to weigh what they have heard during the trial, which is, in large part, social policy. To do otherwise is to force attorneys to emphasize concepts such as proximate cause, foreseeability and remoteness, which will mislead the jury.[159]

Strict liability has emerged out of actions against businesses related to the purpose of the enterprises: selling products. In contrast, negligence was developed largely to handle disputes between individuals. When a corporation was a defendant in a negligence suit, the activity in issue usually was incidental to the purpose of the enterprise, for example, a train setting a field on fire.[160] The court, in deciding the negligence issue, first decided the case and then stated the result in vague terms such as "foreseeability" and "proximate cause."[161]

In deciding strict products liability cases, the courts very early recognized that they were dealing with manufacturers, wholesalers and retailers.[162] They realized that vague phrases were inadequate for dealing with these defendants and, therefore, rested their strict liability decisions on operational factors, such as loss shifting, insurance and modification costs.[163] The functional test implements this unarticulated judicial perception.

The functional test for defect accurately reflects the products liability cases beginning in 1842. It draws a line between negligence and absolute liability, while using a framework that is familiar to the courts. It presents the operative factors that the courts have used in deciding products cases and reestablishes the role of loss shifting that was in place until the erroneous interpretation found in Restatement (Second) of Torts section 402A.

The strengths of the functional approach to defect are that (1) it avoids the vague proximate cause phrases, such as "foreseeable" and "remote"; (2) it points the court toward the operational factors that it should consider in deciding whether to send the case to the jury; (3) it directs the jury toward the factors that they should weigh in deciding whether to hold the defendant liable; (4) it presents a test that is more concrete and predictable than negligence; (5) it retains sufficient flexibility to allow a just result; (6) it recognizes that products liability suits involve highly technical issues; and (7) it strikes a balance among the competing interests of the consumer, the seller, technological development and society.

An important goal of the functional approach to defect is to promote analysis. Appellate court opinions weighing the operational factors will be of predictive benefit to the trial courts and the sellers. If juries are instructed to evaluate the operative factors, they are not as likely to be confused as when they are asked "whether the seller would be negligent if he sold the article knowing of the risk involved," or whether the defendant's product was the "proximate cause" of the injury.

While negligence attempts to balance the consumer against the seller, strict liability works to provide medical care and other compensation to the injured plaintiff. At the same time, extreme cases can be decided on the basis that the operative factors outweigh the policy of loss shifting. Under almost any of the nine tests for strict liability, however, the consumer will likely win more often than under a negligence test.

NOTES

1. W. PROSSER, HANDBOOK OF THE LAW OF TORTS 149-80 (4th ed. 1971) [hereinafter cited as PROSSER].

2. *See* Greenman v. Yuba Power Prods., Inc., 59 Cal. 2d 57, 377 P. 2d 897, 27 Cal. Rptr. 697 (1963).

3. RESTATEMENT (SECOND) OF TORTS § 402A (1965).

4. *Compare e.g.,* Phillips v. Kimwood Mach. Co., 269 Or. 485, 525 P. 2d 1033 (1974) *with* Barker v. Lull Eng'g Co., 20 Cal. 3d 413, 573 P. 2d 443, 143 Cal.

Rptr. 225 (1978); and *compare* Keeton, *Product Liability and the Meaning of Defect*, 5 ST. MARY'S L. J. 30, 37-38 (1973) *with* Donaher, Peihler, Twerski & Weinstein, *The Technological Expert in Products Liability Litigation*, 52 TEX. L. REV. 1303, 1307 (1974).

5. Defects in products are of two kinds: manufacturing defects and design defects. A manufacturing defect is simple to identify because the article can be compared with similar articles made by the same manufacturer—for example, the case of a fly in a soft drink. In the case of a product that is claimed to be defective because of a design defect, the process is not as easy. All the products made to a defective design are the same, such as Volkswagen vans with the engines in the rear. When the plaintiff argues design defect, he raises critical social policy issues.

6. As Dean Keeton has written:

> There are two main points to emphasize. First, when plaintiff seeks to recover for harm resulting from an alleged defective product on a theory of strict liability, rather than negligence, he is not relieved from the burden of showing a defect in the product which was likely present when the maker surrendered possession and control. Second, when negligence is the basis for recovery, proof of the same two requirements will normally serve as circumstantial evidence sufficient for a finding on the part of the jury that the defect was the result of the maker's negligence. . . . Therefore, while strict liability obviates the necessity for convincing the jury as to the existence of negligence, it does not alter in any substantial way the plaintiff's proof problems, and the satisfaction of plaintiff's proof requirements for strict liability will generally result also in a finding of negligence.

Keeton, *Manufacturer's Liability: The Meaning of "Defect" in the Manufacture and Design of Products*, 20 SYRACUSE L. REV. 559, 563 (1969).

"*Improper Design.* There is little difference here between the negligence action and the action for strict liability." Wade, *On the Nature of Strict Tort Liability for Products*, 44 MISS. L. J. 825, 841 (1973).

"Thus, the test for imposing strict liability is whether the product was unreasonably dangerous, to use the words of the Restatement. . . . It may be argued that this is simply a test of negligence. Exactly." Wade, *Strict Tort Liability of Manufacturers*, 19 SW. L. J. 5, 15 (1965).

7. *See, e.g.*, Barker v. Lull Eng'g Co., 20 Cal. 3d 413, 573 P. 2d 443, 143 Cal. Rptr. 225 (1978):

> In *Cronin*, we reviewed the development of the strict product liability doctrine in California . . . and concluded that . . . the "unreasonably dangerous" element which section 402A of the Restatement (Second) of Torts had introduced into the definition of a defective product should not be incorporated into a plaintiff's burden of proof in a product liability action.

Id. at 417, 573 P.2d at 446, 143 Cal. Rptr. at 228.

> The result of the limitation [unreasonably dangerous] . . . has not been merely to prevent the seller from becoming an insurer. . . . Rather, it has burdened the injured plaintiff with proof of an element which rings of negligence. . . . Yet the very purpose of our pioneering efforts in this field was to relieve the plaintiff from problems of proof inherent in pursuing negligence.

Cronin v. J. B. E. Olson Corp., 8 Cal. 3d 121, 132-33, 501 P.2d 1153, 1161-62, 104 Cal. Rptr. 443, 441-42 (1972). "To establish the manufacturer's liability [in strict liability] it was sufficient that plaintiff proved that he was injured . . . as a result of a defect in design and manufacture of which plaintiff was not aware." Greenman v. Yuba Power Prods., Inc., 59 Cal. 2d 57, 64, 377 P.2d 897, 901, 27 Cal. Rptr. 697, 701 (1963).

8. PROSSER, *supra* note 1, at 143, 144, 236-50.

9. 159 F.2d 169 (2d Cir. 1947).

10. *Id.* at 173.

11. Palsgraf v. Long Island R. R. Co., 248 N.Y. 339, 162 N.E. 99 (1928).

12. As Dean Green has noted:

> In later years they [the courts] have become exceedingly timid in discussing the policies which lie at the base of liability based upon negligent conduct. Instead they lower the curtain of "proximate cause" and seldom disclose the policies at the base of their decisions. They seem to think that they are in some way bound by the jury formula of "foreseeability" and that it somehow provides a yardstick for them. . . . Surrender of their rightful function to this shibboleth has become so habitual that the forthright discussion of the limits of liability in a negligence case, out of the thousands reported every year, is almost unheard of. Instead the books are loaded with pages of repetitious and meaningless quotations . . . about "proximate cause" with scarcely a vital thought in volume.

Green, *Proximate Cause in Texas Negligence Law* (pt. 2), 28 TEX L. REV. 621; *id.* (pt. 3), 28 TEX L. REV. 775 (1950). *See generally id.* (pt. 1), 28 TEX L. REV. 471; *id.* (pt. 2), 28 TEX L. REV. 621; *id.* (pt. 3), 28 TEX L. REV. 755 (1950) [hereinafter cited as *Proximate Cause*]. *Compare* Dean Green's position *with* Judge Friendly's in *In re* Kinsman Transit Co., 388 F.2d 281 (2d Cir. 1968).

13. PROSSER, *supra* note 1, at 143.

14. *Id.* at 240.

15. *Proximate Cause* (pt. 1), *supra* note 12, at 474-76.

16. *See* Overseas Tankship (U.K.) Ltd. v. Morts Dock and Eng'g Co. (Wagon Mound No. 1), [1961] A.C. 388; PROSSER, *supra* note 1, at 236.

17. PROSSER, *supra* note 1, at 143.

18. Posner, *A Theory of Negligence*, 1 J. LEGAL STUD. 29, 32 (1972). For a critique of Posner's economic theory of negligence, *see* Epstein, *A Theory of Strict Liability*:

> This common sense approach to torts as a branch of common law stands in sharp opposition to much of the recent scholarship on the subject because it does not regard economic theory as the primary means to establish the rules of legal responsibility. A knowledge of the economic consequences of alternative legal arrangements can be of great importance, but even among those who analyze tort in economic terms there is acknowledgment of certain questions of "justice" or "fairness" rooted in common sense beliefs that cannot be explicated in terms of economic theory.

2 J. LEGAL STUD. 151 (1973).

19. Posner, *supra* note 18, at 29, 32.

20. Epstein, *A Theory of Strict Liability*, 2 J. LEGAL STUD. 151, 154 (1973). Learned Hand may never have fully accepted the *Carroll Towing* formula. In 1962 Laurence H. Eldredge stated at the American Law Institute's Discussion of Restatement (Second) of Torts:

> I remember Judge Learned Hand, Mr. Chairman, at one of our conferences up in Northeast Hartford in the 1930's made a statement that if he could rewrite the tort law of America he would impose a rule of absolute liability in all cases in which a defendant could protect himself by liability insurance.

39 ALI PROCEEDINGS 233 (1962).

21. Posner, *supra* note 18, at 29.

22. *See* Green, *The Duty Problem in Negligence Cases* (pts. 1 & 2), 28 COLUM. L. REV. 1014 (1928), 29 COLUM. L. REV. 255 (1929); *Proximate Cause* (pts. 1-3), *supra* note 12.

23. *Proximate Cause* (pt. 3), *supra* note 12, at 755-56.

24. Green, *The Duty Problem in Negligence Cases* (pts. 1 & 2), 28 COLUM. L. REV. 1014 (1928), 29 COLUM. L. REV. 255 (1929); *Proximate Cause* (pt. 3), *supra* note 12, at 758-59.

25. *See* PROSSER, *supra* note 1, at 244-45; PROXIMATE CAUSE (pt. 1), *supra* note 12, at 473.

26. *See generally* Green, *The Duty Problem in Negligence Cases* (pts. 1 & 2), 28 COLUM. L. REV. 1014 (1928), 29 COLUM. L. REV. 255 (1929).

27. *See* PROSSER, *supra* note 1, at 244-89. For a case applying many of the proximate cause tests at the same time, *see* Martin v. Southern Bell Tel. and Tel. Co., 126 Ga. App. 809, 192 S.E.2d 176 (1972).

28. *See, e.g.*, *In re* Kinsman Transit Co., 338 F.2d 708 (2d Cir. 1964); *In re* Kinsman Transit Co., 388 F.2d 821 (2d Cir. 1968). Judge Coulson was to the point: "General Motors concedes that it could foresee that its products would be

involved in accidents of an infinite variety, including roll-overs. Its argument is that foreseeability cannot be equated with duty. . . . If duty were commensurate with foreseeability, then an automobile manufacturer would be an insurer."

29. *Proximate Cause* (pt. 3), *supra* note 12, at 758.

30. *See Proximate Cause* (pt. 3), *supra* note 12, at 755.

31. Dean Green indicated that the following are some of the factors that can be weighed by the courts in deciding the scope of liability in negligence cases: lack of precedent, flood of litigation, administrative impracticality, no limitation on liability, immorality, hardship, injustice, ability to carry the risk, changed social conditions, economics and prevention. *Proximate Cause* (pt. 3), *supra* note 12, at 757 n. 4; Green, *The Duty Problem in Negligence Cases* (pt. 1), 28 COLUM. L. REV. 1014, 1034-44 (1928).

32. Overseas Tankship (U.K.) Ltd. v. Morts Dock and Eng'g Co., [1961] A.C. 388.

33. *In re* Arbitration Between Polemis and Furness, Withy & Co., [1921] 3 K.B. 560.

34. *Id.* at 575, 577.

35. 197 N.W. 2d 678 (N.D. 1972).

36. *Id.* at 684.

37. 126 Ga. App. 385, 190 S.E. 2d 815 (1972).

38. Professor Posner has suggested:

> It is time to take a fresh look at the social function of liability for negligent acts. . . . In a negligence case, Hand said, the judge (or jury) should attempt to measure three things: the magnitude of the loss if an accident occurs; the probability of the accident's occurring; and the burden of taking precautions that would avert it.

Posner, *A Theory of Negligence*, 1 J. LEGAL STUD. 29, 32 (1972).

> It is fundamental that the standard of conduct which is the basis of the law of negligence is determined by balancing the risk, in the light of the social value of the interest threatened, and the probability and extent of the harm, against the value of the interest which the actor is seeking to protect, and the expedience of the course pursued.

PROSSER, *supra* note 1, at 149.

39. To this extent, the evaluation of factors in strict liability compares with duty analysis as presented by Dean Green. *See generally* Green, *The Duty Problem in Negligence Cases* (pts. 1 & 2), 28 COLUM. L. REV. 1014 (1928), 29 COLUM. L. REV. 255 (1929). Dean Green's work has helped clarify analysis for academicians more than for judges, however. The courts still rely on proximate cause and foreseeability. *See generally Proximate Cause* (pts. 1-3), *supra* note 12.

40. Turner v. General Motors Corp., 514 S.W. 2d 497 (Tex. Civ. App. 1974).

41. *See* Spano v. Perini Corp., 25 N.Y. 2d 11, 250 N.E. 2d 31, 302 N.Y.S. 2d 527, *on remand*, 33 A.D. 2d 516, 304 N.Y.S. 2d 15 (1969). The *Spano* court uses the term "absolute liability," but since the defense of assumption of risk would be available, "strict liability" is a more accurate term. *See* W. PROSSER, J. WADE & V. SCHWARTZ, CASES AND MATERIALS ON TORTS 15 (6th ed. 1976).

42. "The question . . . was not *whether* it was lawful or proper to engage in blasting but *who* should bear the cost of any resulting damage—the person who engaged in the dangerous activity or the innocent neighbor injured thereby." *Spano*, 25 N.Y. 2d 11, 17, 250 N.E. 2d 31, 34, 302 N.Y.S. 2d 527, 532 (1960) (emphasis in original).

43. *See* RESTATEMENT (SECOND) OF TORTS § 520C (1977).

44. 3 H. & C. 774 (Ex. 1865), *rev'd*, [1866] L.R. 1 Ex. 265, *aff'd*, [1868] L.R. 3 H.L. 330.

45. Blasting neatly fits the Section 520 formula. It involves a high degree of risk and great harm, and risk cannot be eliminated by the exercise of reasonable care. It is not a matter of common usage, is often inappropriate to the place where it is carried on and has a substantial value to the community. By comparison, most other activities, such as mountain land development in California, do not quite fit. *See* Beck v. Bel Air Properties, Inc., 134 Cal. App. 2d 834, 286 P. 2d 503 (1955). *But see* Cities Serv. Co. v. State, 312 So. 2d 799 (Fla. Dist. Ct. App. 1975).

46. *See, e.g.*, Spano v. Perini Corp., 25 N.Y. 2d 11, 250 N.E. 2d 31, 302 N.Y.S. 2d 527 (1969). *See also* RESTATEMENT (SECOND) OF TORTS § 520D (1977).

47. *See* Spano v. Perini Corp., 25 N.Y. 2d 11, 250 N.E. 2d 31, 302 N.Y.S. 2d 527 (1969); Rylands v. Fletcher, 3 H. & C. 774 (Ex. 1865), *rev'd*, [1866] L.R. 1 Ex. 265, *aff'd*, [1868] L.R. 3 H.L. 330.

48. Rylands v. Fletcher, 3 H. & C. 774 (Ex. 1865), *rev'd*, [1866] L.R. 1 Ex. 265, *aff'd*, [1868] L.R. 3 H.L. 330, 338-39.

49. *See* F. HARPER & F. JAMES, LAW OF TORTS 28 (4th ed. 1971); Newark, *Non-Natural User and* Rylands v. Fletcher, 24 MOD. L. REV. 557 (1961); Stallybrass, *Dangerous Things and the Non-Natural User of Land*, 3 CAMBRIDGE L. J. 376 (1929).

50. 32 Misc. 2d 955, 223 N.Y.S. 2d 692, *aff'd*, 16 A.D. 2d 659, 226 N.Y.S. 2d 1022, *appeal dismissed*, 11 N.Y. 2d 1053, 184 N.E. 2d 180, 230 N.Y.S. 2d 207 (1961).

51. *See* Spano v. Perini Corp., 25 N.Y.S. 2d 11, 250 N.E. 2d 31, 302 N.Y.S. 2d 527 (1969).

52. Cities Serv. Co. v. State, 312 So. 2d 799, 803 (Fla. Dist. Ct. App. 1975).

53. *See id.* at 804; Spano v. Perini Corp., 25 N.Y.S. 2d 11, 250 N.E. 2d 31, 34, 302 N.Y.S. 2d 527, 532 (1969).

54. Baxter v. Ford Motor Co., 168 Wash. 456, 12 P. 2d 409 (1932).

55. *See, e.g.*, Henningsen v. Bloomfield Motors, 32 N.J. 358, 161 A.2d 69 (1960).

56. *Id.* "In such a marketing milieu his remedies and those of persons who properly claim through him should not depend 'upon the intricacies of the law of sales.' It should rest . . . upon 'the demands of social justice.'" *Id.* at 384, 161 A.2d at 83.

57. *Id.* at 379, 161 A.2d at 81.

58. *See* PROSSER, *supra* note 1, at 650-56.

59. *Id.*

60. 32 N.J. at 379, 161 A.2d at 81 (1960).

61. RESTATEMENT (SECOND) OF TORTS § 402A (1965).

62. *See* Barker v. Lull Eng'g Co., 20 Cal. 3d 413, 573 P.2d 443, 143 Cal. Rptr. 225 (1978); Cronin v. J. B. E. Olson Corp., 8 Cal. 3d 121, 501 P.2d 1153, 104 Cal. Rptr. 443 (1972).

63. RESTATEMENT (SECOND) OF TORTS § 402A comment i states:

> Many products cannot possibly be made entirely safe for all consumption, and any food or drug necessarily involves some risk of harm, if only from over-consumption. Ordinary sugar is a deadly poison to diabetics and castor oil found use under Mussolini as an instrument of torture. That is not what is meant by "unreasonably dangerous" in this Section. The article sold must be dangerous to an extent beyond that which would be contemplated by the ordinary consumer who purchases it, with the ordinary knowledge common to the community as to its characteristics. Good whiskey is not unreasonably dangerous merely because it will make some people drunk, and is especially dangerous to alcoholics; but bad whiskey, containing a dangerous amount of fusel oil, is unreasonably dangerous.

64. *See* Barker v. Lull Eng'g Co., 20 Cal. 3d 413, 425, 573 P.2d 443, 451, 143 Cal. Rptr. 225, 233 (1978).

65. *See* Cronin v. J. B. E. Olson Corp., 8 Cal. 3d 121, 132-33, 501 P.2d 1153, 1162, 104 Cal. Rptr. 433, 442 (1972).

66. Keeton, *Product Liability and the Meaning of Defect*, 5 ST. MARY'S L.J. 30, 32 (1973); Wade, *On the Nature of Strict Tort Liability for Products*, 44 MISS. L.J. 825, 829-38 (1973).

67. *See, e.g.*, Greenman v. Yuba Power Prods., Inc., 59 Cal. 2d 57, 377 P.2d 897, 27 Cal. Rptr. 697 (1963); Escola v. Coca-Cola Bottling Co., 24 Cal. 2d 453, 150 P.2d 436 (1944); Henningsen v. Bloomfield Motors, 32 N.J. 358, 161 A.2d 69 (1960).

68. 38 ALI PROCEEDINGS 87-88 (1961).

69. *See generally* PROSSER, *supra* note 1, at 139-205.

70. Wade, *On the Nature of Strict Tort Liability for Products*, 44 MISS. L.J. 825, 831 (1973).

71. *Id.*

72. *See* Keeton, *Products Liability–Design Hazards and the Meaning of Defect*, 10 CUM. L. REV. 293, 313 (1979). *See also* Wade, *On the Nature of Strict Tort Liability for Products*, 44 MISS L.J. 825, 828, 835 (1973).

73. Keeton, *Product Liability and the Meaning of Defect*, 5 ST. MARY'S L.J. 30, 37-38 (1973) (emphasis in original). *See* Wade, *On the Nature of Strict Tort Liability for Products*, 44 MISS. L.J. 825, 830-38 (1973). *But see* Donaher, Piehler, Twerski & Weinstein, *The Technological Expert in Products Liability Litigation*, 52 TEX. L. REV. 1303, 1307 (1974).

74. Keeton, *Products Liability–Design Hazards and the Meaning of Defect*, 10 CUM L. REV. 293, 314 (1979).

75. *Id.* at 314.

76. *Id.*

77. The California court recognized in 1972 that the Restatement's "unreasonably dangerous" test would force the plaintiff to prove negligence. Cronin v. J. B. E. Olson Corp., 8 Cal. 3d 121, 132-33, 501 P. 2d 1153, 1162, 104 Cal. Rptr. 433, 442 (1972). This was affirmed in 1978. Barker v. Lull Eng'g Co., 20 Cal. 3d 413, 433, 573 P. 2d 443, 456, 143 Cal. Rptr. 225, 238 (1978).

78. Keeton, *Products Liability–Design Hazards and the Meaning of Defect*, 10 CUM. L. REV. 293, 314-15 (1974).

79. Barker v. Lull Eng'g Co., 20 Cal. 3d 413, 432, 573 P. 2d 443, 455-56, 143 Cal. Rptr. 225, 237-38 (1978).

80. *Id.* at 433, 573 P. 2d at 456, 143 Cal. Rptr. at 238.

81. *Id.*

82. Wade, *On the Nature of Strict Tort Liability for Products*, 44 MISS. L.J. 825, 825, 829 (1973).

83. *Proximate Cause* (pt. 3), *supra* note 12, at 758-59.

84. *See* Wade, *On the Nature of Strict Tort Liability for Products*, 44 MISS. L.J. 825, 837-41 (1973).

85. Phillips v. Kimwood Mach. Co., 269 Or. 485, 492, 525 P. 2d 1033, 1036 (1974).

86. *See* Keeton, *Manufacturer's Liability: The Meaning of "Defect" in the Manufacture and Design of Products*, 20 SYRACUSE L. REV. 559, 568 (1969); Wade, *Strict Tort Liability of Manufacturers*, 19 SW. L.J. 5, 15-16 (1965).

87. Wade, *Strict Tort Liability of Manufacturers*, 19 SW. L.J. 5, 15 (1965).

88. Keeton, *Manufacturer's Liability: The Meaning of "Defect" in the Manufacture and Design of Products*, 20 SYRACUSE L. REV. 559, 568 (1969).

89. *See* discussion in Phillips v. Kimwood Mach. Co., 269 Or. 485, 492 n. 6, 525 P. 2d 1033, 1036 n. 6 (1974).

90. *See e.g.*, Barker v. Lull Eng'g Co., 20 Cal. 3d 413, 573 P. 2d 443, 143 Cal. Rptr. 225 (1978); Cronin v. J. B. E. Olson Corp., 8 Cal. 3d 121, 501 P. 2d 1153, 104 Cal. Rptr. 433 (1972).

91. *See* Prosser, *The Fall of the Citadel (Strict Liability to the Consumer)*, 50 MINN. L. REV. 791, 840–45 (1966).

92. *See* Barker v. Lull Eng'g Co., 20 Cal. 3d 413, 573 P. 2d 443, 143 Cal. Rptr. 225 (1978); Cronin v. J. B. E. Olson Corp., 8 Cal. 3d 121, 501 P. 2d 1153, 104 Cal. Rptr. 443 (1972).

93. *See* Sindell v. Abbott Labs., 26 Cal. 3d 588, 607 P. 2d 924, 163 Cal. Rptr. 132, *cert. denied*, 449 U.S. 912 (1980).

94. *Id.*

95. *See* Borel v. Fiberboard Paper Prods. Corp., 493 F. 2d 1076 (5th Cir. 1973), *cert. denied*, 419 U.S. 869 (1974).

96. *See* Cipollone v. Liggett Group, Inc., 789 F. 2d 181 (3d Cir. 1986).

97. Green, *Strict Liability Under Sections 402A and 402B: A Decade of Litigation*, 54 TEX. L. REV. 1185, 1188 (1976).

98. *Id.* at 1191.

99. *Id.*

100. *Id.* at 1190.

101. Some of the most conceptually difficult products liability cases are those brought by bystanders. *See, e.g.*, Elmore v. American Motors Corp., 70 Cal. 2d 578, 451 P. 2d 84, 75 Cal. Rptr. 652 (1969).

102. *See* Borel v. Fiberboard Paper Prods. Corp., 493 F. 2d 1076 (5th Cir. 1973), *cert. denied*, 419 U.S. 869 (1974); Burch v. Amsterdam Corp., 366 A. 2d 1079 (D.C. 1976); Michael v. Warner/Chilcott, 91 N.M. 651, 579 P. 2d 183 (Ct. App. 1978).

103. *See generally* G. CALABRESI, THE COSTS OF ACCIDENTS (1970); Calabresi and Hirschoff, *Toward a Test for Strict Liability in Torts*, 81 YALE L. J. 1055 (1972).

104. Calabresi & Hirschoff, *Toward a Test for Strict Liability in Torts*, 81 YALE L.J. 1055, 1077 (1972). Professor Calabresi has criticized sellers for suggesting a products liability crisis. The sellers want to shift the loss to the consumers or the government, but Professor Calabresi argues that this violates a basic principle of economics: taking risks is what corporations do best. Calabresi, *Product Liability: Curse or Bulwark of Free Enterprise*, 27 CLEV. ST. L. REV. 313, 321 (1978).

Professor Posner appears to define strict liability as absolute liability: "Even if strict liability had no effect whatever on safety, it would have an economic effect: it would compel the manufacturer to insure consumers against accidents resulting from nonnegligent defects in his product." R. POSNER, ECONOMIC ANALYSIS OF LAW 137 (2d ed. 1977). He then criticizes strict liability, thus defined, because it fails to balance cost against benefit. In products cases Professor Posner clearly prefers the negligence approach as defined by Learned Hand. In an apparent oversight, he evaluates contributory negligence and mishandling as defenses to strict liability, but fails to consider the economic impact of assumption of risk in products liability cases. *Id.* at 137–42. *But see id.* at 127–28.

105. Calabresi & Hirschoff, *Toward a Test for Strict Liability in Torts*, 81 YALE L. J. 1055, 1077 (1972).

106. *Id.* at 1075.

107. *Id.* at 1060 (emphasis in original).

108. *Id.* at 1069.

109. *Id.*

110. Atlanta Journal, July 20, 1988, at 8D, col. 1. New York State Supreme Court Justice Carmen Ciparick said: "San Diego violated the spirit of the deed of gift" and ordered the America's cup forfeited to New Zealand. Atlanta Journal, March 29, 1989, at 1A, col. 5.

111. *Id.*

112. 24 Cal. 2d 453, 150 P. 2d 436 (1944).

113. *Id.* at 461, 150 P. 2d at 440 (Traynor, J., concurring).

114. *Id.* at 462, 150 P. 2d at 441.

115. Calabresi & Hirschoff, *Toward a Test for Strict Liability in Torts*, 81 YALE L. J. 1055, 1056 (1972). "General insurance was not the rule in classical instances of strict liability, such as ultrahazardous activities, or in legislatively mandated instances, such as workmen's compensation, and it is not the rule in the recent instances of application such as products liability." *Id.*

116. Keeton, *Product Liability and the Meaning of Defect*, 5 ST. MARY'S L. J. 30, 30–33 (1973).

117. *See, e.g.*, Barker v. Lull Eng'g Co., 20 Cal. 3d 413, 417, 573 P. 2d 443, 446, 143 Cal. Rptr. 225, 228 (1978); Phillips v. Kimwood Mach. Co., 269 Or. 581, 525 P. 2d 1033 (1974).

118. Keeton, *Product Liability and the Meaning of Defect*, 5 ST. MARY'S L. J. 30, 33, 39 (1973).

119. Epstein, *A Theory of Strict Liability*, 2 J. LEGAL STUD. 151, 165 (1973).

120. *Id.* at 160.

121. *Id.* at 160–89. *See also* Epstein, *Defenses and Subsequent Pleas in a System of Strict Liability*, 3 J. LEGAL STUD. 165 (1974).

122. Epstein, *A Theory of Strict Liability*, 2 J. LEGAL STUD. 151, 173 (1973).

123. *Id.* at 165–66.

124. *Id.* at 168–69. *Cf.* Brown v. Kendall, 60 Mass. (6 Cush.) 292 (1850): "These *dicta* are no authority . . . for holding, that damage received by a direct act of force from another will be sufficient to maintain an action of trespass, whether the act was lawful or unlawful, and neither willful, intentional, or careless." *Id.* at 295. Indeed, Professor Epstein reflects the tort law of 1466: "[I] f a man does a thing he is bound to do it in such a manner that by his deed no injury or damage is inflicted upon others." Anonymous, Y.B. 5 Edw. 4, f. 7, pl. 18 (K.B. 1466).

125. *See Proximate Cause* (pts. 1 & 3), *supra* note 12, at 474-90, 771-76.

126. *See* Barker v. Lull Eng'g Co., 20 Cal. 3d 413, 573 P. 2d 443, 143 Cal. Rptr. 225 (1978); Greenman v. Yuba Power Prods., Inc., 59 Cal. 2d 57, 377 P. 2d 897, 27 Cal. Rptr. 697 (1963).

127. *See* Leichtamer v. American Motors Corp., 67 Ohio St. 2d 456, 424 N.E. 2d 568 (1981); Turner v. General Motors Corp., 514 S.W. 2d 497 (Tex. Civ. App. 1974).

128. Grimshaw v. Ford Motor Co., No. 19-77-61 (Orange County (Cal.) Super. Ct., March 30, 1978); Harris, *Why the Pinto Jury Felt Ford Deserved $125 Million Penalty*, Wall St. J., Feb. 14, 1978, at 1, col. 4; Bruck, *How Ford Stalled the Pinto Litigation*, Am. Law., June, 1979, at 23.

129. Dreisonstok v. Volkswagenwerk, A. G., 489 F. 2d 1066 (4th Cir. 1977).

130. In Schemel v. General Motors Corp., 384 F. 2d 802 (7th Cir. 1967), the court apparently wanted to avoid deciding the appropriate maximum speed for a car. The goal was to avoid this administrative quagmire.

131. *See Proximate Cause* (pt. 1), *supra* note 12, at 475.

132. *See* Schwinn Sales South v. Waters, 126 Ga. App. 385, 190 S.E. 2d 815 (1972).

133. This policy was enunciated in Greenman v. Yuba Power Prods., Inc., 59 Cal. 2d 57, 377 P. 2d 897, 27 Cal. Rptr. 697 (1963), and in Escola v. Coca-Cola Bottling Co., 24 Cal. 2d 453, 150 P. 2d 436 (1944).

134. *See, e.g.*, discussion of the boxy Volkswagen van in Dreisonstok v. Volkswagenwerk, A. G., 489 F. 2d 1066 (4th Cir. 1977).

135. *See, e.g.*, the controversy over the location of the Pinto gas tank, Grimshaw v. Ford Motor Co., No. 19-77-61 (Orange County (Cal.) Super. Ct., March 30, 1978); a steam vaporizer with a lid that falls off, with the result that a child is scalded by boiling water, McCormack v. Hankscraft Co., 278 Minn. 322, 154 N.W. 2d 488 (1967); and a fondue pot handle that permits the pot to rotate when hot (and filled with oil), Ellis v. Rich's, Inc., 233 Ga. 573, 212 S.E. 2d 373 (1975).

136. For example, is there a substitute for "red dye number two" as a food coloring? Are there other less dangerous drugs that accomplish the same result? In contrast, there is no substitute for blood. Hines v. St. Joseph's Hosp., 86 N.M. 763, 527 P. 2d 1075 (1974).

137. For example, there is a substantial likelihood of injury from a vaporizer with a nonlocking lid. McCormack v. Hankscraft Co., 278 Minn. 322, 154 N.W. 2d 488 (1967).

138. If there is an injury, will it be minor or serious? Jagged threads on a drum of gasoline are likely to produce an explosion and serious injuries. Gulf Refining Co. v. Williams, 183 Miss. 723, 185 So. 234 (1938).

139. *See* Schwinn Sales South v. Waters, 126 Ga. App. 385, 190 S.E. 2d 815 (1972). Reflectors could be placed on a child's bike by the manufacturer for a few cents.

140. The seller may be liable for failure to include an adequate warning. *See* Crane v. Sears Roebuck & Co., 218 Cal. App. 2d 855, 32 Cal. Rptr. 754 (1963). *See generally* Noel, *Products Defective Because of Inadequate Directions or Warnings*, 23 SW. L. J. 256 (1969); Twerski, Weinstein, Donaher & Piehler, *The Use and Abuse of Warnings in Product Liability–Design Defect Litigation Comes of Age*, 61 CORNELL L. REV. 495 (1976).

141. *See* Greenman v. Yuba Power Prods., Inc., 59 Cal. 2d 57, 377 P. 2d 897, 27 Cal. Rptr. 697 (1963); Henningsen v. Bloomfield Motors, 32 N.J. 358, 161 A. 2d 69 (1960). *See generally* G. CALABRESI, THE COSTS OF ACCIDENTS: A LEGAL AND ECONOMIC ANALYSIS 39-60, 103-25, 168-284, 313-14 (1970).

142. *See* Green, *Proximate Cause* (pt. 3), *supra* note 12, at 757. *See generally* Schemel v. General Motors Corp., 384 F. 2d 802 (7th Cir. 1976).

143. For example, "it is also true . . . of many new or experimental drugs as to which, because of lack of time and opportunity for sufficient medical experience, there can be no assurance of safety . . . but such experience as there is justifies the marketing and use of the drug notwithstanding a medically recognizable risk." RESTATEMENT (SECOND) OF TORTS § 402A comment k (1965). With any experimental product, clear and detailed warnings of risks would, of course, be necessary.

144. *See generally* Schwinn Sales South v. Waters, 126 Ga. App. 385, 190 S.E. 2d 815 (1972).

145. *See* Winnett v. Winnett, 57 Ill. 2d 7, 310 N.E. 2d 1 (1974).

146. Dreisonstok v. Volkswagenwerk, A. G., 489 F. 2d 1066, 1074 (4th Cir. 1974).

147. *See* notes 7, 40, 67, 130, 133.

148. *See generally Proximate Cause* (pts. 1-3), *supra* note 12.

149. *See* Calabresi & Hirschoff, *Toward a Test for Strict Liability in Torts*, 81 YALE L. J. 1055, 1060-68 (1972); Keeton, *Product Liability and the Meaning of Defect*, 5 ST. MARY'S L. J. 30, 30, 33 (1973).

150. *See* Barker v. Lull Eng'g Co., 20 Cal. 3d 413, 427-29, 573 P. 2d 443, 452-53, 143 Cal. Rptr. 225, 234-35 (1978); Phillips v. Kimwood Mach. Co., 269 Or. 485, 499-501, 525 P. 2d 1033, 1040-41 (1974); Keeton, *Product Liability and the Meaning of Defect*, 5 ST. MARY'S L. J. 30, 35-36 (1973).

151. Wade, *Strict Tort Liability of Manufacturers*, 19 SW. L. J. 5, 17 (1965).

152. *See generally* Green, *Strict Liability Under Sections 402A and 402B: A Decade of Litigation*, 54 TEX. L. REV. 1187, 1218-20 (1976); Keeton, *Product Liability and the Meaning of Defect*, 5 ST. MARY'S L. J. 30 (1973).

153. Cronin v. J.B.E. Olson Corp., 8 Cal. 3d 121, 133, 501 P. 2d 1153, 1162, 104 Cal. Rptr. 443, 442 (1972).

154. Barker v. Lull Eng'g Co., 20 Cal. 3d 413, 573 P. 2d 443, 143 Cal. Rptr. 225 (1978).

155. *Id.* at 417, 573 P. 2d at 446, 143 Cal. Rptr. at 228.

156. *Id.* at 426-27, 573 P. 2d at 452, 143 Cal. Rptr. at 234.

157. *See supra* text accompanying notes 133-46.

158. *See* Donaher, Piehler, Twerski & Weinstein, *The Technological Expert in Products Liability Litigation*, 52 TEX. L. REV. 1303, 1310-12 (1974).

159. An alternative to asking the jury to weigh the operative factors presented in this chapter is to ask, "Was the product defective?" This is clear and would force the jury to focus on the product and whether it was defective. It has the value of eliminating the reasonable-man test, avoiding the proximate cause quagmire, and directing the testimony of witnesses toward the operative factors rather than toward how much care the manufacturer exercised. The purpose behind this alternative is to permit the jury to answer the question of defect based on the jurors' experiences in society. This is comparable to the negligence approach in that the question of defectiveness is given to the jury. In a negligence case the question of whether the defendant exercised the care of a reasonable man is given to the jury.

Under this approach there are several important differences between strict liability and negligence. The most important difference is that the jury is asked to look at the product and decide whether it was defective, rather than to look at the conduct of the seller. Another difference is that reasonable care on the part of the seller is, of course, no defense. *See* Cronin v. J.B.E. Olson Corp., 8 Cal. 3d 121, 501 P. 2d 1153, 104 Cal. Rptr. 433 (1972).

160. Anderson v. Minneapolis, St. P & S.ST. M. R.R. Co., 146 Minn. 430, 179 N.W. 45 (1920).

161. *See* PROSSER, *supra* note 1, at 244-70.

162. This is a fair description of the defendants discussed in text accompanying notes 6-32 *supra*.

163. *See* notes 7, 40, 67, 129, 133.

BIBLIOGRAPHY

Bruck, "How Ford Stalled the Pinto Litigation." *Am. Law.* (June, 1979).

Calabresi, G., *The Costs of Accidents: A Legal and Economic Analysis.* (1970).

Calabresi, "Product Liability: Curse or Bulwark of Free Enterprise." 27 *Clev. St. L. Rev.* 313 (1978).

Calabresi & Hirschoff, "Toward a Test for Strict Liability in Torts." 81 *Yale L. J.* 1055 (1972).

Donaher, Peihler, Twerski & Weinstein, "The Technological Expert in Products Liability Litigation." 52 *Tex. L. Rev.* 1303 (1974).

Epstein, "Defenses and Subsequent Pleas in a System of Strict Liability." 3 *J. Legal Stud.* 165 (1974).

Epstein, "A Theory of Strict Liability." 2 *J. Legal Stud.* 151 (1973).

Green, "The Duty Problem in Negligence Cases," (pts. 1-2). 28-29. *Colum. L. Rev.* 1014, 255 (1928, 1929).

Green, "Proximate Cause in Texas Negligence Law" (pts. 1-3). 28 *Tex. L. Rev.* 471, 621, 755 (1950).

Harper, F., & F. James. *Law of Torts* (4th ed. 1971).

Harris, "Why the Pinto Jury Felt Ford Deserved $125 Million Penalty." *Wall St. J.*, Feb. 14, 1978, at 1, col. 4.

Keeton, "Manufacturer's Liability: The Meaning of 'Defect' in the Manufacture and Design of Products." 20 *Syracuse L. Rev.* 599 (1969).

Keeton, "Product Liability and the Meaning of Defect." 5 *St. Mary's L.J.* 30 (1973).

Keeton, "Products Liability–Design Hazards and the Meaning of Defect." 10 *Cum. L. Rev.* 293 (1979).

Newark, "Non-Natural User and *Rylands v. Fletcher.*" 24 *Mod. L. Rev.* 557 (1961).

Noel, "Products Defective Because of Inadequate Directions or Warnings." 23 *SW. L. J.* 256 (1969).

Posner, R. *Economic Analysis of Law* (2d ed. 1977).

Posner, "A Theory of Negligence." 1 *J. Legal Stud.* 29 (1972).

Prosser, "The Fall of the Citadel (Strict Liability to the Consumer)." 50 *Minn. L. Rev.* 791 (1966).

Prosser, W., *Handbook of the Law of Torts* (4th ed. 1971).

Prosser, W., J. Wade, & V. Schwartz, *Cases and Materials on Torts* (6th ed. 1976).

Restatement (Second) of Torts (1965).

Stallybrass, "Dangerous Things & the Non-Natural User of Land." 3 *Cambridge L. J.* 376 (1929).

Twerski, Weinstein, Donaher & Piehler, "The Use and Abuse of Warnings in Products Liability–Design Defect Litigation Comes of Age." 61 *Cornell L. Rev.* 495 (1976).

Wade, "On the Nature of Strict Tort Liability for Products." 44 *Miss L. J.* 825 (1973).

Wade, "Strict Tort Liability of Manufacturers." 19 *Sw. L. J.* 5 (1965).

5

Problems with Negligence-Efficiency Theory and with Traditional Negligence

In order to understand why the courts have become attracted to strict liability, it is necessary to examine the problems with negligence theory. Two branches of negligence will be explored: Judge Posner's economic concept of negligence and traditional negligence. The purpose of this chapter is to manifest that Posner's thesis is wrong in regard to torts. The first section of the chapter addresses Posner's theory; the second section deals with traditional negligence. The conclusion reached is that because the efficiency theory is seriously flawed and traditional negligence is biased against the consumer, strict liability is deserving of serious consideration.

POSNER'S ECONOMIC CONCEPT OF NEGLIGENCE

The essence of Judge Richard A. Posner's negligence-efficiency theory is as follows:

> The essential clue, I believe, is provided by Judge Learned Hand's famous formulation of the negligence standard. . . . In a negligence case, Hand said, the judge (or jury) should attempt to measure three things: the magnitude of the loss if an accident occurs; the probability of the accident's occurring; and the burden of taking precautions that would avert it. If the product of the first two terms exceeds the burden of precautions, the failure to take those precautions is negli-

gence. Hand was adumbrating, perhaps unwittingly, an economic meaning of negligence. . . . If the cost of safety measures . . . exceeds the benefit in accident avoidance to be gained by incurring that cost, society would be better off, in economic terms, to forego accident prevention. . . . Furthermore, overall economic value or welfare would be diminished . . . by incurring a higher accident-prevention cost in order to avoid a lower accident cost.[1]

His position that one merely calculates the costs and the benefits of an activity to decide whether an injurer was negligent is superficial, and his stand that no values are involved in efficiency theory is inaccurate. Because of Posner's embrace of the negligence theory and the impact of his efficiency analysis on personal injury scholarship, there is a need to examine his theory and its foundations.

Efficiency Calculations Involve Value

Posner argues that his efficiency model is value free and therefore unchallengeable.[2] This is wrong. Because our most important values lack a market and cannot be assigned a price, it is not possible to engage in efficiency analysis in regard to personal injuries. That is, since it is not possible to discover a price for love, pain, depression, loss of a child, the burden of raising an unwanted child, supporting the handicapped, or encouraging children to explore, efficiency analysis rests upon speculation. Efficiency also ignores other basic goals: lowering the cost of accidents, compensating victims, and reaching a just result. Further, the price assigned to important values by Posner is certain to reflect the examiner's biases. The costs must be worked out carefully beforehand in order for the desired conclusion to be obtained. Efficiency analysis is loaded with value decisions. Professor Polinsky, an economist, summarizes:

Probably the most difficult problem in undertaking an economic analysis of a legal rule or policy is putting dollar values on the relevant costs and benefits.

. . . .

[T]he practical implementation of economic analysis will usually require a somewhat arbitrary method to determine the value of losses and gains involving nonmarketed or nonstandardized items.

The problem of assigning dollar values to costs and benefits is particularly difficult when life or limb is involved.

. . . .

. . . [C]ritics have suggested that because of the difficulty of quantifying certain costs or benefits, the economic analyst will tend to substitute his own subjective values for these items, and therefore the analysis may simply "confirm" his prior beliefs.[3]

The result of the absence of markets, and therefore prices, for important values is that economic analysis has little to say about personal injury law or policy.[4] Indeed, when an economist enters into the area, he has become a philosopher or politician and is making statements based on his beliefs and feelings. He should be treated with the same dignity reserved for other social scientists, such as historians, psychiatrists and sociologists.[5] In regard to personal injury, it is not clear what insights have been provided through economics, and this is after more than seventeen years of research and numerous law and economics articles and books.

Transaction Costs

One of the pillars underlying Posner's theory is the Coase Theorem.[6] In its barest form, "it states that if transaction costs are zero, then efficiency will be achieved regardless of which party is assigned the property right in a situation of conflicting uses."[7] A transaction cost is any cost involved in the striking of a bargain by two parties.[8] Attorneys' fees, information costs, interest rates, inflation, willingness to discuss a problem, love of the land, feelings toward a neighbor and communication costs are examples of transaction costs. Posner realizes the problem of transaction costs, but does not allow for them in his model.[9] This is strange because these costs are decisive in many situations. Lawyers and economists know that if two neighbors have a conflict, and attorneys' fees, a transaction cost, are substantial, the injured party may either do nothing or engage in self-help, including armed conflict.[10] Transaction costs may often be determinative. Reflecting this, Professor Polinsky concludes: "If there are positive transaction costs, the efficient outcome may not occur under every legal rule."[11] Because Posner assumes away the costs of transactions, his theory is critically flawed.

Externalities

Posner's efficiency calculation includes an unrealistic assumption that externalities need not be considered.[12] An externality is anything that does not directly affect the bargaining positions of each party.[13] Years ago, smoke pollution was viewed as an externality because it did not directly impact the decision of the purchaser of steel or the manufacturer of steel. Today, however, externalities are recognized as being enormously important. An entire law school course, Environmental Law, is devoted to the study of externalities. It considers, for example, water pollution, air pollution, the impact of federal projects upon the environment, and toxic substances.

Proximate cause is the most challenging decision in torts, and the most important element of the proximate cause decision is the impact of the legal rule upon society. In proximate cause analysis it is often not the damages between the parties that are crucial, but rather the impact of the legal decision upon society, an externality. Negligent infliction of mental distress is also an example. The important issue there is the effect on society if victims are permitted to recover for pain that is negligently inflicted. Posner's theory ignores all of this. As a result, Professor Rizzo rejects the artificiality of Posner's position:

> There are a whole array of externalities that the law of torts must . . . consider. Often external costs (or benefits) cannot be measured in a way "which is acceptably objective and nonarbitrary." . . . These externalities cannot be dismissed merely because they are hard to measure. Minimization of social costs differs from the minimization of private costs precisely because there is an absence of complete markets, and this absence is exactly what makes measurements so difficult.[14]

The Flawed Wealth-Maximization Explanation

The foundation of Posner's efficiency theory is wealth maximization.[15] If legal decisions are based on efficiency, then nothing will be wasted and the wealth of the country will be at its maximum. It follows, Posner reasons, that everyone will then be better off.[16] The Achilles' heel of the theory is that in order to conduct efficiency analysis, everything must have a price or be capable of having a price assigned.[17] In truth, there are no markets for personal injury damages. Professor Coleman therefore rejects wealth maximization:

> Unfortunately, the system of wealth maximization has its fair share of drawbacks–many of which arise because of the conceptual or logical connection of wealth maximization to the existence of prices. First, because the reliance on prices is necessary and not merely contingent, the system of wealth maximiza-

tion cannot tell us anything about right conduct where no prices exist. Second, prices are in part the result of demand, demand the result of prior entitlements. Consequently, wealth maximization cannot generate an initial set of entitlements.[18]

Further examination of Coleman's second point is enlightening. Wealth maximization may only be defined within an institutional framework that sets initial allocations of wealth, property and permissible conduct. There is no unique maximization of wealth since different initial institutional arrangements–including legal rules–vary.[19] Samuels and Mercuro, noting the difficulty of using wealth maximization as a basis for determining liability, have argued:

> The problem is not that we do not have the data with which to use wealth maximization. The problem is that wealth maximization does not and cannot itself (even with complete data) determine rights. The rights must be antecedently determined in order to pursue wealth maximization and this antecedent determination is a matter of social control accomplished in the legal area by judicial choice.[20]

Further, even if wealth could be maximized, it does not follow that everyone will be better off, as Posner suggests. There will be losers, perhaps in large numbers.[21]

In contrast to Posner's theory, strict liability has developed as a means of providing compensation to injured persons. It permits the free-market economic system to function and has nothing to do with wealth maximization.

Failure of the Consent Rationale

Because of these problems, Judge Posner was forced to develop a new explanation for efficiency. Recently Posner has argued that the basis for his negligence theory is consent: "[W]ealth maximization . . . derives support from the principle of consent. . . ."[22] Unable to find any way of determining express consent by the injured party to the negligence action, Posner quickly retreated to implied consent: "If there is no reliable mechanism for eliciting express consent . . . we should look for implied consent. . . . This procedure resembles a judge's imputing the intent of parties to a contract that fails to provide expressly for some contingency."[23]

Professor Dworkin rejects Posner's consent explanation as irrelevant:

> Since Posner's argument from consent depends entirely on counterfactual consent ["I would have consented had I been asked"], and since counterfactual consent is in itself irrelevant to political justification, the argument from consent wholly fails. Posner's appeal to "autonomy"—and his associated claim to have captured what is most worthwhile in "Kantian" theories—is wholly spurious.[24]

It appears that Posner has painted himself into a corner in regard to consent. An element of first-year contracts is that implied consent is not consent in fact; it is consent implied by law.[25] Implied consent is whatever the judge says it is and for whatever reasons the judge wishes.[26] In deciding the question of implied consent, the judge can consider the problems of the plaintiff, the nature of consideration and the impact of the decision upon a third party, the law or society. In short, in weighing implied consent, the judge can weigh all sorts of values.[27] Posner has therefore embraced, through implied consent, the devil he wished to avoid: open-ended consideration of social values. Because he has done this, his efficiency position now rests upon a weighing of values, just like traditional negligence.

Efficiency Theory Is Political

Efficiency theory provides predictable political results. Professor Englard notes this in discussing Posner and others:

> Legal formalism bestows upon the rules of law an appearance of being self-contained, apolitical, and logical. The conceptual framework with its inherent pre-established value decisions tends to exclude new policy discussions by reducing the judicial process to a mere rule application. Legal formalism thus may become a tool for legal conservatism in preventing the instrumental use of the law for attaining redistributional goals.[28]

More to the point: "[Efficiency] will now appear as a way to drive *the left* crazy by showing that its naive hopes of reconciling social justice with material plenty are inconsistent with elementary economic laws."[29] Experience has shown this to be true, particularly in regard to environmental reforms, strict liability, products liability and punitive damages.

Also disturbing is the negative impact of efficiency theory upon individual freedom. For example, an individual must surrender his right to bodily security if cheap gas tanks are found to be beneficial to society.[30]

Clearly efficiency theory favors the rich at the expense of the poor: "[T]he [wealth maximization criterion] is inherently biased in favor of wealthier individuals."[31] Professor Dworkin explains with the example of automobile drivers and pedestrians:

> But is is not true that everyone's actual welfare will be improved. For there will be some who will not, in fact, take out the appropriate insurance, and who will be unlucky. They will suffer so much uncompensated loss from nonnegligent accidents that they would have been better off . . . had the court laid down a regime of strict liability. . . .
>
> . . . .
>
> . . . [Y]ou lost more than you gained.[32]

Several examples will manifest how Posner's negligence-efficiency theory makes "tort-feasors" richer at the expense of victims. First, in arriving at prices to be used in Posner's cost-benefit model, it is much easier to develop prices for modification costs, lost sales and reduced profits than for human values such as pain, death and the cost of raising an unwanted child. Indeed, it is likely that attempts to quantify abstract costs, such as damage to quality of life from smoke pollution or encouraging the blind to go about in society, will receive sneers. As a result, the damage side of the equation ("benefits") will tend to be underpriced. The simple conclusion will be that the injurer should not be found negligent.

Second, if we assume that (1) the poor purchase less expensive cars, (2) less expensive cars tend to be more dangerous (even though, admittedly, there are some very expensive sports cars that are less safe than some cheaper cars such as station wagons), and (3) that more of the less expensive cars are sold, then more of the poor than the wealthy will be injured and recover nothing because the manufacturer was not negligent. This analysis will work for most products.

Third, if we assume that the wealthy tend to be the doers (builders, investors and manufacturers), they will benefit from a negligence-efficiency standard. There are two reasons for this: many negligence suits will not be brought because of too little damage, and many will be lost because negligence is hard to prove. Posner's efficiency theory has a built-in preference for the wealthy.

Justice Is the Goal

The core problem with efficiency theory is that it assumes that wealth maximization is the goal of law. It is not. The goal of law is justice.[33] Justice is a much broader and more open-ended inquiry than efficiency. One suspects that the difficulty in devising a formula for justice is a major reason for economists limiting their inquiries to mere efficiency. Of those writing in law and economics, only Calabresi clearly articulates this:

> I have always believed that efficiency and distributional language does not translate directly into justice language; that there are components of the just society that could only be encompassed in the terms efficiency and distribution if these terms were given meaning far different from their ordinary ones.
>
> . . . .
>
> . . . Clearly, the relationship between the instruments (efficiency, distribution) and the goal (justice) needs to be studied.
>
> . . . .
>
> I believe that law-and-economics is concerned with the road signs.[34]

If Judge Posner were to suggest that he never intended actual prices to be used in his cost-benefit formula,[35] it would still be flawed, because Posner's negligence-efficiency theory does not identify the difficult task of a judge: reaching a just result. His formula does not provide a method for addressing the tough questions, such as which direction society should take. It provides no method for dealing with critical issues involving justice, such as, Should children receive special protection?[36] Should a fledgling industry be subsidized?[37] Should lives be favored over highway construction?[38] Should rescues be encouraged?[39] Should the handicapped receive special consideration?[40] Should the insane be liable for their torts?[41]

Failure of the Market Assumption

Posner's efficiency theory rests upon the assumption that victims know all risks and evaluate them before engaging in activities or buying products.[42] Therefore, market analysis can be used to evaluate torts. The truth is that victims usually are unaware of risks connected with their activities or purchases. Over twenty years ago, Calabresi wrote that an "all knowing, all rational economic world . . . does not exist."[43] This is easy to manifest. Ask a nonexpert to explain an automobile differential, a boom vang, or a disc brake caliper. A passenger on an airplane that later crashes has no knowledge of the defect in the engine. Pinto purchasers did not know of the dangerous nature of the car's gas tank. Few patients know of the risks involved in surgery unless they are informed by the physician. Polinsky, an economist, agrees: "This assumption [that consumers have perfect information about expected accident losses] seems especially inappropriate for products that cause harm very infrequently."[44]

Efficiency Analysis Produces Pop Answers

A disturbing aspect of Posner's efficiency theory is that it encourages users of the theory, by plugging numbers into formulas, to give pop answers to serious issues that have troubled society and the legal profession for hundreds of years.[45] The analysis is superficial and the conclusions questionable.[46]

After analyzing Posner's theories, and others, Professor Kelman concluded:

> I . . . firmly believe that the neoclassical orthodoxy that has provided the most significant spark of light in fancy legal academic writing . . . has served a mystifying, obscuring function . . . misleading lawyers and law students through its simplistic elegance not only into what strikes me as a relatively minor sin–misunderstanding law–but a rather serious one as well–misunderstanding social life in general.[47]

Consumers Will Purchase Too Much Under a Negligence Rule

Because consumers often lack knowledge of risks, they will purchase too much under a negligence rule. If they knew of the risks and knew that they would not be compensated for injuries where the seller exercised reasonable care, they would purchase less. This is strong criticism of the negligence rule because it suggests that negligence skews the market toward too much consumption. Reflecting that, Professor Polinsky argues:

> The important point about negligence when consumers underestimate product risks is that . . . consumers will buy too much of the good because they will not fully take into account the accident losses. . . .

. . . .

. . . When consumers underestimate product risks, only the rule of strict liability is efficient both with respect to the care exercised by firms and the purchase decisions of consumers. The rule of negligence can induce producers to take appropriate care, but consumers will purchase too much of the good. . . . Thus, strict liability is, in effect, a substitute for perfect consumer information.[48]

This discussion assumes that consumers are capable of evaluating risk in the first place. That may be false. It may be more accurate to say that people cannot evaluate risk unless it is rather dramatic. What does it mean, for example, to say that an activity is risky? In addition, many have no choice except to engage in risky ventures. The poor often cannot afford a "safe" car or a more experienced doctor.

Efficiency Is Not Related to the Real World

Posner's efficiency theory has little value in dealing with "real-world" problems. Professor Rizzo concludes:

[T]he substantial information requirements that must be satisfied in order to identify efficient legal rules make efficiency impractical as a standard. Unless the efficiency theorists can show how courts can overcome the difficulties outlined here they will continue to argue for a norm that has little operational content. It is all too easy to show that efficiency leads to desirable results within simplified constructs; it is quite another thing to show what this has to do with the world in which we live.[49]

Professor Polinsky suggests that important questions lie outside the training and experience of the economist: "Thus the [efficiency] paradigm reduces questions of public policy to the determination of the most desirable distribution of income. This decision involves a value judgment about whether one person's welfare should be increased at the expense of another's, a judgment outside the scope of the economist's professional expertise."[50]

Professor Kelman is more critical: "[T]he pop version of economics has deluded more people than it has enlightened, and . . . once one moves beyond the pop version, economics gives very little guidance in real disputes."[51]

Efficiency Fails to Address Proximate Cause Issues

Proximate cause is the concept used to address the most challenging questions in tort law. Yet the efficiency theory suggested by Judge Posner fails to address proximate cause issues such as whether damages are foreseeable, direct, remote or natural.[52] In addition, it fails to grapple with criticial, but less obvious, proximate cause issues, such as the impact of the legal decision on third parties or society. Efficiency also fails to ask which party is best able to obtain insurance.[53]

Posner fails to indicate what costs are to be included in the cost-benefit calculation. If all costs of every nature (and all benefits) that result from the activity are to be considered—negligent infliction of mental distress, birth of unwanted child, stock market loss due to being hospitalized as a result of being hit by the injurer's car, Rembrandt painting in trunk of plaintiff's car—then the theory collapses under its own weight. The calculations will be too numerous and far-ranging. Inability to deal with proximate cause issues is a further example of the ivory-tower nature of efficiency theory.

Negligence Is Predictable: Victims Lose

Negligence favors the injurer because the victim has to prove negligence, a heavy burden. What may not be quite so obvious grows out of the goal of negligence to put both parties at equal advantage. A study of negligence manifests that the law struggles to place each party on equal footing. The result of this is that victims are often going to lose. There are several reasons for this. First, many victims will not have sufficient funding to bring a suit (the attorney may refuse to take the case on a contingent fee). Second, the damages may be too small to be worth suing (adding up large numbers of small damages may yield a great savings to injurers, however). Third, the victim may lack the time or be unable to find qualified experts (for a malpractice action, for example) to bring a suit. Fourth, the victim may be unable to discover evidence of negligence.

With the adoption of negligence, it is predictable that victims are going to lose substantially more often than injurers. This realization has persuaded the courts to adopt strict liability.

TRADITIONAL NEGLIGENCE AND PRACTICAL PROBLEMS WITH EFFICIENCY THEORY

This section's purpose is to manifest that there is little relationship between Judge Posner's theory of negligence and the negligence used by traditional scholars and the courts. Let us examine the negligence presented by traditional scholars. Prosser defines it as follows:

> Negligence is a matter of the risk . . . of recognizable danger of injury. It has been defined as "conduct which involves an unreasonably great risk of causing damage," or . . . conduct "which falls below the standard established by law for the protection of others against unreasonably great risk of harm."
>
> . . . .
>
> It is fundamental that the standard of conduct which is the basis of the law of negligence is determined by balancing the risk in light of the social value of the interest threatened and the probability and extent of harm, against the value of the interest which the actor is seeking to protect. . . . For this reason, it is seldom possible to reduce negligence to any definite rules: it is "relative to the need and the occasion. . . ."[54]

From this definition we see that negligence involves a balancing process. In fact, both Posner and Prosser quote Judge Hand.[55] The key difference between Posner's theory and traditional negligence as presented by Prosser is that Prosser does not suggest that the entire negligence process can be reduced to a comparison of numerical costs. The terms used by the traditional authors are vague and unquantifiable: risk, danger, unreasonable, standard established by law, social value, relative, prudent person, foresight, likelihood, seriousness. Indeed, Judge Hand was cognizant that the operative elements of negligence could not be assigned a cost.[56]

Answering the negligence question resembles more closely a philosophical inquiry than solving a calculus formula.[57] It is an open-ended value inquiry, and there are no numbers (costs) because each element of the negligence question, except perhaps cause in fact, involves "incommensurables."[58] There are also no formulas or rules for the negligence inquiry.[59] The main distinction between Posner's formula and traditional negligence is that Posner believes that every important issue in a negligence case can be reduced to a dollar amount and inserted into the cost-benefit formula.[60] Traditional negligence is a balancing process, to be sure, but a balancing of relative social values that have no price: life, love, pain and suffering, for example. When Posner suggests that costs and benefits are to be calculated,[61] he apparently means that numbers should be assigned to costs and benefits, with the result determining whether the plaintiff recovers. The cases reject this.

No negligence case has used the mathematical approach suggested by Posner.[62] An examination of three well-known negligence cases will illustrate the careful weighing of values by the courts—but without any attempt to assign numbers to costs. *Palsgraf*[63] is the best-known case in torts. Mrs. Palsgraf claimed to have been injured when scales fell on her while she was waiting for a train. It appears that when a guard tried to help a stranger onto a train, the stranger dropped a package containing fireworks and they exploded. Mrs. Palsgraf argued that the concussion from the fireworks knocked the scales onto her. No attempt was made by the court to place numbers on the costs and the benefits.[64] (Indeed, it would have been quite a formidable task to identify the costs and benefits in *Palsgraf.*) Posner apparently concedes the point in his torts casebook by avoiding any attempt at applying numbers to the activities involved in *Palsgraf.*[65]

In *Petition of Kinsman Transit Company*[66] the court used a traditional negligence approach and avoided a cost-based solution. In *Kinsman* a huge ship broke loose from its moorings and slammed into another large ship, which also broke loose. The two ships then collided with a bridge and dammed the Buffalo River, which was filled with ice. As a result, the river flooded and the plaintiff's riverside property was damaged. Judge Friendly, in finding for the plaintiff, echoed Judge Hand's theory, but rejected a numerical approach:

> We see little similarity between the Palsgraf case and the situation before us. . . . In contrast, a ship insecurely moored in a fast flowing river is a known danger. . . . The shipowner and wharfinger in this case having thus owed a duty of care to all within the reach of the ship's known destructive power, the impossibility of advance identification of the particular person who would be hurt is without legal consequences.[67]

An identification of all of the damages and the related costs that could have occurred, prior to the event, would have been a superhuman task.[68]

The most damaging case is Posner's own keystone example, *Carroll Towing*,[69] in which an unmanned barge broke away from its moorings. After presenting the quota that Posner states is the linchpin of law and economics,[70] Judge Hand continues:

In the case at bar the barges left at five o'clock in the afternoon of January 3rd, and the flotilla broke away at about two o'clock in the afternoon of the following day, twenty-one hours afterwards. . . . At the locus in quo—especially during the short January days and in the full tide of war activity—barges were being constantly "drilled" in and out. Certainly it was not beyond reasonable expectation that, with the inevitable haste and bustle, the work might not be done with adequate care. In such circumstances we hold . . . that it was a fair requirement that the Conners Company should have had a bargee aboard . . . during the working hours of daylight.[71]

Hand carefully avoided inserting actual costs into his formula. That is not surprising in view of his earlier statement in *Conway v. O'Brien*:

The degree of care demanded of a person by an occasion is the resultant of three factors: the likelihood that his conduct will injure others, taken with the seriousness of the injury if it happens, and balanced against the interest which he must sacrifice to avoid the risk. *All these are practically not susceptible of any quantitative estimate, and the second two are generally not so, even theoretically. For this reason a solution always involves some preference, or choice between incommensurables*, and it is consigned to a jury because their decision is thought most likely to accord with commonly accepted standards, real or fancied.[72]

Judge Hand is saying that it is impossible to derive costs for concepts such as likelihood, seriousness and the interests sacrificed. Indeed, that is one reason for juries.

Judge Hand had little use for the "Hand" formula. In 1962 Laurence H. Eldredge stated at the American Law Institute's discussion of *Restatement (Second) of Torts*:

I remember Judge Learned Hand . . . at one of our conferences up in Northeast Hartford in the 1930's made a statement that if he could rewrite the tort law of America he would impose a rule of absolute liability in all cases in which a defendant could protect himself by liability insurance.[73]

The previous discussion has shown that the courts endorse a balancing approach in resolving negligence cases and avoid a quantified cost-benefit formula. The next case is presented to manifest that in contemporary torts cases the values are too vague, too far-reaching and too complex to be assigned costs, and therefore Posner's negligence theory is impractical.

In *Kelly v. Gwinnell*[74] Zak served Gwinnell as many as thirteen drinks[75] in Zak's home and then watched as Gwinnell drove away. On the way home, Gwinnell was involved in a head-on collision with Kelly, who was seriously injured. The suit was brought against the social host, Zak. The question was whether the social host was liable in negligence for the damages to Kelly.

The point is that the costs involved in an actual torts case such as *Kelly* are too vague and too interrelated with other concepts and bound up with values to be assigned a price. For example, what is the price of "enjoyment, relaxation, and camaraderie that accompany social gatherings at which alcohol is served. . . ?"[76] What is the cost of the intrusion through anticipated litigation into a private social setting such as a small party among friends? If the social host is held liable, which course of conduct will be selected and what is the cost of each: no parties, fewer parties, less alcohol served, parties without alcohol, the volume of alochol served and consumed is monitored, host makes certain a nondrinker will drive, host provides a ride, a taxi is called, taking the intoxicated driver's keys, threatening to call the police, calling the police? What is the cost of losing friends or associates because less alcohol is served or drinks are cut off? How do you attach a price to the policies of compensating the victim and deterring drunk driving, for example? Does insurance cover the host's loss? What price is to be assigned if insurance does or does not cover this loss by the social host?[77] What costs are involved in social hosts obtaining sufficient insurance?

Assigning prices to benefits[78] is equally impossible. How do you calculate prices for the "misery, death and destruction caused by the drunken driver,"[79] for example? What are all of the damages that flow from drunk driving? How many deaths will be prevented by holding the social host liable? How much misery? How much destruction? What, for example, is the value of a child killed by a drunk driver?[80] Attempting to put a price on one of these "benefits" involves numerous other inquiries and relationships with other vague concepts.

This partial list demonstrates two points. First, the costs involved in a real negligence case are never-ending and therefore cannot be computed, and second, any attempt to arrive at specific costs will involve an injection of the examiner's values. For example, the "costs" in the *Kelly* case would surely reflect the examiner's personal values on alcohol.

This chapter manifests that the elements involved in a personal injury suit cannot be assigned a numerical price. It has made clear that Judge Posner's efficiency theory and traditional negligence are different concepts and that there is a need for someone to demonstrate the overlap, if any, between them. Posner's theory misrepresents reality to the extent that it suggests that value-free numbers can be pulled out of the air and plugged into a formula.[81] Additionally, it provides no method for addressing critical justice issues. No fine-tuning concept such as duty or proximate cause exists in his theory.

Judge Posner's theory is impractical. Applying it to several well-known cases and to *Kelly v. Gwinnell* demonstrates that, unlike marauding cattle[82] and sparking trains,[83] contemporary torts cases defy attempts to assign numbers to concepts. In view of the serious theoretical and practical flaws in the ngeligence-efficiency theory, and the difficulty of proving traditional negligence, as well as the fact that negligence is biased against the consumer, this chapter supports the further expansion of strict liability.

NOTES

1. Posner, *A Theory of Negligence*, 1 J. LEGAL STUD. 29, 29, 32-34 (1972).

2. *Id.* at 33.

3. A. POLINSKY, AN INTRODUCTION TO LAW AND ECONOMICS 123-26 (1983).

4. *See* Knetsch, *Legal Rules and the Basis for Evaluating Economic Losses*, 4 INT'L REV. L. & ECON. 5, 9 (1984).

5. Professor Henry Manne's position that law is economics is an overstatement. Opening presentation by Professor Henry G. Manne, Emory University Law and Economics Center for Economics Institute for Law Professors (July 12, 1981). In like fashion, Posner argues: "[T]he logic of law is really economics." Posner, *The Economic Approach to Law*, 53 TEX. L. REV. 757 (1975).

6. *See* A. POLINSKY, *supra* note 3, at 11, 12.

7. Polinsky, *Economic Analysis as a Potentially Defective Product: A Buyer's Guide to Posner's Economic Analysis of Law*, 87 HARV. L. REV. 1655, 1660 (1974).

8. *Id.* at 1667 n. 67.

9. *See id.* at 1665. *See also id.* at 1660, 1664.

10. A. POLINSKY, *supra* note 3, at 13.

11. *See id.*

12. *See* Rizzo, *Law amid Flux: The Economics of Negligence and Strict Liability in Tort*, 9 J. LEGAL STUD. 291, 298 (1980).

13. A substantial amount of literature has been devoted to the subject of when an externality exists. See, for example, Demsetz, *Toward a Theory of Property Rights*, 57 AMERICAN ECONOMIC REVIEW 347 (1967).

14. Rizzo, *supra* note 12, at 296, 299.

15. Posner, *Utilitarianism Economics and Legal Theory*, 8 J. LEGAL STUD. 103 (1979).

16. *See* Posner, *The Ethical and Political Basis of the Efficiency Norm in Common Law Adjudication*, 8 HOFSTRA L. REV. 487 (1980).

17. *See* R. POSNER, TORT LAW: CASES AND ECONOMIC ANALYSIS 2-3 (1982).

18. Coleman, *Efficiency, Utility, and Wealth Maximization*, 8 HOFSTRA L. REV. 509, 526 (1980).

19. *See* Samuels & Mercuro, *Posnerian Law and Economics on the Bench*, 4 INT'L REV. L. & ECON. 107, 108, 112, 114, 116, 123 (1984).

20. *Id.* at 112.

21. *See* Bebchuk, *The Pursuit of a Bigger Pie: Can Everyone Expect a Bigger Slice?*, 8 HOFSTRA L. REV. 671, 672 (1980).

22. Posner, *supra* note 16, at 488.

23. *Id.* at 494.

24. Dworkin, *Why Efficiency? A Response to Professors Calabresi and Posner*, 8 HOFSTRA L. REV. 563, 575 (1980).

25. *See* A. CORBIN, CORBIN ON CONTRACTS § 19, at 46 (1983).

26. *See id.*

27. *See id.*

28. Englard, *The System Builders: A Critical Appraisal of Modern American Tort Theory*, 9 J. LEGAL STUD. 27, 31-32 (1980).

29. Kennedy, *Cost-Benefit Analysis of Entitlement Problems: A Critique*, 33 STAN. L. REV. 387, 445 (1981).

30. Professor Owen notes: "Ford had a particular problem with the design of the fuel system of the Pinto. To save about $10 per vehicle, Ford's management decided to avoid a design alternative that would have dramatically improved the safety of the fuel system. . . ." W. KEETON, D. OWEN & J. MONTGOMERY, PRODUCTS LIABILITY AND SAFETY 422 (1980).

31. Bebchuk, *supra* note 21, at 672.

32. Dworkin, *supra* note 24, at 581.

33. *See* 2 F. HARPER & F. JAMES, THE LAW OF TORTS 743 (1956); Calabresi, *About Law and Economics: A Letter to Ronald Dworkin*, 8 HOFSTRA L. REV. 553, 559-60 (1980).

34. Calabresi, *supra* note 33, at 559-60.

35. *See supra* note 16.

36. *See* RESTATEMENT (SECOND) OF TORTS § 339 (1965); Goll v. Muscara, 211 Pa. Super. 93, 235 A. 2d 443 (1967).

37. *See* Davison v. Snohomish County, 149 Wash. 109, 270 P. 422 (1928).

38. *See* Bartlett v. N. Pac. R. Co., 74 Wash. 2d 881, 447 P. 2d 735 (1968).

39. *See* Wagner v. Int'l Ry. Co., 232 N.Y. 176, 133 N.E. 437 (1921).

40. *See* Hill v. City of Glenwood, 124 Iowa 479, 100 N.W. 522 (1904).

41. *See* Johnson v. Lambotta, 147 Colo. 203, 363 P. 2d 165 (1961).

42. *See* Polinsky, *supra* note 7, at 1671.

43. Calabresi, *Some Thoughts on Risk Distribution and the Law of Torts*, 70 YALE L. J. 499, 506 (1961).

44. A. POLINSKY, *supra* note 3, at 97-98.

45. *See* Kelman, *Misunderstanding Social Life: A Critique of the Core Premises of "Law and Economics,"* 33 J. LEGAL EDUC. 274, 278 (1983).

46. Kelman argues that some of Posner's conclusions are "rather comic." *Id.* at 274.

47. *Id.*

48. A. POLINSKY, *supra* note 3, at 98-99.

49. Rizzo, *The Mirage of Efficiency*, 8 HOFSTRA L. REV. 658 (1980).

50. Polinsky, *supra* note 7, at 1669.

51. Kelman, *supra* note 45, at 278.

52. Rizzo concludes: "[T]he efficiency criterion cannot explain the result in re *Polemis.* The defendants were not economically negligent with respect to the harm that actually came to pass and hence ought not to have been held liable." Rizzo, *supra* note 12, at 296.

53. *See* Calabresi, *supra* note 43, at 506.

54. W. PROSSER, HANDBOOK OF THE LAW OF TORTS 145, 149 (4th ed. 1971).

55. Posner, *supra* note 1, at 32-34; W. PROSSER, *supra* note 54, at 149.

56. Conway v. O'Brein, 111 F. 2d 611, 612 (2d Cir. 1940), *rev'd on other grounds*, 312 U.S. 492 (1941).

57. For examples of the calculus or math approach, *see* Brown, *Toward an Economic Theory of Liability*, 2 J. LEGAL STUD. 323 (1973).

58. *See Conway*, 111 F. 2d at 612.

59. *See* Green, *Proximate Cause in Texas Negligence Law* (pts. 1-3), 28 TEX. L. REV. 471, 621, 755 (1950). *See also* Green, *The Duty Problem in Negligence Cases* (pt. 2), 29 COLUM. L. REV. 255 (1929).

60. *See,* for example, Polinsky, *supra* note 7.

61. *See* Posner, *supra* note 1, at 32.

62. *But see* Wilson v. Piper Aircraft Corp., 282 Or. 61, 69-70, 577 P. 2d 1322, 1327 (1978).

63. Palsgraf v. Long Island R.R., 248 N.Y. 339, 162 N.E. 99 (1928).

64. 248 N.Y. at 340-41, 162 N.E. at 99.

65. *See* R. POSNER, *supra* note 17, at 586.

66. 338 F. 2d 708 (2d Cir. 1964).

67. *Id.* at 721-22.

68. *See* Petition of Kinsman Transit Co., 338 F. 2d 821, 824 (2d Cir. 1968).

69. United States v. Carroll Towing, 159 F.2d 169 (2d Cir. 1947).

70. *See supra* note 1 and accompanying text.

71. *Carroll Towing*, 159 F.2d at 173-74.

72. Conway, *supra* note 56 at 612 (emphasis added).

73. 39 ALI PROCEEDINGS 233 (1962).

74. 96 N.J. 538, 476 A.2d 1219 (1984).

75. 96 N.J. at 541, 476 A.2d at 1220.

76. 96 N.J. at 548, 476 A.2d at 1224.

77. 96 N.J. at 549-551, 476 A.2d at 1225.

78. "Benefits" refers to damages that will not occur if safety modifications are made. For example, less alcohol is served, or the intoxicated guest is driven home by the sober host. *See* Posner, *supra* note 1, at 32-34.

79. *Kelly*, 96 N.J. at 558, 476 A.2d at 1229.

80. "We hold that the measure of damages for the wrongful death of a minor child should be extended to include the loss of the society, comfort, and companionship of the child." Selders v. Armentrout, 190 Neb. 275, 207 N.W.2d 686 (1973).

81. *See* 54 U.S.L.W. 2174 (Oct. 1, 1985) (reviewing L. TRIBE, CONSTITUTIONAL CHOICES (1985)).

82. *See* Coase, *The Problem of Social Cost*, 3 J. L. & ECON. 1 (1960).

83. *See* Posner, *Strict Liability: A Comment*, 2 J. LEGAL STUD. 206 (1973).

BIBLIOGRAPHY

Bebchuk, "The Pursuit of a Bigger Pie: Can Everyone Expect a Bigger Slice?" 8 *Hofstra L. Rev.* 671 (1980).

Brown, "Toward an Economic Theory of Liability." 2 *J. Legal Stud.* 323 (1973).

Calabresi, "About Law and Economics: A Letter to Ronald Dworkin." 8 *Hofstra L. Rev.* 553 (1980).

Calabresi, "Some Thoughts on Risk Distribution and the Law of Torts." 7 *Yale L. J.* 499 (1961).

Coase, "The Problem of Social Cost." 3 *J. L. & Econ.* 1 (1960).

Coleman, "Efficiency, Utility, and Wealth Maximization." 8 *Hofstra L. Rev.* 509 (1980).

Corbin, A., *Corbin on Contracts* (1983).

Demsetz, "Toward a Theory of Property Rights." 57 *American Economic Review* 347 (1967).

Dworkin, "Why Efficiency? A Response to Professors Calabresi and Posner." 8 *Hofstra L. Rev.* 563 (1980).

Englard, "The System Builders: A Critical Appraisal of Modern American Tort Theory." 9 *J. Legal Stud.* 27 (1980).

Green, "The Duty Problem in Negligence Cases" (pt. 2). 29 *Colum. L. Rev.* 255 (1929).

Green, "Proximate Cause in Texas Negligence Law" (pts. 1-3). 28 *Tex. L. Rev.* 471, 621, 755 (1950).

Harper, F., & F. James, *The Law of Torts*, vol. 2 (1956).

Keeton, W., D. Owen & J. Montgomery, *Products Liability and Safety* (1980).

Kelman, "Misunderstanding Social Life: A Critique of the Core Premises of 'Law and Economics.'" 33 *J. Legal Educ.* 274 (1983).

Kennedy, "Cost-Benefit Analysis of Entitlement Problems: A Critique." 33 *Stan. L. Rev.* 387 (1981).

Knetsch, "Legal Rules and the Basis for Evaluating Economic Losses." 4 *Int'l Rev. L. & Econ.* 5 (1984).

Polinsky, "Economic Analysis as a Potentially Defective Product: A Buyer's Guide to Posner's Economic Analysis of Law." 87 *Harv. L. Rev.* 1655 (1974).

Polinsky, A., *An Introduction to Law and Economics* (1983).

Posner, "The Economic Approach to Law." 53 *Tex. L. Rev.* 757 (1975).

Posner, "The Ethical and Political Basis of the Efficiency Norm in Common Law Adjudication." 8 *Hofstra L. Rev.* 487 (1980).

Posner, "Strict Liability: A Comment." 2 *J. Legal Stud.* 206 (1973).

Posner, "A Theory of Negligence." 1 *J. Legal Stud.* 29 (1972).

Posner, R., *Tort Law: Cases and Economic Analysis* (1982).

Posner, "Utilitarianism Economics and Legal Theory." 8 *J. Legal Stud.* 103 (1979).

Prosser, W., *Handbook of the Law of Torts* (4th ed. 1971).

Restatement (Second) of Torts (1965).

Rizzo, "Law amid Flux: The Economics of Negligence and Strict Liability in Tort." 9 *J. Legal Stud.* 291 (1980).

Rizzo, "The Mirage of Efficiency," 8 *Hofstra L. Rev.* 658 (1980).

Samuels & Mercuro, "Posnerian Law and Economics on the Bench." 4 *Int'l Rev. L. & Econ.* 107 (1984).

6

The Present Scope of Strict Liability

The purpose of this chapter is to indicate the existing reach of the cause of action in strict liability. It is intended to be an outline of those cases to which strict liability has already been applied. The chapter will conclude with a discussion of the frontier of strict liability: those cases involving products such as handguns, cigarettes, alcohol and blood, where there is currently substantial disagreement whether strict liability should apply. This chapter lays the foundation for the next chapter, which involves the most challenging question in the application of strict liability: Should strict liability be applied to professionals—those who exercise a high degree of discretion in their work?

Food was the first product to which strict liability was applied. In the 1913 case of *Mazetti*,[1] a customer contracted food poisoning from eating canned tongue served at a restaurant. The suit was brought against Armour, the manufacturer of the tongue. The court decided that an implied warranty ran from the manufacturer to the consumer. Today the case would rest on strict liability. *Escola v. Coca-Cola* (1944)[2] involved a waitress who was injured by an exploding Coca-Cola bottle. Suit was brought against the manufacturer. The majority of the court decided the case on the basis of res ipsa loquitur, but Judge Traynor, in a concurring opinion, urged that the manufacturer should be held strictly liable.[3] Although strict liability has been widely applied to manufacturers and sellers of food, it was not applied to a case where several women prepared turkey sandwiches to be sold at a church bazaar.[4] The underlying rationale in that case was that the women who prepared the sandwiches were in no better position to bear the loss than the purchasers who contracted salmonella.[5]

One of the most popular areas for the application of strict liability is automobiles and other machinery. In *Henningsen v. Bloomfield Motors*[6] the purchaser's wife was driving a new Plymouth at the time of the crash. As she was proceeding down the road, something went wrong with the front end of the car and it collided with a wall. In that 1960 case the New Jersey Supreme Court held that implied warranty extended to the manufacturer of the automobile. The cause of action would be strict liability today. *Henningsen* includes an excellent discussion of the social policy reasons for strict liability as well as the arguments for disregarding manufacturers' disclaimers.

Strict liability was applied in *Elmore v. American Motors Corp.*[7] In that case the front end of the drive shaft dropped to the ground, and the AMC vehicle was catapulted into the air and the oncoming traffic. The plaintiff was the driver of the car in the other lane of traffic that was hit by the AMC vehicle. The court in *Elmore* did not hesitate to reject the defendant's privity argument (the plaintiff had no contract with AMC) and adopt strict liability against AMC, the manufacturer of the defective drive shaft.[8] In *Cronin v. Olson* the defendant assembled a bakery van.[9] The driver of the van, while passing another vehicle, went off the road. The van came to an abrupt stop, and the bread storage rack, because of a defective hasp, slid forward and caused substantial injury to the driver. The plaintiff argued that strict liability should apply to the assembler of the van. The court held that strict liability applied to the assembler, but refused to adopt the definition of strict liability contained in section 402A of the Restatement, because it resembled negligence too closely.[10] The California Supreme Court applied strict liability to a defective high-lift loader in the keystone case of *Barker v. Lull Engineering Company* (1978).[11] The decision in *Barker* is discussed extensively at another point in this book.[12]

Strict liability has been applied to a broad range of home appliances. In the classic case of *Greenman v. Yuba Power Products* the California Supreme Court applied strict liability against the manufacturer of a Shopsmith, an all-purpose lathe. It contained a defective mechanism for holding the wood to the spinning portion of the lathe.[13] In *Hankscraft*[14] the court applied strict liability to a defective vaporizer. In that case a four-year-old child got up in the middle of the night to go to the bathroom. She stumbled into the steam vaporizer, which had been placed on a chair. Unknown to the parents, the vaporizer contained boiling water, and it splashed over the child, causing serious burns. The court in *Hankscraft* found the manufacturer strictly liable because it would have been very inexpensive to put threads on the top of the vaporizer or to provide a locking mechanism so that when the vaporizer was knocked over, the water would not gush out the top.[15]

Strict liability has been applied to various forms of clothing and pharmaceuticals. In *LaGorga v. Kroger Company*[16] strict liability was applied against Kroger, which sold lightweight children's windbreakers. A minor child was wearing one of the jackets that had been purchased at Kroger's. While the plaintiff, John LaGorga, was poking sticks through a metal barrel used to incinerate trash, the jacket caught fire and exploded into flames. The appellate court upheld the jury verdict for the plaintiff.[17]

In *Ellsworth v. Sherne Lingerie, Inc.*,[18] the Maryland Court of Appeals applied strict liability to a woman's nightgown. The plaintiff wore her nightgown into the kitchen to make coffee. She admitted that she was wearing the nightgown inside out and, as a result, two pockets at the side were protruding and flapping. As she put a tea kettle on the front burner of her electric stove, she reached above the stove for a coffee filter. Her nightgown ignited and she was severely burned. The court of appeals approved the trial court's application of strict liability against the manufacturer of the nightgown.[19]

Because of the extensive role of the Food and Drug Administration in the premarketing approval of pharmaceuticals, strict liability, based on design, is rarely applied to cases involving drugs. Instead, the question is usually whether a warning was required for the particular drug or, if there was a warning, whether it was adequate.

An example of a recent pharmaceutical case is *Reyes v. Wyeth Laboratories.*[20] In that case an eight-month-old child was administered two drops of Sabin oral polio vaccine by eyedropper at a county health clinic in Texas. The vaccine was given to Anita Reyes by a licensed practical nurse. There were no doctors present. Anita's mother certified that she was not warned of any possible dangers associated with the vaccine. About two weeks later, young Anita became ill and was diagnosed as having paralytic poliomyelitis. Anita became paralyzed from the waist down. The issue was whether Wyeth was under a duty to warn the parents of Anita Reyes that there was a possibility that she might contract polio from the drug designed to immunize her. Wyeth argued that it had warned the Texas State Department of Health. The court held "that in the case of a prescription drug, which is unavoidably unsafe, and as to which there is a certain or small risk throughout the population, there must be either a warning or an individualized medical judgment that this treatment or medication is necessary and desirable for the patient."[21] Since there was no individualized medical judgment in Anita's case, the administration of the Sabin vaccine was held to be defective in the absence of a warning.[22]

Asbestos has been a fertile ground for the application of strict liability. In *Borel v. Fiberboard Paper Products Corporation*[23] the plaintiff developed pulmonary asbestosis and eventually a form of lung cancer known as mesothelioma from inhalation of asbestos dust over the thirty-three years he worked as an industrial insulation worker. The suit was in strict liability against manufacturers of insulation materials containing asbestos for their failure to warn of the dangers of asbestos dust inhalation. The jury returned a verdict for Borel, the worker, and this was affirmed by the Fifth Circuit Court of Appeals.[24]

In *Beshada v. Johns-Manville Products Corporation*[25] the plaintiffs were survivors of deceased workers who claimed to have been exposed to asbestos for varying periods of time. They alleged that as a result of their exposure they contracted asbestosis, mesothelioma and other asbestos-related illnesses. The actions were brought against manufacturers and distributors of asbestos products. The issue in the case was whether, in a products liability case based on strict liability for failure to warn, defendants may raise a "state-of-the-art" defense.[26] In the "state-of-the-art" defense the manufacturer argues that it did everything that was known to science at the time of manufacture to make the product safe. The court found in favor of the plaintiff and rejected the "state-of-the-art" defense. The court assumed that the manufacturer did not know of the defect in asbestos at the time of manufacture. It nevertheless concluded that because the basic rationale of strict liability is loss shifting, the manufacturer should be strictly liable for failure to warn.[27] It is highly likely, however, that *Beshada* will be limited to asbestos cases and not expanded to personal injury cases in general.[28]

The courts have had substantial difficulty in applying strict liability to situations where the defendant was not the manufacturer or seller, or the product was used. In *Cintrone v. Hertz Truck Leasing*[29] the court held the lessor of a truck strictly liable. It reasoned:

> A bailor for hire, such as a person in the U-Drive-It business, puts motor vehicles in the stream of commerce in a fashion not unlike a manufacturer or retailer, [and exposes] the bailee, his employees, passengers and the traveling public . . . to a greater *quantum* of potential danger of harm from defective vehicles than usually arises out of sales by the manufacturer.[30]

The court also stressed that the leasing of vehicles is a huge business today.[31]

When an individual is injured by a product that has been purchased in a used condition, this raises substantial problems for the court. First, there are issues of cause in fact; that is, did the seller of the used product cause the injury? Second, there may be a disclaimer involved in the case; that is, the seller may have sold the used product "as is." Finally, when someone purchases a used product, he may not expect it to be in good condition.[32] However, in *Turner v. International Harvester Company*[33] the plaintiff was able to bring strict liability against the seller of a used truck. While the plaintiff was working on the engine, the raised cab fell on the plaintiff because of a defective latch.[34] In *Turner* the court rejected the "as is" argument and held the dealer in used equipment strictly liable to the injured consumer.[35] This is not always the result, however. In *Peterson v. Lou Backrodt Chevrolet Co.*[36] two children were killed when the brakes on a car failed. The used car had been purchased from the defendant car dealer. The court refused to apply strict liability because the plaintiff had failed to prove that the defects in the brakes had been caused by the manufacturer or the used-car dealer.[37]

The remainder of this chapter will deal with frontier cases, those on the cutting edge of products liability. They involve the question whether strict liability should apply to the manufacturers of cigarettes, alcohol and handguns, as well as the providers of blood.

One of the most challenging cases in products liability involved the application of strict liability to a manufacturer of handguns, Saturday night specials. The reason such an application is noteworthy is because the injured party was not the consumer and the handgun was used exactly as it was intended, that is, to kill people. In *Richman v.*

Charter Arms Corp.[38] a female medical student was raped and murdered by a thug. The mother of the medical student brought this suit against Charter Arms, the manufacturer of the handgun used in the crime. The court in *Richman* decided in favor of the plaintiff and held that the manufacturer of the handgun was strictly liable on the basis that the manufacture and sale of such a product is an abnormally dangerous activity.[39] In *Perkins v. F.I.E. Corp.*,[40] which is the appellate case for *Richman v. Charter Arms*, the United States Fifth Circuit Court of Appeals decided in favor of Charter Arms and held that strict liability does not apply to the manufacturer of a handgun. It rejected the theory that the manufacture and sale of a handgun is an abnormally dangeorus activity because that theory applies only where the defendant's activity is related to land. The court also held that in order for strict liability to apply, there must be something wrong with the product.[41]

In *Kelley v. R. G. Industries*[42] Kelley was injured when a thug shot him in the chest during an armed robbery of a grocery store where he was employed. Kelley sued the manufacturer of the Saturday night special used in the attack. The Maryland Court of Appeals examined and rejected the usual theories of strict liability. However, it held, in a confusing opinion, that the manufacturer of the Saturday night special was strictly liable, apparently on the theory that federal and state legislation severely restricts the sale of such guns.[43] Maryland has recently become the first state to ban the sale of Saturday night specials.[44]

Some of the most important contemporary products litigation involves suits brought against the manufacturers of cigarettes. Rose Cipollone began smoking in 1942 and later developed lung cancer. Her husband brought an action against the Liggett group shortly before her death.[45] In that suit Mr. Cipollone contended that the cigarette manufacturer was strictly liable for failure to warn of the addictive nature of cigarettes. The issue squarely raised was whether the Federal Cigarette Labeling and Advertising Act preempts any or all of the state common law claims brought by Mr. Cipollone and his wife. The act provides:

> No requirement or prohibition based on smoking and health shall be imposed under state law with respect to the advertising or promotion of any cigarettes, the packages of which are labeled in conformity with the provisions of this chapter.[46]

The United States Court of Appeals for the Third Circuit held in 1986 that the Cipollones' strict liability for failure to warn action was preempted by the Federal Cigarette Labeling Act.[47] By refusing to review the court of appeals decision, the United States Supreme Court has approved the decision in regard to preemption.[48] However, the Minnesota Court of Appeals recently held that the Federal Cigarette Labeling and Advertising Act does not preempt tort actions against tobacco manufacturers at the state level.[49] A recent decision by the United States District Court held that the Cipollones' claims, based on failure to warn and negligence in regard to advertising and promotion before 1966 (date of the Cigarette Labeling Act), remain viable and capable of being litigated. The district court also found that the federal act did not preempt the Cipollones' claims based on strict liability that are premised on improper design or negligent research or testing.[50]

In June, 1988, a Newark, New Jersey, jury returned a verdict of $400,000 for the husband of Rose Cipollone. The jury based its decision on breach of express warranty and held that Liggett, the cigarette manufacturer, should have warned Rose Cipollone about the risks of smoking before 1966.[51] This is a most important personal injury verdict. With "more than 100 smokers' suits pending," it is likely that cigarette litigation will become as sizable and important as asbestos.[52]

The next frontier for strict liability is alcohol. In December, 1987, the Third Circuit Court of Appeals held that a case resting on strict liability for failure to warn of the danger of pancreatitis should go to the jury.[53] Mr. Hon consumed two to three cans of Stroh's beer each night for several years. He died from pancreatitis at age twenty-six. Mrs. Hon argued that based on the Restatement of Torts, section 402A, Stroh's should be held strictly liable for failure to warn of the dangers from excessive consumption.[54] This is the first case involving beer to go before a jury.

A challenging question involving the scope of strict liability is whether or not a blood bank or a hospital can be held liable for supplying defective blood. An early case, *Cunningham v. MacNeal Memorial Hospital*,[55] held that a patient who suffered severe injury because of the transfusion of blood containing the hepatitis virus was able to sue the hospital and recover in strict liability. The court rejected the arguments that blood was human tissue and not a product, that the sale of blood fell within the exception to strict liability for "unavoidably unsafe" products and that the provision of blood was a service, not a sale. *Cunningham* was later superseded by an act of the Illinois legislature, however.[56] Other courts have rejected the *Cunningham* approach and have held that neither the hospital nor the blood bank can be strictly liable for providing blood that contains the hepatitis virus.[57] *Brody v. Overlook Hospital*,[58] for example, held that the relationship between the hospital, the county blood bank and the decedent was not a commercial enterprise, and therefore strict liability was inappropriate. It also held that the provision of blood was an unavoidably unsafe activity within the meaning of comment k to the Restatement Second, section 402A. Comment k provides that unavoidably unsafe products, particularly drugs, which in the present state of human knowledge are incapable of being made safe for their intended and ordinary use, are not defective products. Such products, properly prepared and accompanied by proper directions and warnings, are not unreasonably dangerous, and the seller thereof is not to be held strictly liable under comment k.[59] It is highly likely, however, that in the next few years hospitals and blood banks will be held strictly liable to patients who contract AIDS from blood transfusions. The reason is that hospitals and blood banks are the cheapest cost avoiders, as compared with the patient, and it makes more sense for the hospitals and blood banks to bear the loss than the patient.

Economic loss is a continuing problem of tort law. It can be defined as commerical loss, that is, loss that does not involve personal injury or property damage. The traditional approach has been to say that economic loss cannot be recovered in strict liability, but may be recovered under express warranty.[60] A 1986 decision by the United States Supreme Court continues the distinction between strict liability and warranty. In *East River Steamship Corporation v. Transamerica Delaval*[61] the Supreme Court was faced with an economic loss claim resting on strict liability. In that case the defendant designed, manufactured and supervised the installation of huge turbines that would be the main propulsion units for four oil-transporting supertankers constructed by the shipbuilder. After each ship was completed, it was chartered to one of the petitioners. When the ships were put into service, the turbines on all four ships malfunctioned due to design and manufacturing defects. Only the products themselves were damaged.[62] The Court held that whether stated in negligence or strict liability, no products liability claim lies in admiralty when a commercial party alleges injury only to the product itself—

purely economic loss. The reasoning behind the decision was that such a claim is most naturally understood as arising in express warranty.[63]

We have seen in this chapter the breadth and depth of application of strict liability. The last few examples illustrate the courts' weighing whether strict liability should apply to cases at the fringe. Although it is clear that strict liability applies to defective food, automobiles, machinery, vaporizers, pharmaceuticals and clothing, it has not yet been decided whether strict liability will apply to manufacturers of handguns, cigarettes and alcohol, and to those who supply blood, such as hospitals and blood banks. The examination of these cases has prepared us for a look at the most demanding cases: those involving professionals. The assumption in the next chapter is that if sound arguments can be presented for the application of strict liability to professionals, then a foundation has been laid for applying strict liability far beyond the products cases. That will be the goal of the following chapter—to manifest that it is appropriate for courts to apply strict liability to medical doctors, lawyers, architects and beyond.

One question that arises is, should strict liability apply to all personal injury cases? The answer is no, and a good example of the type of case to which strict liability should not apply is automobile crashes brought about because of the absence of care by one or more of the drivers. There are several reasons. The key is knowledge. Both parties know, when they step into a car, that there is a possibility of a collision. Everybody who drives knows that automobile crashes are common.

In regard to loss shifting, each party is presumptively able to bear the loss. At a minimum, each driver can purchase insurance. Indeed, automobile crashes are so common that many states require automobile owners to purchase insurance. Many states require no-fault insurance for automobile drivers. In automobile crashes there are no inequities in bargaining power between parties, such as those we saw between consumer and seller in the products area. Finally, strict liability is not applicable because negligence is neither too expensive nor too difficult to prove in most of these cases. The vast majority are settled.

NOTES

1. Mazetti v. Armour, 75 Wash. 622, 135 P. 633 (1913).
2. Escola v. Coca-Cola Bottling Co., 24 Cal. 2d 453, 150 P. 2d 436 (1944).

3. *Id.*
4. Samson v. Riesing, 62 Wis. 2d 698, 215 N.W. 2d 662 (1974).
5. *Id.*
6. Henningsen v. Bloomfield Motors, 32 N.J. 358, 161 A. 2d 69 (1960).
7. Elmore v. American Motors, 70 Cal. 2d 578, 451 P. 2d 84 (1969).
8. *Id.*
9. Cronin v. J.B.E. Olson Corp., 8 Cal. 3d 121, 501 P. 2d 1153, 104 Cal. Rptr. 433 (1972).
10. *Id.*
11. Barker v. Lull Eng'g Co., 20 Cal. 3d 413, 573 P. 2d 443, 143 Cal. Rptr. 239 (1978).
12. *See* chapter 4.
13. Greenman v. Yuba Power Prods., Inc., 59 Cal. 2d 57, 377 P. 2d 897, 27 Cal. Rptr. 697 (1963).
14. McCormack v. Hankscraft Co., 278 Minn. 322, 154 N.W. 2d 488 (1967).
15. *Id.*
16. LaGorga v. Kroger Co., 275 F. Supp. 373 (W.D. Pa. 1967).
17. *Id.*
18. Ellsworth v. Sherne Lingerie, Inc., 303 Md. 581, 495 A. 2d 348 (1985).
19. *Id.*
20. Reyes v. Wyeth Laboratories, 498 F. 2d 1264, *cert. denied*, 419 U.S. 1096, 95 S. Ct. 687 (5th Cir. 1974).
21. *Id.*
22. *Id.*
23. Borel v. Fiberboard Paper Products Corp., 493 F. 2d 1076, *cert. denied*, 419 U.S. 869, 95 S. Ct. 127 (1974).
24. *Id.*
25. Beshada v. Johns-Manville Products Corp., 90 N.J. 191, 447 A. 2d 539 (N.J. S. Ct. 1982).
26. *Id.*
27. *Id.*
28. *See* Feldman v. Lederle Laboratories, 97 N.J. 429, 479 A. 2d 374 (1984).
29. Cintrone v. Hertz Truck Leasing, 45 N.J. 434, 212 A. 2d 769 (1965).
30. *Id.*
31. *Id.*
32. Turner v. International Harvester Co., 133 N.J. Super. 277, 336 A. 2d 62 (1975).
33. *Id.*
34. *Id.*
35. *Id.*
36. Peterson v. Lou Backrodt Chevrolet Co., 61 Ill. 2d 17, 329 N.E. 785 (1975).
37. *Id.*

38. Richman v. Charter Arms Corp., 571 F. Supp. 192 (1983).

39. *Id.*

40. Perkins v. F. I. E. Corp., 762 F. 2d 1250 (5th Cir. 1985).

41. *Id.*

42. Kelley v. R. G. Industries, 304 Md. 124, 497 A. 2d 1143 (1985).

43. *Id.*

44. Atlanta Journal, May 23, 1988, at 6-A.

45. Cipollone v. Liggett Group, Inc., U.S. Ct. App., 3d Cir. (April 7, 1986).

46. *Id.*

47. *Id.*

48. Cipollone v. Liggett Group, Inc., U.S. Sup. Ct., No. 86-563 (Jan. 12, 1987).

49. Forster v. R. J. Reynolds Tobacco, Minn. Ct. App., No. C1-87-2170 (May 3, 1988).

50. Cipollone v. Liggett Group, Inc., D.C. N.J. (Dec. 9, 1986).

51. 74 AM. BAR ASSOC. J. 28 (August 1988).

52. *Id.*

53. Hon v. Stroh Brewery, U.S. Ct. App. (3d Cir. Dec. 21, 1987).

54. *Id.* In Brune v. Brown Forman Corp., No. 13-87-445-CV (Tex. Ct. App. Aug. 31, 1988), 1988 Tex. App. Lexis 2254, the court remanded in favor of the plaintiff, where an eighteen-year-old died from drinking tequila shots. The plaintiff argued failure to warn based on negligence and strict liability.

55. Cunningham v. MacNeal Memorial Hospital, 47 Ill. 2d 443, 266 N.E. 2d 897 (S. Ct. 1970).

56. *See* ILL. CODE ANN. ch. 91, §§ 181-184 (1971).

57. Brody v. Overlook Hospital, 127 N.J. Super. 331, 317 A. 2d 392, *aff'd*, 66 N.J. 448, 332 A. 2d 596 (1975).

58. *Id.*

59. *Id.*

60. *See* Seely v. White Motor Co., 63 Cal. 2d 9, 403 P. 2d 145 (1965).

61. East River Steamship Corp. v. Transamerica Delaval, 106 S. Ct. 2295 (June 16, 1986).

62. *Id.*

63. *Id.*

7

Applying Strict Liability to Professionals: Doctors and Lawyers

Although strict liability has been expanding over the past few years,[1] no court has held that strict liability controls the result in a case involving a professional.[2] Tort policies support applying the theory to professionals and beyond, however.[3] The purpose of this chapter is to examine, from both economic and legal perspectives, the appropriateness of extending strict liability to professionals.

The complexity of the subject matter, the availability of appellate cases and the continuing failure of injured patients to prevail in professional negligence cases call for an examination of medical doctors' liability.[4] The failure to recover is due to the need for an expert witness,[5] the difficulties involved in proving negligence[6] and the hesitancy of juries to attach the negligence label to a physician.[7] If it can be shown that strict liability should apply to physicians, then a strong case can be made that strict liability should apply to other professionals and beyond. This chapter will emphasize the pure service cases,[8] not those involving products, commonly referred to as sales-service hybrids.[9]

ECONOMIC CONSIDERATIONS

The arguments against suing physicians are often economic in nature: doctors will leave the profession[10] or move to a less risky specialty,[11] malpractice insurance rates will increase[12] and suits will raise the costs of medical treatment beyond the reach of the poor.[13] These arguments will likely be raised to counter the application of strict liability to physicians. This section's goal is to discover what light economic analysis sheds upon the issue of whether strict liability should apply to physicians.

A Tax on Automobile Sales Compared to the Application of Strict Liability to Professionals

It will be helpful at this point to examine a model: a tax on automobile sales. This model suggests that if strict liability is applied to only one doctor, he will have to bear the cost himself. Once strict liability is applied to all physicians, however, the patients, the doctor and other medical employees will share the cost. The model indicates that if the physician can control the supply of doctors, he will be able to pass the entire cost through to the patients, however.

Tax with a Fixed Supply

Assume that there are seven cars and that a buyer is willing to spend $500 for a car. Assume further that the demand and supply schedules are fixed.[14]

Now the legislature imposes a tax of $200 on the sale of a car. This is represented in Figure 7.1. Because supply is fixed at seven cars and a buyer is only willing to spend $500, the entire tax falls upon the seller.[15] He keeps $300 and sends $200 to the state. As Professor Alchian states, "The upper demand curve is a smoothed version of the demand by consumers and the lower demand curve, exactly $200 lower, is the net of tax demand that sellers retain after the government tax."[16] The tax does not alter the price paid by the car buyers; instead, it reduces the portion retained by the seller by $200.[17] This result, of course, is dictated by the assumption that supply and demand are fixed. If the seller tried to raise his price to $700, fewer cars would be sold and the unsold cars would then be bid down in price back to the old $500 per car.[18] If the supply of physicians is fixed and the demand for medical treatment is fixed, then the application of strict liability to medical malpractice will mean that the cost of that liability will be borne entirely by the doctor.

Figure 7.1.
Tax with a Fixed Supply

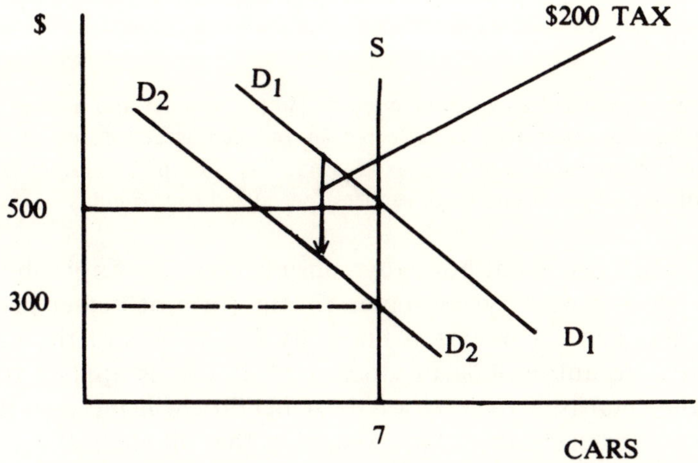

Source: From EXCHANGE AND PRODUCTION: COMPETITION, COORDINATION, AND CONTROL, 2/E by Armen Alchian and William R. Allen ©1977, 1964, 1967, 1969 by Wadsworth Publishing Company, Inc. Reprinted by permission of the publisher.

If the $200 tax on cars were used to improve highways to the extent of $200, then car purchasers might be willing to pay more than $500 for the cars because of the additional value of the improved roads.[19] If we assume that strict liability results in the patient receiving more from the physician (compensation for iatrogenic[20] injuries), then the doctor will be able to increase his fees to some extent, and the patients will pay more because of the increased value received.[21]

Tax on All Producers in an Industry

It will now be helpful to look at a model of the entire automobile industry. As with the previous model, assume that the legislature imposes a tax of $200 on the sale of automobiles. This tax increases each car dealer's marginal costs by $200 and adds $200 to the average cost of each car.[22] If we add together the new higher marginal-cost curves of all the dealers in the country, we obtain a higher-cost supply curve.[23] Before the tax, the price of a car was $500. Each dealer, now operating on a higher marginal-cost curve, would reduce its supply at the old price from X_1 to X_2.[24] The reduced total supply of cars would push up the price, which would induce each dealer to restrain its supply reduction to X_3.[25] The supply curve for the automobile industry shifts upward to reflect taxes of $200 per car.[26] This forces the price up to $600.[27] Professor Alchian notes:

> Part of tax is revealed as a higher price to [*sic*] consumer and a smaller rate of consumption; another part is reflected in reduced wealth value of resources specialized in production of this taxed good. Tax is borne by consumers and by owners of capital goods and labor services specialized to this industry.[28]

The entire tax is not borne by consumers of the automobiles. Part of the tax is borne by consumers in the form of higher prices and fewer cars. The other part is borne by the owners of the resources specialized to automobile production.[29] If this is applied to physicians, the increased expense of strict liability will increase the marginal costs for each physician. Assuming that all medical doctors are subject to strict liability over time, the price of medical treatment will rise and fewer services will be available. The costs of strict liability will be shared by patients, doctors and those who provide resources and labor services specialized to medical treatment.[30]

Tax on One Car Dealer Only

Assume that the tax is applied to only one automobile dealer. This is represented in Figure 7.2. The market supply for all car dealers (the industry) would not shift substantially, because there is no tax on the other dealers.[31] The car dealer who receives the tax has no way to "recoup part of his wealth by a higher price."[32] If he attempted to raise his price, purchasers would go to other dealers.[33]

If this is applied to physicians, the first new doctors who are forced to pay under strict liability will bear the entire loss themselves. But as more doctors are subject to strict liability, they will raise their prices and thus cover part of their losses. Indeed, as already noted, if the patient received substantial benefits through strict liability, the doctor could completely cover the increased expense.[34] That is, the patient would be willing to pay more for the medical service because he received more.

There is one sure method for the car dealer to pass the tax to the consumer: "If you could exclude competitors (whose supply in the market makes your selling price lower), you could raise your price."[35]

Figure 7.2.
Tax on One Automobile Dealer Compared with a Tax on All Automobile Dealers

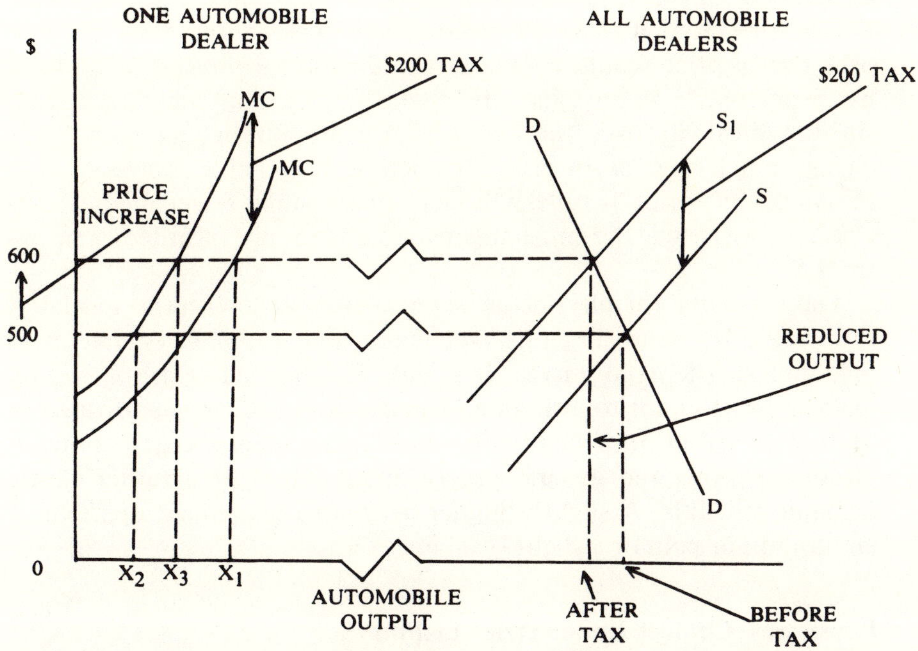

Source: From EXCHANGE AND PRODUCTION: COMPETITION, COORDINATION, AND CONTROL, 2/E by Armen Alchian and William R. Allen ©1977, 1964, 1967, 1969 by Wadsworth Publishing Company, Inc. Reprinted by permission of the publisher.

An example in the medical context would be limiting the number of competitors by controlling the size of medical schools.[36]

Elasticity of the Physicians' Demand Curve

The concept of elasticity indicates how responsive the quantity demanded is to a change in price.[37] If the demand for medical services is very elastic, a small increase in physicians' prices will lead to a substantial loss of physicians' total revenue.[38] On the other hand, if the demand schedule for these services is inelastic, then a small increase in price will lead to a corresponding small loss in total revenue.[39]

The impact of an increase in the price of medical services brought on by the adoption of strict liability will depend upon the elasticity of the demand curve facing the physician. Professor Alchian cautions, however: "Elasticities of demand with respect to prices are extremely difficult to estimate."[40] Nevertheless, he suggests that the elasticity of demand for physicians is less than one.[41] This means, for example, that if the elasticity for physicians were eight-tenths, then a 1 percent rise in price would decrease the demand for physicians' services by .8 percent.[42] In response, the medical profession might argue that since medical care is a "necessity,"[43] the amount demanded will not change much with an increase in price. It is arguable, however, that at some high price people will elect to consume fewer medical services, even though the most urgent are commonly regarded as necessities.[44]

The elasticity for physicians' services may vary with the specialty. For example, neurosurgeons and emergency room physicians may face inelastic demand curves. It is unlikely that many people would make a decision not to visit an emergency room or have neurosurgery performed based on a small percentage increase in price. In contrast, plastic surgeons and general practitioners may face a rather elastic demand schedule. A slightly higher price may encourage a patient to endure minor pain or a slight scar, for example.

Physicians' Choices Under Strict Liability

With the expansion of strict liability to medical doctors, they will be paying more in damages or in insurance premiums than under a negligence cause of action. There are several choices open to the physician in response to the increased cost brought on by strict liability.

Some physicians will claim that if they are going to be held strictly liable, they will quit the practice or shift to a less risky specialty. Some will no doubt state that they would rather sing country music, wait tables or go sailing than be subject to strict liability. Others may go on strike as a means of protest.[45] On the other hand, many doctors will likely work with the American Medical Association and Congress for the legislative overturn of strict liability.[46]

Most physicians will remain in practice and devise means to shift the increased costs to the patients, however. The most obvious method for accomplishing this is to increase fees or purchase sufficient insurance to cover strict liability and add the cost to the fee. The increase may not be substantial. One study indicates that medical malpractice insurance costs $1.50 per patient visit.[47] Finally, the physician could require the patient to purchase insurance covering strict liability as a condition to treatment.[48]

The sky may not be falling, and the prediction of physician strikes, shifts to less risky specialties and mass resignations may be inaccurate. It is doubtful that many patients inquire about the fee before obtaining medical services, or if they do ask, that they make their decision based on an increased cost of several dollars.[49] Most patients would not consider a small amount determinative, and it is unlikely that the application of strict liability will cause a substantial decrease in the demand for medical services. Because of this, few doctors will seriously consider resigning or moving to a less risky specialty because of the impact of strict liability.

Efficiency Considerations

Judge Posner argues that "the dominant function of the fault system is to generate rules of liability that . . . will bring about . . . the efficient—the cost-justified—level of accidents and safety."[50] He suggests that the appropriate statement of the relationship between law and economics is contained in Judge Learned Hand's early formulation of the negligence standard.[51] His reason for endorsing the Hand negligence formula is to increase overall economic value or welfare.[52]

Posner criticizes the theory of strict liability for failing to maximize the joint value of the interfering activities and argues again that the Hand formulation of negligence leads to the most efficient results.[53] His thesis touches upon fundamental theories of negligence, strict liability and economics. It therefore deserves more attention, particularly as applied to medical malpractice.

Judge Posner uses "the now familiar example of the railroad engine that emits sparks which damage crops along the railroad's right of way."[54] He concludes:

> The value-maximizing solution may turn out to involve changes by both parties in their present behavior; for example, the railroad may have to install a good but not perfect spark arrester and the farmer may have to leave an unplanted buffer space between the railroad right of way and his tilled fields. Or, the value-maximizing solution may involve changes by the railroad only, by the farmer only, or by neither party.[55]

There are several reasons why Posner's criticism of strict liability, as applied to medical malpractice cases, is invalid. In most medical malpractice cases the patient can do nothing to prevent the injury. For example, where a doctor ties an artery rather than a Fallopian tube or the wrong drug is prescribed, the patient can do nothing to avoid the injury. Posner argues that negligence is superior to strict liability because it encourages the injured party to take preventive measures.[56] In the sparking train example, the farmer may be in the best position to take preventive action. For example, the farmer could plant a nonflammable crop beside the tracks or leave a buffer zone unplanted.[57] There are few medical situations, however, where the patient can take steps to avoid the injury.

The doctor is usually in the best position to prevent the injury. He can select another procedure, prescribe a different drug or exercise more care during surgery. Moreover, the American Medical Association is in an excellent position to fund injury-prevention research.[58] The conclusion that a doctor should be held strictly liable for iatrogenic injuries follows from Professor Calabresi's strict liability test: "[W]hich of the parties to the accident *is in the best position to make the cost-benefit analysis between accident costs and accident avoidance costs. . . .*"[59] In medical malpractice, because of the technical material and his or her superior education, the doctor is in the best position to make the cost-benefit evaluation. The patient retains the authority to approve of the risk, the procedure or the drug, of course.[60]

The railroad example upon which Judge Posner bases his theory is inapplicable to medical cases. The relationship between doctor and patient is one of trust and confidence, a fiduciary relationship.[61] The doctor has an obligation to inform the patient of all material risks.[62] Posner may be able to suggest that the railroad should be permitted to cause substantial damage to the landowner, without liability, for efficiency reasons.[63] This is invalid as applied to the physician, however. Because of the fiduciary relationship, the doctor must avoid substantial damage to the patient. Certainly there is no suggestion that a doctor could inflict injury upon a patient for efficiency reasons.[64] If injury to the patient is to be anticipated, a different course of action must be selected, or the patient warned.[65]

The physician is in the best position to purchase insurance. In Judge Posner's example of the sparking train, he assumes that either the railroad or the farmer could with equal ease purchase insurance.[66] In contrast, the doctor, because of experience and ability to foresee the hazards involved, is best able to purchase insurance. Often the patient will be extremely anxious, unconscious or poor. The doctor may either purchase insurance or require the patient to purchase it as a condition to treatment.[67] When strict liability is adopted, the cost of insurance will become a normal part of the patient's bill.

The physician has reasons for not warning of risks or discussing a more expensive treatment in some cases.[68] If he did, the patient would become aware of the dangers and might not purchase the treatment or surgery. In light of this information gap, Judge Posner argues in favor of strict liability:

> If a product hazard is small, or perhaps great but for some reason not widely known . . . consumers may not be aware of it. In these circumstances a seller may be reluctant to advertise a safety improvement, because the advertisement will contain an implicit representation that the product is hazardous. . . . But make the producer liable for the consequences of a hazardous product, and no question of advertising safety improvements to consumer will arise. He will adopt cost-justified precautions not to divert sales from competitors but to minimize liability to injured consumers.[69]

Therefore, if the physician is held strictly liable, he will likely warn the patient of the risks.

The problem of setting the monetary value for benefits and burdens of medical injuries suggests that the cost-benefit discussion may be more philosophical than economic. That is, it may be possible to set a price for an acre of hay or a train's spark arrester,[70] but it is impossible to set a price for the birth of an unwanted child,[71] death due to an inappropriate drug or the suffering caused by a failure to diagnose cancer. Because these costs are not subject to monetization, the opposition to strict liability may in fact rest on values.[72]

This examination suggests that an exception exists to the Posner-Hand negligence formula: the strict liability rule should apply when the injured party was helpless to prevent the injury. This reasoning has been followed in cases involving ultrahazardous activities. For several hundred years strict liability has applied in blasting cases, where the landowner was helpless to avoid the damage.[73] Strict liability has also been applied in many products liability cases where the consumer is helpless to avoid the effects of the defective product.[74] Indeed, the law expressly recognizes this helplessness. If the product consumer is not helpless and can prevent the injury but fails to, then the defenses of misuse or assumption of risk may apply.[75]

LEGAL ANALYSIS

The application of strict liability to professionals raises a challenging legal question: how do you draw a line between injuries for which a plaintiff will be able to recover and those for which no recovery will be permitted? This section will consider that question and apply strict liability to cases involving professionals. Detailed discussions of the policy reasons for applying strict liability to physicians may be found elsewhere.[76]

The Compensable Event

A threshold issue in applying strict liability to professionals is how to draw the line between injuries for which the claimant will be able to recover in strict liability and other injuries. A line must be drawn at some point, because strict liability theory does not intend, in dealing with professionals or product sellers, for the defendant to be held liable for all injuries he causes.[77] Strict liability is not absolute liability.[78] Several commentators have suggested that there is no feasible method to draw such a line when considering professionals.[79] However, this section will evaluate several approaches for determining the compensable event, that is, when the claimant can recover from a professional in strict liability.

Proximate Cause and Duty

Proximate cause is the term used for resolving the scope of liability issue under the negligence cause of action.[80] Several tests have been used to answer the complex question of where to draw the line in negligence cases: foreseeability,[81] remoteness,[82] natural cause, direct cause,[83] the foreseeable small risk[84] and the foreseeable plaintiff.[85] All suffer from extreme vagueness and serve to mask the true social policies that motivate the judge to decide that liability should end at a particular point.[86] Because of these shortcomings, it promotes clear analysis to use the duty approach in negligence cases rather than proximate cause.[87]

Dean Leon Green has pioneered an analytical approach to the scope of liability issue that rests on the duty concept and eliminates the issue of proximate cause.[88] In weighing that issue, he urges the courts to consider several factors: flood of litigation, administrative impracticality, no limitation on liability, immorality, hardship, injustice, ability to carry the risk, changed social conditions, economics and prevention.[89] The duty approach avoids "squid function" words such as foreseeability[90] and directs the court to consider the operative social policies.

The great value of Green's approach is that it points us to the important policies. There are several problems, however, in applying it to strict liability and professionals. First, it fails to indicate that cases dealing with abnormally dangerous activities and products liability have held that the primary reason for strict liability is loss shifting.[91] Second, the duty approach was developed over fifty years ago and fails to reflect recent judicial developments in strict liability.[92]

Cheapest Cost Avoider

Professor Calabresi suggests that strict liability be imposed on whichever "of the parties to the accident *is in the best position to make the cost-benefit analysis between accident costs and accident avoidance costs and to act on that decision once it is made.*"[93] Several reasons suggest the application of this test to medical doctors:

> Implicit in the test is the notion that strict liability should place fault wherever a marked differential in ability to perform the cost-benefit analysis relevant to the maloccurrence is evident between identifiable categories of parties. . . . Presumably health care providers, as a category, have more information or better access to information than their patients and are therefore in a better position to perform the cost-benefit analysis as to what procedures to follow in diagnosing and treating ailments. Moreover, strict liability seems to promise a savings in administrative costs comparable to that expected under no-fault automobile insurance plans or under strict products liability.[94]

There are several problems with the "cheapest cost avoider" test. When applied to doctors, the result is absolute liability, because in most medical cases the doctor possesses superior knowledge.[95] Because the "cheapest cost avoider" approach leads to absolute liability, there may be a substantial increase in insurance costs and related administrative expenses.[96] Finally, the author of the test has never endorsed its application to professionals.[97] He prefers a type of workers' compensation in this area.[98]

New Zealand's Social Insurance

In 1972 New Zealand abolished tort claims for personal injury damages.[99] This was replaced with a system of social insurance. The main features of the system are straightforward:[100] "[T]he system generally covers all cases of 'personal injury by accident' without inquiry into fault, without inquiry into cause, and for the most part, without other qualifying requirements that would delay or complicate the payment of benefits." The Accident Compensation Act states that "personal injury by accident" includes "medical, surgical, dental, or first aid misadventure."[101] Medical misadventure is defined as follows: "(a) [A] person suffers bodily or mental injury or damage in the course of, and as part of, the administering to that person of medical aid, care or attention, and (b) such injury or damage is caused by mischance or accident, unexpected and undesigned, in the nature of medical error or medical mishap."[102]

The compensable event for strict liability could track the New Zealand plan. There are several drawbacks to relying on the New Zealand approach, however. First, in New Zealand the term "medical misadventure" "clearly excludes the normal risks of operative or other medical procedures."[103] Second, there is an "uncertainty about the extent to which tort claims are abolished."[104] Third, in New Zealand "medical misadventure" covers most, but not all, negligence, and therefore doctors still carry liability insurance.[105] Fourth, tough cases involving an absence of diagnosis, a wrong diagnosis or adverse consequences from proper treatment have created substantial difficulties.[106] For example, coverage has been rejected for cases involving postoperative infection.[107] Coverage will likely be rejected in New Zealand for treatment that "does not improve the patient's condition . . . or where the change results from . . . bodily reaction, or other complication."[108] These problems suggest that the New Zealand approach is inadequate for defining the compensable event for strict liability.

Consumer's Reasonable Expectations

One professor suggests that a service should be considered defective "if it fails to meet the reasonable expectations of the consumer."[109] He qualifies this by stating: "In service transactions . . . it is not always possible to attain the consumer's goal, and when this is so, an expectation of perfection is not reasonable."[110]

A serious flaw is present in this test: many professional-service transactions, particularly those of doctors, lawyers and architects, are too technical and specialized for consumers to form reasonable expectations. In the products area Dean Wade stated that the expectations of the ordinary consumer cannot be used as a standard for evaluating design defectiveness because "in many situations . . . the consumer would not know what to expect, because he would have no idea how safe the product could be made."[111] This suggests that the consumer's reasonable expectations test will not be helpful in determining the compensable event.

The Inouye-Kennedy Approach

Senators Inouye and Kennedy proposed strict liability for medical injuries in 1975.[112] The bill provided for no-fault compensation "for loss from any injury suffered as a result of health care services provided by an insured to [any] beneficiary."[113] The compensable event was defined as follows:

> [A] n injury "results" from the provision of health care services when it is more probably associated in whole or in part with the provision of such services than with the condition for which such services were provided.
>
> . . . .
>
> . . . "[H] ealth care services" means the rendering, as well as the omission, of any care, treatment, or services. . . .[114]

This answers the critics who argue that no test can be devised for the compensable event.[115] There is a major problem with using this particular test: the phrase "more probably associated . . . with the provision of such services" is extremely vague and will only be answered through case-by-case litigation. Such extensive litigation may consume the savings brought about through strict liability.[116]

A Functional Test

From this analysis it is clear that a test for determining the compensable event is needed that combines generality and specificity, while indicating appropriate factors for consideration. Modifications to the design-defect test noted earlier[117] produce a functional test that accomplishes these goals. The purpose of the functional test is to set forth the factors that have been identified by the courts as important in deciding two related questions: first, should strict liability apply to these facts; second, if strict liability applies, should this defendant be held liable?

The test for the court in deciding whether a professional should be held strictly liable involves a balancing of operative factors. First, and of primary importance, the court must consider that the reasons for strict liability are to shift the loss from the injured person to the professional and that the loss should be borne by the person who created it.[118] Second, the court should weigh (1) the social utility of the service performed by the professional, including whether it was trivial or necessary;[119] (2) the modified procedures that could have been used to accomplish the same result;[120] (3) possible substitute services;[121] (4) the likelihood of injury;[122] (5) the nature of the injury;[123] (6) the cost of making the service less risky;[124] (7) the value and opportunity of providing the patient or client with a warning of the risks;[125] (8) the ability of the professional to obtain insurance or otherwise carry the loss;[126] (9) the impact upon society of finding the professional strictly liable for this service;[127] (10) the experimental nature of the service;[128] (11) the amount of judgment required of the professional in making the decision;[129] and (12) the time available to make the decision.[130] The court may, of course, consider other factors that it deems relevant.

The test states that priority should be given to the primary reason for strict liability: loss shifting.[131] No priority is given to the twelve secondary factors because the weight given to each will vary with the facts of each case.

Application of the Functional Test

This section will apply the functional test to reported cases dealing with the medical profession and attorneys. The purpose is to make it clear that the functional test is workable and produces appropriate results.

Physicians

The following three cases deal with a strict liability suit against a physician for injuries from a service where no product was involved. In *Helling v. Carey*[132] the plaintiff developed glaucoma because the defendant, an ophthalmologist, failed to test for it. The doctor was following the professional standard for ophthalmologists: the glaucoma test was usually not given to persons under forty years of age. The court expressly rejected the standard of the medical profession and found the ophthalmologist negligent. The court reasoned that the test was simple, inexpensive and harmless; thus it should have been given.[133] There was "no judgment factor involved."[134]

In applying the functional test to *Helling*, the simple, inexpensive and harmless nature of the glaucoma test, as well as the ministerial nature of the decision, argue that strict liability should apply. To be sure, the concurring opinion in *Helling* suggested that the case rested on strict liability.[135] It also emphasized the role of insurance: "[S]trict liability serves a compensatory function in situations where the defendant is, through use of insurance, the financially more responsible person."[136]

In *Hoven v. Kelble*[137] a surgeon, an anesthesiologist, the hospital and the insurance carrier were sued. The patient suffered cardiac arrest while undergoing a lung biopsy. After considering strict liability, the court rejected it, because "the consequences of the step the plaintiffs urge cannot be predicted with sufficient clarity."[138] The court permitted a count in res ipsa loquitur, however.

There were insufficient facts presented in *Hoven* to decide whether, under the functional test, strict liability was appropriate. For example, the following questions need to be answered before the test can be applied: Could the procedure have been modified? Were other services available? What was the likelihood of the injury and the cost of making the service less risky? Was there an opportunity to provide the patient with a warning? How much judgment was involved in the decision? Was there an emergency?

Clark v. Gibbons[139] presents the most clearly stated judicial discussion of the application of strict liability to professionals. The patient suffered injury from premature termination of a fracture reduction. The anesthesia wore off before the surgery was completed. The patient sued the anesthesiologist and the orthopedic surgeon. The majority applied res ipsa, but Judge Tobriner, in a concurring opinion, argued for the application of strict liability:

> A system openly imposing liability without any pretense of negligence . . . can avoid unwarranted imputations of fault while permitting the rational development of badly needed doctrine. Simultaneously, such a system can insure that the burdens of unexplained accidents will not fall primarily upon the helpless but will be borne instead by those best able to spread their cost among all who benefit from the surgical operations in which those misfortunes occur.[140]

Tobriner added that strict liability will encourage settlements[141] and avoid the destruction of reputations that flows from a finding of negligence.[142] He concluded: "[B]asic error lies in primary reliance upon the concept of *negligence* and . . . the courts should undertake a fundamental re-assessment of the largely fictitious and often futile search for fault which presently characterizes medical injury litigation. . . ."[143]

The doctors would be liable in *Clark* if the functional test were applied. Several different procedures could have been used by the anesthesiologist,[144] there was substantial likelihood of injury if the anesthetic wore off,[145] the cost of extending the duration of the anesthetic was small,[146] the doctors failed to communicate with each other and therefore failed to exercise the judgment they possessed[147] and there was no emergency.[148] These factors weigh in favor of holding the physicians strictly liable.

Products have been present in several of the many important cases dealing with strict liability and a professional service. In *Magrine v. Krasnica* a patient sued a dentist for damages suffered when a hypodermic needle broke off in the patient's jaw.[149] On appeal, the New Jersey Superior Court affirmed the Hudson County court's decision in favor of the dentist.[150] The court rejected the application of strict liability: "[The dentist] . . . neither created the defect nor possessed any better capacity or expertise to discover or correct it. . . . Defendant dentist did not put the needle in the stream of commerce. . . . [P]rofessional services and skill [are] the *essence* of the relationship. . . ."[151]

Under the functional test *Magrine* was wrongly decided because the dentist was in the best position to spread the loss and to prevent the injury. If his insurance did not presently cover such losses,[152] it would in the future.[153] His ability to purchase insurance and spread the loss was the primary factor.[154] Also, the dentist was in the best position to prevent the injury.[155] He will note the needle's manufacturer[156] and select a more reliable manufacturer the next time. Indeed, he could have cheaply prevented the breakage by not using each needle eight times.[157] The cost of using a fresh needle each time, in relation to the potential injury, was low. Another important factor is that the dentist's decision was ministerial in nature.[158] Finally, the dissent makes a telling point in support of strict liability: "Dentistry as an enterprise should pay its own way. Denying compensation is to require an injured person who bears the loss alone to subsidize the risk-creating activity by which others profit."[159]

The Superior Court of New Jersey in *Newmark v. Gimbel's, Inc.*,[160] limited the scope of *Magrine* when it held that strict liability applied to a beautician who caused the plaintiff to contract dermatitis by applying a permanent wave solution to the plaintiff's hair: "[T]he transaction here . . . consisting of the supplying of a product for use in the administration of a permanent wave to plaintiff, carried with it an implied warranty that the product used was reasonably fit for the purpose for which it was to be used."[161] On appeal, in *Newmark*, the New Jersey Supreme Court was faced with a challenging argument: "[T]here is no doctrinal basis for distinguishing the services rendered by a beauty parlor operator from those rendered by a dentist or a doctor."[162] That is, because of *Magrine*, strict liability should not apply. The court rejected the argument:

> On the contrary there is a vast difference in the relationships. The beautician is engaged in a commercial enterprise; the dentist and doctor in a profession. The former caters publicly not to a need but to a form of aesthetic convenience or luxury. . . . The dentist or doctor does not and cannot advertise for patients. . . .[163]

This reasoning has been severely undermined by the recent Supreme Court decisions that advertising by doctors[164] and lawyers[165] is commercial speech and cannot be prohibited. These decisions remove the basis for distinguishing the beautician in *Newmark* from the dentist in *Magrine*, suggesting that strict liability should apply to both.[166]

Attorneys

Strict liability has not been applied by a court to attorneys. Two cases have noted the issue, however. One stated, in dicta, that implied warranty may apply to an attorney. Another merely referred to the issue.[167] *Broyles v. Brown Engineering* is the only case that offers specific reasons why an attorney should not be held strictly liable:

> Interpretation of law . . . cannot be an exact and accurate science. There is generally no formula to follow. Even when Code forms are used in the drafting of a complaint, questions often arise as to whether or not the correct form for the client's case has been used. The courts from state to state, and among the judges on a particular court, often disagree in their interpretation as to the effect of judicial pronouncements or legislative enactments. Trial lawyers are dependent on the reactions of jurors to factual presentations and the application of law thereto. . . . [A]s a whole, lawyers are dealing with factors that are beyond their control and under such circumstances, common dealings would reasonably suggest the absence of any implied guaranty of results.[168]

Some activities of an attorney should be subject to strict liability under the functional test. In finding strict liability here the important factors might be the likelihood of injury if too few witnesses were used, the low cost involved in checking the statute for the correct number of witnesses, the ability of the attorney to insure against the risk as compared with the client, the small amount of judgment involved in the activity,[169] and the time available to research the law. Thus in routine matters the factors favoring the imposition of strict liability apply to attorneys. On the other hand, strict liability would not apply to many areas of an attorney's work. For example, a great deal of judgment is involved in litigation decisions about who to depose and who to call as witnesses at trial.

STRICT LIABILITY, CONTRACT AND NO-FAULT

Professor Richard Epstein suggests that a physician employ contractual provisions to avoid strict liability.[170] This theory has been soundly rejected by the courts because it fails to reflect the inherent imbalance in the physician-patient relationship. The patient likely knows little about the medical procedure involved[171] and lacks bargaining power.[172] However, the physician has considerable market power and lacks the incentive to draft an individualized contract. He would probably resort to forms.[173] Unfortunately, the patient would likely underestimate the risk of the medical procedure.[174] Epstein apparently intends no real quid pro quo and appears to favor a contract where the patient would surrender his or her right to sue for large amounts in damages in return for a slight decrease in the physician's fee.[175] Finally, the courts have uniformly struck down disclaimers of liability in health care cases[176] such as this because they violate public policy.[177]

A problem with the contract solution is that much would be surrendered (the damage action) in return for very little (a slight decrease in the fee). A stronger case for contract would be presented if the doctor promised to pay for all out-of-pocket expenses arising from an iatrogenic injury in return for the patient's promise to relinquish his right to recover in tort.

Professor Jeffrey O'Connell has proposed that no-fault insurance be adopted for injuries arising from medical treatment.[178] He suggests that a professional "should be able to elect . . . to pay for injuries he causes on a no-fault basis, thereby foreclosing claims based on fault or defect."[179] The no-fault solution would, of course, involve a contract, but an agreement much more generous to the patient than the Epstein proposal: "[P]ayment under elective no-fault liability would be limited to out-of-pocket losses above any amounts payable from collateral sources such as Blue Cross and sick leave. Payment would . . . not be made for pain and suffering."[180]

The reason for the failure of the no-fault solution to be widely adopted is clear: there is little incentive for a physician to elect no-fault, because he or she stands an excellent chance of winning most malpractice cases.[181] The strict liability approach would provide an incentive for no-fault, however. If the doctor failed to offer no-fault to his patient, he would often be strictly liable if the patient suffered injury.

Strict liability has several advantages over elective no-fault. It would, for example, have a more substantial deterrent effect than no-fault.[182] As noted by economics Professors Polinsky and Shavell,[183] strict liability, rather than no-fault, would lead to medical services reflecting the socially correct price. It should also be noted that the patient's recovery under no-fault is substantially less than under strict liability. Finally, elective no-fault must await action by the physician. In contrast, strict liability is independent of any physician-patient contract.

Traditional economic analysis suggests that a professional should not be treated differently from a product seller for the purposes of imposing liability. Indeed, recent economic studies that argue that strict liability should apply to product sellers suggest that strict liability is also appropriate for professionals.[184]

Legal analysis also supports the application of strict liability to professionals. Tests for dealing with the core question of where to draw the line are available. Admittedly they are not neat, but neither are basic tort concepts such as negligence or proximate cause. This chapter proposes that courts adopt the functional test. Applying the functional test for strict liability to decided cases manifests that it is workable and will assist the courts in addressing the operative social policies. Indeed, the case analysis section of this chapter makes it clear that strict liability is applicable to physicians, attorneys and beyond.

NOTES

1. *See* Keeton, *Products Liability–Design Hazards and the Meaning of Defect*, 10 CUM. L. REV. 293 (1979); Prosser, *The Fall of the Citadel*, 50 MINN. L. REV. 791 (1961); Wade, *On the Nature of Strict Tort Liability for Products*, 44 MISS. L. J. 825 (1973).

2. *See infra* notes 132-69.

3. *See* Greenfield, *Consumer Protection in Service Transactions–Implied Warranties and Strict Liability in Tort*, 1974 UTAH L. REV. 661, 688; Franklin, *Tort Liability for Hepatitis: An Analysis and a Proposal*, 24 STAN. L. REV. 439, 472 (1972).

4. J. O'CONNELL, ENDING INSULT TO INJURY 29 (1975).

5. *See* W. PROSSER, HANDBOOK OF THE LAW OF TORTS 161-66 (1971) [hereinafter cited as PROSSER].

6. J. O'CONNELL, *supra* note 4, at 29.

7. *See* Helling v. Carey, 83 Wash. 2d 514, 519 P. 2d 981 (1974); Clark v. Gibbons, 66 Cal. 2d 399, 426 P. 2d 525, 58 Cal. Rptr. 125 (1967).

8. A pure service involves only a service, or primarily a service, where there is no material issue of whether a defective product caused the injury. An example of a pure service is ophthalmology. *See, e.g.*, Helling v. Carey, 83 Wash. 2d 514, 519 P. 2d 981 (1974), where an ophthalmologist was held liable for failing to test a patient for glaucoma.

9. For a classic example of a sales-service hybrid, *see* Newmark v. Gimbel's, Inc., 54 N.J. 585, 258 A. 2d 697 (1969), where a beauty parlor was held strictly liable for the damage caused by a permanent wave it had applied.

10. Sepler, *Professional Malpractice Litigation Crises: Danger or Distortion?*, 15 FORUM 493, 500 (1980).

11. *Id.*

12. *Id. at 502.*

13. *Id.* at 501. *See also* Aitken, *Medical Malpractice: The Alleged "Crisis" in Perspective*, 1976 INS. L. J. 90, 90-97.

14. This hypothetical case is adapted from A. ALCHIAN & W. ALLEN, EXCHANGE AND PRODUCTION: COMPETITION, COORDINATION, AND CONTROL 88 (2d ed. 1977) [hereinafter cited as ALCHIAN & ALLEN].

15. *Id.* at 89.

16. *Id.*

17. *Id.*

18. *See id.* at 90.

19. *See id.* at 91.

20. "Iatrogenic" is defined as referring to "any condition in a patient occurring as the result of treatment by a physician or surgeon." DORLAND'S ILLUSTRATED MEDICAL DICTIONARY (24th ed. 1965).

21. In the auto example, if the taxes were burned (not used for something of value to the car buyer), people would not be willing to pay more than $500 for a car. If, on the other hand, some of the taxes were put into road improvement, people would pay more than $500 for a car because they received more in return (better roads). If all of the $200 tax was put into roads, people might be willing to pay more than $700 ($500 + $200) because they valued the new roads more than $200. Application of this theory to doctors suggests that they may be able to increase their fees more than the cost of added insurance (to cover strict liability) if the value of the potential strict liability recovery to the patient is greater than the cost of the insurance to the physician.

22. *See* ALCHIAN & ALLEN, *supra* note 14, at 278-79.

23. *Id.*

24. *Id.* We have dropped here the assumption in the previous example that supply and demand curves are fixed.

25. *Id.*

26. *Id.*

27. "Price rises by less than tax because, at smaller output, marginal and average costs are lower." *Id.* at 277. "[E]ven if every supplier is affected, price will not rise as much as the cost because (1) the demand schedule is negatively sloped—less will be sold when price is raised; and (2) the supply schedule is positively sloped." *Id.* at 281.

28. *Id.* at 281.

29. *Id.*

30. *See* Shavell, *Strict Liability Versus Negligence*, 9 J. LEGAL STUD. 1, 4 (1980). *See also* A. M. Polinsky & W. P. Rogerson, Products Liability, Consumer Misperceptions, and Market Power (May 1982) (working paper available from Frank J. Vandall); Brown, *Toward an Economic Theory of Liability*, 2 J. LEGAL STUD. 323 (1973); Spence, *Consumer Misperceptions, Product Failure and Producer Liability*, 44 REV. ECON. STUD. 561 (1977).

31. ALCHIAN & ALLEN, *supra* note 14, at 281.

32. *Id.*

33. *Id.*

34. *See supra* notes 19-21 and accompanying text.

35. ALCHIAN & ALLEN, *supra* note 14, at 281.

36. Reder, *Medical Malpractice: An Economist's View*, 1976 AM. B. FOUND. RESEARCH J. 511, 559.

37. ALCHIAN & ALLEN, *supra* note 14, at 59.

38. *See* P. A. SAMUELSON, ECONOMICS 358 (11th ed. 1980).

39. *Id.* at 360.

40. ALCHIAN & ALLEN, *supra* note 14, at 63 (noting that "the total change in amount bought will not be the result only of a change in price along a fixed demand"). Variables other than price may have shifted the demand curve itself.

41. *Id.*

42. *Id.*

43. Professor Alchian addresses this argument when he comments that "'[n]eed' is a word often used to suggest absolute minimum requirements, when in fact the amount 'needed' depends on the cost of having more." ALCHIAN & ALLEN, *supra* note 14, at 74.

44. For example, as the price of medical services increases, such uses as cosmetic surgery and visits for preventive treatment (flu shots, routine checkups and so on) will most likely be reduced.

45. *See* Redish, *Legislative Response to the Medical Malpractice Insurance Crisis: Constitutional Implications*, 55 TEX. L. REV. 759, 760 (1977).

46. For a discussion of the AMA's proposed Model Informed Consent Statute, *see* Meisel & Kabnick, *Informed Consent to Medical Treatment: An Analysis of Recent Legislation*, 41 PITT. L. REV. 407, 409-17 (1980).

47. Note, *Comparative Approaches to Liability for Medical Maloccurrences*, 84 YALE L. J. 1141, 1156 n. 78 (1975) [hereinafter cited as *Comparative Approaches*].

48. For example, Pilot Life Insurance Co. offers comprehensive accident insurance to parents of grade-school children for $8.00 per year.

49. Assume, for example, that the cost of strict liability is double the cost of existing malpractice insurance. That would still only amount to $3.00 per visit. *See Comparative Approaches*, *supra* note 47, at 1156 n. 78.

50. Posner, *A Theory of Negligence*, 1 J. LEGAL STUD. 29 (1972).

51. *Id.*

52. *Id.*

53. Posner, *Strict Liability: A Comment*, 2 J. LEGAL STUD. 205 (1973).

54. *Id.*

55. *Id.* at 206.

56. *Id.*

57. *Id.*

58. *See generally* Reder, *Medical Malpractice: An Economist's View*, 1976 AM. B. FOUND. RESEARCH J. 511, 544-45.

59. Calabresi & Hirschoff, *Toward a Test for Strict Liability in Torts*, 81 YALE L. J. 1055, 1060 (1970) (emphasis added).

60. Scholendorf v. Society of N.Y. Hosp., 211 N.Y. 125, 105 N.E. 92 (1914).

61. Miller v. Kennedy, 11 Wash. App. 272, 522 P.2d 852 (1974), *aff'd*, 85 Wash. 2d 151, 530 P.2d 334 (1975).

62. *Id.*

63. Posner, *supra* note 53.

64. In an emergency, however, a physician may select either of two available courses of action when both will lead to injury. PROSSER, *supra* note 5, at 168-69.

65. Miller v. Kennedy, 11 Wash. App. 272, 522 P.2d 852 (1974), *aff'd*, 85 Wash. 2d 151, 530 P.2d 334 (1975).

66. Posner, *supra* note 53.

67. The doctor may also self-insure if he believes that he is particularly careful.

68. *Contra*, Miller v. Kennedy, 11 Wash. App. at 286, 522 P.2d at 862 ("There is no room for paternalism").

69. Posner, *supra* note 53, at 211.

70. *Id.*

71. "When the parents say their child should not have been born, they make it impossible for a court to measure their damages in being the mother and father of a defective child." Gleitman v. Cosgrove, 49 N.J. 22, 29-30, 227 A.2d 689, 693 (N.J. 1967).

72. *See* Dworkin, *Is Wealth a Value?*, 9 J. LEGAL STUD. 191 (1980).

73. *See* Spano v. Perini Corp., 25 N.Y.2d 11, 250 N.E.2d 31, 302 N.Y.S.2d 527 (1969); PROSSER, *supra* note 5, at 513–14. *But see* Foster v. Preston Mill Co., 44 Wash. 2d 440, 268 P.2d 645 (1954) (creating an exception of the imposition of liability where the plaintiff's use of his own land could be characterized as unusual or extraordinary).

74. *See, e.g.*, Stevens v. Parke-Davis, 9 Cal. 3d 51, 507 P.2d 653, 107 Cal. Rptr. 45 (1973) (extensive overpromotion of chloromycetin); Henningsen v. Bloomfield Motors, 32 N.J. 358, 161 A.2d 69 (1960) (purchaser's wife injured when car suddenly veered off the road and into a wall).

75. "The seller is entitled to have his due warnings and instructions followed; and when they are disregarded, and injury results, he is not liable." PROSSER, *supra* note 5, at 669.

76. *See* Franklin, *supra* note 3, at 472.

77. Justice Traynor's suggestion for imposition of absolute liability in Escola v. Coca-Cola Bottling Co., 24 Cal. 2d 453, 463, 150 P.2d 436, 440 (1944), has not been followed by courts.

78. *See* chapter 4.

79. *See Comparative Approaches, supra* note 47, at 1153.

80. *See* PROSSER, *supra* note 5, at 236–37.

81. *See* Overseas Tankship (U.K.) Ltd. v. Mort Dock and Eng'g Co. (Wagon Mound No. 1), [1961] A.C. 388.

82. *See In re* Kinsman Transit Co., 388 F.2d 821 at 824 (2d Cir. 1968).

83. *See In re* Arbitration Between Polemis and Furness, Withy & Co., [1921] 3 K.B. 560 (C.A.).

84. *See* Overseas Tankship (U.K.) Ltd. v. Miller Steamship Co. (Wagon Mound No. 2), [1967] 1 A.C. 617.

85. *See* Palsgraf v. Long Island R.R. Co., 248 N.Y. 339, 162 N.E. 99 (1928).

86. *See* Green, *Proximate Cause in Texas Negligence Law* (pt. 3), 28 TEX. L. REV. 755, 758 (1950) [hereinafter cited as Green].

87. Green argues that the judge should determine the defendant's duty to the plaintiff, considering "the policies which enter into the allocation of risks such as may be involved in the particular case." *Id.* at 773-74.

88. *Id.* at 773.

89. *Id.* at 757 n. 4; Green, *The Duty Problem in Negligence Cases* (pt. 1), 28 COLUM. L. REV. 1014, 1034-44 (1928).

90. *See* Green, *supra* note 86.

91. *See* chapter 2.

92. *See, e.g.*, Dreisonstok v. Volkswagenwerk, A.G., 489 F.2d 1066 (4th Cir. 1977); Greenman v. Yuba Power Products, Inc., 59 Cal. 2d 57, 377 P.2d 897, 27 Cal. Rptr. 697 (1963); Escola v. Coca-Cola Bottling Co., 24 Cal. 2d 453, 150 P.2d 436 (1944); McCormack v. Hankscraft Co., 278 Minn. 322, 154 N.W. 2d 488 (1967).

93. Calabresi & Hirschoff, *supra* note 59, at 1060.

94. *Comparative Approaches, supra* note 47, at 1152.

95. "According to its originators, this test would be applied to broad categories, and not to individuals on a case-by-case basis." *Id.* at 1151-52.

96. *Id.* at 1154-55.

97. Calabresi, *The Problem of Malpractice: Trying to Round Out the Circle*, 27 U. TORONTO L.J. 131 (1977) [hereinafter cited as Calabresi, *The Problem of Malpractice*]. Calabresi here discusses the problems of compensation for injuries due to medical malpractice, but without ever recommending, indeed hardly mentioning, the cheapest cost avoider approach.

98. Calabresi states that he considers "the most promising attempt at reform . . . that tried by Havighurst & Tancredi." *Id.* at 137. The approach is described in Havighurst & Tancredi, *Medical Adversity Insurance–A No-Fault Approach to Medical Malpractice and Quality Assurance*, 1974 INS. L.J. 69, 71.

99. T. ISON, ACCIDENT COMPENSATION 13 (1980).

100.

> Stated over-simply, the main features of the system are as follows: A statutory body, the ACC, is the administering agency and adjudicating tribunal. The main revenues of the system are derived in three ways and recorded in three funds.
>
> 1. Levies on employers and the self-employed are collected by the Inland Revenue (a collecting agent for the ACC), and paid into an "earners' fund." The rate of levy payable in respect of employees ranges from 50 cents to $5.00 per $100.00 of payroll (as of 1 April 1979), depending on the risk classification of the employment. For the self-employed there is a standard rate of $1.00 per $100.00 of earnings.
>
> 2. Levies on motor vehicles are collected by the Post Office (a collecting agent for ACC) as part of the motor vehicle license fee. These levies are paid into a "motor vehicle fund." The rate of levy for an ordinary motor car is $14.20 per annum, with other rates applying to other types of motor vehicles.

> 3. A "supplementary fund" is created from general government revenues to provide benefits in respect of injuries not covered by either of the other two funds, for example, housewives injured at home.

Id. at 14.

101. *Id.*

102. *Id.* at 36.

103. *Id.*

104. *Id.*

105. *Id.*

106. G. PALMER, COMPENSATION FOR INCAPACITY 256 (1979).

107. *Id.* at 257.

108. *Id.* at 258.

109. Greenfield, *supra* note 3, at 697.

110. *Id.*

111. Wade, *On the Nature of Strict Tort Liability for Products*, 44 MISS. L.J. 825, 829 (1973).

112. S. 215, 94th Cong., 1st Sess., 121 CONG. REC. 681 (1975).

113. *Id.* § 1711(a).

114. *Id.* § 1721(8), (11).

115. *See, e.g.*, Greenfield, *supra* note 3, at 697–98; *Comparative Approaches, supra* note 47, at 1153–54.

116. Savings would probably result, however, if special hearing officers developed expertise in making determinations using the test. *See*, *Comparative Approaches, supra* note 47.

117. *See* chapter 4.

118. This rationale was stated in Greenman v. Yuba Power Prods, Inc., 59 Cal. 2d 57, 377 P. 2d 897, 27 Cal. Rptr. 697 (1963), and in Escola v. Coca-Cola Bottling Co., 24 Cal. 2d 453, 150 P. 2d 436 (1944).

119. For example, was the doctor performing neurosurgery to remove a malignant tumor or was he removing a mole for cosmetic reasons?

120. For example, could a less risky drug have been prescribed? Could the technique or surgery have been less invasive?

121. Could rest and diet have accomplished the same result as surgery? Could the attorney have settled the case without going to trial?

122. Should the physician have anticipated a substantial chance of adverse results? Should the attorney have been able to anticipate that he might lose the case?

123. Is the resultant injury trivial, substantial or very serious?

124. Could the service have been made substantially less risky by a small expenditure of time or money?

125. Was the patient very young or in an emergency situation so that a warning would be inappropriate? Could the patient or client comprehend the warning?

126. In medical malpractice cases the doctor will usually have insurance. Sometimes, however, the patient will have insurance. In malpractice cases involving attorneys, however, it is unlikely that the client will have insurance that covers the injury. In malpractice cases involving architects, an uninsured third party often will be injured. In contrast, insurance is readily available to architects. Note, *Architect Tort Liability in Preparation of Plans and Specifications*, 55 CAL. L. REV. 1386 (1967). In Helling v. Carey, 83 Wash. 2d 514, 520, 519 P. 2d 981, 985 (1974), the concurring judge argued that strict liability "serves a compensatory function in situations where the defendant is, through the use of insurance, the financially more responsible person."

127. Is this service so vital to society that any real and prolonged decrease in its availability would adversely affect society as a whole? In this vein, there is evidence that the medical malpractice crisis never existed. *See generally* Sepler, *Professional Malpractice Litigation Crises: Danger or Distortion?* 15 FORUM 493 (1980).

128. Was this an important experiment that should receive the encouragement and support of society? *See* RESTATEMENT (SECOND) OF TORTS § 402A, comment k. Was the patient fully informed of the risks of the experiment? *See* Canterbury v. Spence, 464 F. 2d 772 (D.C. Cir. 1972).

129. *See* Mallor, *Liability Without Fault for Professional Services: Toward a New Standard of Professional Accountability*, 9 SETON HALL L. REV. 474, 493-94 (1978).

130. Professionals often find themselves confronted with an emergency. There is little time for reflection, and a decision must be made. When a professional is confronted with an emergency, negligence is the preferred cause of action. In most products cases, however, the manufacturer has time to evaluate the various courses of action. *See, e.g.*, Dreisonstok v. Volkswagenwerk, 489 F. 2d 1066 (4th Cir. 1974); Evans v. General Motors, 359 F. 2d 822 (7th Cir.), *cert. denied*, 385 U.S. 836 (1966).

131. *See* Helling v. Carey, 83 Wash. 2d 514, 519 P. 2d 981, 984-85 (1974).

132. 83 Wash. 2d 514, 519 P. 2d 981 (1974).

133. *Id.* at 518, 519 P. 2d at 983.

134. *Id.*

135. *Id.* at 520, 519 P. 2d at 984.

136. *Id.* at 521, 519 P. 2d at 985.

137. 79 Wis. 2d 444, 256 N.W. 2d 379 (1977).

138. 79 Wis. 2d at 472, 256 N.W. 2d at 393.

139. 66 Cal. 2d 399, 426 P. 2d 515, 58 Cal. Rptr. 125 (1967).

140. 66 Cal. 2d 399, 426 P. 2d at 539, 58 Cal. Rptr. at 139 (Tobriner, J., concurring).

141. *Id.* at 540.

142. *Id.*

143. *Id.* at 538.

144. *Id.* at 528–29. Other anesthetics or other modes of administration could have been used.

145. *Id.* at 529.

146. *Id.*

147. *Id.*

148. *Id.* at 528–29, 58 Cal. Rptr. at 128–29.

149. Magrine v. Krasnica, 94 N.J. Super. 228, 227 A. 2d 539 (Hudson County Ct. 1967), *aff'd sub nom.* Magrine v. Spector, 100 N.J. Super. 223, 241 A. 2d 637 (Super. Ct. App. Div. 1968), *aff'd* 53 N.J. 259, 250 A. 2d 129 (1969).

150. *See id.*, Magrine v. Krasnica.

151. *See id.*, Magrine v. Krasnica, at 234–35.

152. The insurance carrier here was denying coverage, apparently on the grounds that the case involved implied warranty, a contract claim, rather than a covered malpractice claim. *Id.* at 239, 227 A. 2d at 545.

153. *See* Franklin, *supra* note 3, at 439, 472.

154. The refusal of courts to visit large losses upon small businesses has, in part, rested on the idea that it would put them out of business. Contemporary insurance equalizes the loss-spreading ability of large and small businesses, however. Applying this to professionals, then, the dentist is just as able to purchase malpractice insurance as the large or small business is able to purchase products liability insurance.

155. He could have used the needle only once or purchased a better grade of needle (if that was the problem).

156. The dissent in Magrine v. Spector notes that strict liability "may encourage greater caution in purchasing equipment and examining for defects." 100 N.J. Super. at 232, 241 A. 2d at 642.

157. 94 N.J. Super. at 230, 227 A. 2d at 540.

158. Compare the judgment factor with the discretionary functions exception in administrative law. The discretionary functions exception to the Federal Torts Claim Act protects the official from suit. The purpose of the exception is to avoid dampening the ardor of the official. K. DAVIS, ADMINISTRATIVE LAW TEXT § 26.01–.02 (3rd ed. 1972).

159. 100 N.J. Super. at 240–41, 241 A. 2d at 647.

160. 102 N.J. Super. 279, 246 A. 2d 11 (1968), *aff'd*, 54 N.J. 585, 258 A. 2d 697 (1969).

161. 102 N.J. Super. at 286, 246 A. 2d at 15.

162. 54 N.J. at 596, 258 A. 2d at 702.

163. *Id.*

164. Virginia Pharmacy Bd. v. Virginia Consumer Council, 425 U.S. 748 (1976); Bigelow v. Virginia, 421 U.S. 809 (1975).

165. Bates v. State Bar of Ariz., 433 U.S. 350 (1977).

166. In the other cases where a product and a professional service have been involved, the courts have generally rejected the application of strict liability. For

example, in Batiste v. American Home Prod. Corp., 32 N.C. App. 1, 231 S.E. 2d 269 (Ct. App. 1967), a doctor was sued for prescribing an oral contraceptive that caused a stroke. The "essence" of the transaction was held to be a service and not the sale of a good.

167. Hoven v. Kelble, 79 Wis. 2d 444, 467, 256 N.W. 2d 379, 390 (1979).

168. *Broyles*, 275 Ala. at 39, 151 So. 2d 767, at 771. Further discussion of reasons why an attorney should not be held strictly liable is found in Mallor, *supra* note 129.

169. The "standardized" nature of the service has been suggested as a key to applying strict liability to a lawyer. *See supra* note 133.

170. Epstein, *Medical Malpractice: The Case for Contract*, 1976 AM. B. FOUND. RESEARCH J. 87, 105.

171. Cobbs v. Grant, 8 Cal. 3d 229, 242, 502 P. 2d 1, 9-10, 104 Cal. Rptr. 505, 513 (1972).

172. *Id.*

173. Epstein appears to consider general standardized forms as valuable in giving the physician "necessary discretion." Epstein, *supra* note 170, at 124.

174. Cobbs v. Grant, 8 Cal. 3d at 242-45, 502 P. 2d at 9-11, 104 Cal. Rptr. at 513-15.

175. *See* Epstein, *supra* note 170. In fact, Professor Epstein never sets out what the contract should contain.

176. *See, e.g.*, Tunkl v. Regents of Univ. of Calif., 60 Cal. 2d 93, 383 P. 2d 441, 32 Cal. Rptr. 33 (1963). *See also* Porubiansky v. Emory Univ., 156 Ga. App. 602, 275 S.E. 2d 163 (1980), *aff'd*, 248 Ga. 391 (1981).

177. Tunkl, *supra* at 101, 383 P. 2d at 447, 32 Cal. Rptr. at 39.

178. J. O'CONNELL, *supra* note 4, at 29.

179. O'Connell, *No-Fault Insurance for Injuries Arising from Medical Treatment: A Proposal for Elective Coverage*, 24 EMORY L. J. 21, 34 (1975).

180. *Id.* at 35.

181. O'Connell points to the New Zealand plan as accomplishing some of the goals of elective no-fault. J. O'CONNELL, *supra* note 4, at 73. However, he also notes that as of 1978 in the United States, "no-fault reform is stuck. No state has enacted a new law since 1975." O'Connell, *Harnessing the Liability Lottery: Elective First-Party No-Fault Insurance Financed by Third-Party Tort Claims*, 1978 WASH. U. L. Q. 693, 695.

182. *See supra* notes 4-7.

183. It seems likely that strict liability would result in more cases being lost by the physician, with higher damage awards than under no-fault; the desire to avoid these results would lead to greater care on the part of the physician under strict liability.

184. Shavell, *supra* note 30, at 4.

BIBLIOGRAPHY

Alchian, A., & W. Allen, *Exchange and Production: Competition, Coordination, and Control* (2d ed. 1977).

Aitken, "Medical Malpractice: The Alleged 'Crisis' in Perspective." 1976 *Ins. L.J.* 90.

"Architect Tort Liability in Preparation of Plans and Specifications." 55 *Cal. L. Rev.* 1386 (1967).

Brown, "Toward an Economic Theory of Liability." 2 *J. Legal Stud.* 323 (1973).

Calabresi, "The Problem of Malpractice: Trying to Round Out the Circle." 27 *U. Toronto L. J.* 131 (1977).

Calabresi & Hirschoff, "Toward a Test for Strict Liability in Torts." 81 *Yale L.J.* 1055 (1970).

"Comparative Approaches to Liability for Medical Maloccurrences." 84 *Yale L.J.* 1141 (1975).

Davis, K., *Administrative Law Text* (3rd ed. 1972).

Dworkin, "Is Wealth a Value?" 9 *J. Legal Stud.* 191 (1980).

Epstein, "Medical Malpractice: The Case for Contract." 1976 *Am. B. Found. Research J.* 87.

Franklin, "Tort Liability for Hepatitis: An Anlaysis and a Proposal." 24 *Stan. L. Rev.* 439 (1972).

Green, "The Duty Problem in Negligence Cases" (pt. 1). 28 *Colum. L. Rev.* 1014 (1928).

Green, "Proximate Cause in Texas Negligence Law" (pt. 4). 28 *Tex. L. Rev.* 755 (1950).

Greenfield, "Consumer Protection in Service Transactions–Implied Warranties and Strict Liability in Tort." 1974 *Utah L. Rev.* 661.

Havighurst & Tancredi, "Medical Adversity Insurance–A No-Fault Approach to Medical Malpractice and Quality Assurance." 1974 *Ins. L. J.* 69.

Ison, T., *Accident Compensation* (1980).

Keeton, "Products Liability–Design Hazards and the Meaning of Defect." 10 *Cum. L. Rev.* 292 (1979).

Mallor, "Liability Without Fault for Professional Services: Toward a New Standard of Professional Accountability." 9 *Seton Hall L. Rev.* 474 (1978).

Meisel & Kabnick, "Informed Consent to Medical Treatment: An Analysis of Recent Legislation," 42 *Pitt. L. Rev.* 407 (1980).

O'Connell, J., *Ending Insult to Injury* (1975).

O'Connell, "Harnessing the Liability Lottery: Elective First-Party No-Fault Insurance Financed by Third-Party Tort Claims." 1978 *Wash. U. L. Q.* 693.

O'Connell, "No-Fault Insurance for Injuries Arising from Medical Treatment: A Proposal for Elective Coverage." 24 *Emory L. J.* 21 (1975).

Palmer, G., *Compensation for Incapacity* (1979).

Polinsky, A. M., & W. P. Rogerson, "Products Liability, Consumer Misperceptions, and Market Power" (May 1982) (working paper available from Frank J. Vandall).

Posner, "Strict Liability: A Comment." 2 *J. Legal Stud.* 205 (1973).

Posner, "A Theory of Negligence." 1 *J. Legal Stud.* 29 (1972).

Prosser, "The Fall of the Citadel (Strict Liability to the Consumer)." 50 *Minn. L. Rev.* 791 (1961).

Prosser, W., *Handbook of the Law of Torts* (4th ed. 1971).

Reder, "Medical Malpractice: An Economist's View." 1976 *Am. B. Found. Research J.* 511.

Redish, "Legislative Response to the Medical Malpractice Insurance Crisis: Constitutional Implications." 55 *Tex. L. Rev.* 759 (1977).

Restatement (Second) of Torts, § 402A (1965).

Samuelson, P. A., Economics (11th ed. 1980).

Sepler, "Professional Malpractice Litigation Crises: Danger or Distortion?" 15 *Forum* 493 (1980).

Shavell, "Strict Liability Versus Negligence." 9 *J. Legal Stud.* 1 (1980).

Spence, "Consumer Misperceptions, Product Failure and Producer Liability." 44 *Rev. Econ. Stud.* 561 (1977).

Wade, "On the Nature of Strict Tort Liability for Products." 44 *Miss. L. J.* 825 (1973).

8

Applying Strict Liability to Professionals Having Little Discretion: Pharmacists

This chapter is an examination of the liability of pharmacists for civil damages in strict liability suits brought by injured patients or third parties. In discussing this topic, actions in negligence and strict liability will be considered, although the main thrust will be to consider the application of strict liability to pharmacists. Strict liability may be raised in a case where the pharmacist dispenses a defective drug, mistakenly dispenses one drug for another, omits a warning label or refills a prescription without physician approval, for example.

The pharmacist occupies a unique position in the health care market. The physician prescribes the drugs and the pharmacist fills the precise prescription. Few pharmacists manufacture drugs. Instead, they are purchased from pharmaceutical companies. The pharmacist has little discretion to vary from the exact language of the prescription.

The application of strict liability to pharmacists is important in the development of strict liability theory because it raises the question whether someone should be held liable when he was not careless and has done nothing "wrong." That is, should the pharmacist be held liable because of loss shifting, because he is better able to absorb the loss, spread it or obtain insurance, than the patient?

One of the very first recorded cases in American law deals with a negligence action brought against a pharmacist. In *Thomas v. Win-*

chester (1852)[1] the plaintiff requested extract of dandelion for his wife, but the pharmacist supplied a potentially toxic substance, belladonna. The defendant was a manufacturing pharmacist engaged in the production and sale of vegetable extracts for medicinal purposes. He was held liable for damages resulting from his negligence in putting the label of a harmless medicine on a bottle containing a potentially toxic substance. The court stated that the rule of privity, which generally led to nonliability, did not apply to products that were inherently dangerous to human life. *Thomas* manifests that early in the development of American jurisprudence, the courts recognized that the pharmacist should be held liable for mistakes in dealing with pharmaceuticals.

TESTS FOR STRICT LIABILITY AS APPLIED TO PHARMACISTS

Restatement (Second) of Torts, Section 402A

The Restatement takes the position that "[o]ne who sells any product in a defective condition unreasonably dangerous to the user or consumer or to his property is subject to liability for physical harm thereby caused to the ultimate user or consumer."[2] Under the Restatement any user can recover from a seller. The privity argument is no longer controlling. If a pharmacist sold a drug that was defective and caused an injury to the consumer, the consumer could bring a suit against the pharmacist and recover in strict liability. Comment k to the Restatement will be discussed later in the chapter.

Risk-Benefit Test

Dean Keeton's position is that since strict liability is not insurance or absolute liability, any evaluation of a defective product must involve the weighing of danger against utility.[3] My critique is that this is a negligence test. The only distinction is that under the risk-benefit test as applied to strict liability, the danger as proven at the time of trial determines whether or not the product is defective. The risk-benefit test would produce the same result as the negligence test in most cases involving a pharmacist.

California Test

California developed a two-part test for strict liability in *Barker v. Lull* (1978):

> First, a product may be found defective in design if the plaintiff establishes that the product failed to perform as safely as an ordinary consumer would expect when used in an intended or reasonably foreseeable manner. Second, a product may alternatively be found defective in design if the plaintiff demonstrates that the product's design proximately caused his injury and the defendant fails to establish, in light of the relevant factors, that on balance, the benefits of the challenged design outweigh the risk of danger inherent in such design.[4]

The first branch of the *Barker* test would not likely be applied to pharmacists. The court would not hold that a consumer could recover for an injury any time the drug failed to perform as an ordinary consumer would expect. The reason is that the patient always expects the drug to perform as prescribed. The only time a court might follow the consumer expectation test is when the warning on the drug was insufficient.

The second part of the *Barker* test is more likely to be applied to pharmacists. If a consumer can prove that he was injured by a drug purchased from a pharmacist, a court might hold that that is sufficient for the consumer to take the case to the jury, and the pharmacist then has the burden of proving that the benefits of the pharmacist's activity (selling the particular drug) outweighed the risk of danger inherent in such activity.

Negligence with Imputed Knowledge

Phillips v. Kimwood Machine Company has adopted a test based upon a modification of the traditional negligence approach:

> A dangerously defective article would be one which a reasonable person would not put into the stream of commerce if he had knowledge of its harmful character. The test, therefore, is whether the seller would be negligent if he sold the article knowing of the risk involved. Strict liability imposes what amounts to constructive knowledge of the condition of the product.[5]

This is a negligence test, although labeled as a strict liability test. Under *Phillips* the jury is asked to find whether the pharmacist was negligent.

Cheapest Cost Avoider

Professor Calabresi has developed the following test for strict liability:

> The strict liability test we suggest does not require that a government institution make such a cost-benefit analysis. It requires of such an institution only a decision as to which of the parties to the accident is in the best position to make the cost-benefit analysis between accident costs and accident avoidance costs and to act on that decision once it is made. The question for the court reduces to a search for the cheapest cost avoider.[6]

A pharmacist would almost always be the cheapest cost avoider because he has superior education, has knowledge of the risks and the benefits of the drug and will almost always be in a better position than the consumer to do something in regard to the pharmaceutical.

However, if a suit were brought against both the pharmacist and the doctor, where the doctor had prescribed the drug and the pharmacist sold it, the pharmacist could argue that the doctor was the cheapest cost avoider. The doctor was the one best able to evaluate the costs and the benefits of the particular drug.

COMPENSABLE EVENT

In applying strict liability to pharmacists, a problem arises as to how to draw the line between injuries for which the consumer will be able to recover in strict liability and other injuries, such as those brought about by the illness for which the customer purchased the drug. This line must be drawn because there is no policy to turn strict liability into absolute liability.

In chapter four it has been suggested that the courts should adopt a functional test for determining the compensable event.[7] In deciding whether pharmacists should be held strictly liable, the court must balance important factors. First, the court must consider that the reasons for strict liability are to shift the loss from the injured person and that the loss should be borne by the person who caused it. Second, the court should weigh the other factors to see whether in this case it is appropriate to find the pharmacist strictly liable. Is there an important offsetting policy, for example? The functional test makes clear that priority should be given to the basic reason for strict liability, loss shifting. It retains the cost-benefit approach, but puts it in a secondary role. Under the functional test the pharmacist will be held liable more often than under a negligence test.

APPLICATION OF DISCLAIMERS TO PHARMACISTS

It might be argued that a pharmacist should be able to disclaim all liability in return for a reduction in price on the part of the drugs sold.[8] If a pharmacist were to adopt a contractual disclaimer, it would be likely to be rejected by the courts because it fails to recognize the substantial advantage that the pharmacist has as compared to the consumer. It is clear that the pharmaceutical consumer knows little about the drug in question. That is why he is purchasing it from a pharmacist. Also, the consumer lacks bargaining power. The pharmacist is licensed by the state and has a form of monopoly. In giving up his right to sue, the patient would likely underestimate the risk involved in the drug. Some drugs are relatively innocuous; others are enormously toxic. The pharmaceutical consumer has little expertise in deciding which are safe and which are hazardous. Finally, the courts have uniformly struck down disclaimers of liability in health care cases as violations of public policy.[9] The problem with the contract solution to pharmacist liability is that something of substantial value would be surrendered (the right to sue for damages) in return for a slight decrease in the price of the drug.

DEFENSES

This section will survey the defenses that might be available to a pharmacist who is sued in a strict liability cause of action. The particular defenses available will depend on the facts in each case, and the list is, therefore, not intended to be complete.

Assumption of Risk

In a strict liability suit assumption of risk is a defense, although contributory negligence is not.[10] The theory behind assumption of risk is that if the plaintiff knows the risk and voluntarily assumes it, he has consented to the injury. It is important, in arguing assumption of risk, for the defendant to show that plaintiff subjectively knew the specific risk and had choices available to him when he assumed it. If the plaintiff was not aware of the risk or if he was buying the drugs because of an emergency, the defense of the assumption of risk would not be available. The point is that in most suits against pharmacists, assumption of risk is not a viable defense because the consumer neither knew the risk nor had alternatives.

Cause in Fact

Cause in fact[11] is fundamental to all personal injury suits. The plaintiff must show that the defendant's conduct was a cause in fact of his injury. The defendant's conduct must have been a "substantial factor" in bringing about the plaintiff's damages, or the injury would not have occurred "but for" defendant's conduct. If the plaintiff was consuming drugs that had been purchased from the defendant pharmacist at the time the plaintiff (not the pilot) was killed in an airplane crash, the pharmacist would have available the defense of absence of cause in fact. The drugs being consumed had nothing to do with the plaintiff's death in the crash. Similarly, if the customer's death was brought about by a preexisting illness, then the pharmacist might be able to defend on the basis that the drugs were not a substantial factor in causing death. At this point the functional test for the compensable event would be employed.

Proximate Cause

Social policy is the key to proximate cause.[12] It is the concept developed by the courts in order to allow them to control the jury. The function of proximate cause is to determine the scope of liability. The courts use it to determine the damages they will permit the jury to consider. Under proximate cause the task is ascertaining where to draw the line. The most popular test used to determine proximate cause is foreseeability: Were the damages foreseeable to the pharmacist at the time of injury? Could he or she have anticipated the injury that occurred?

A pharmacist could defend on the basis of no proximate cause where the drug manufacturer had not informed the pharmacist of the risks involved in the particular drug, and therefore the pharmacist had not informed the consumer. In that case the pharmacist could argue that the damages were not foreseeable. If the customer used the drug for treating an illness for which the drug was not intended, the pharmacist would have the defense of proximate cause or misuse.

One branch of proximate cause is the defense of superseding cause.[13] A superseding cause is one that comes after the defendant's conduct and from a different source than the defendant. An example of a superseding cause is the Tylenol case. In that case a criminal third party opened the Tylenol containers and inserted poison into the capsules. The manufacturer of Tylenol was able to defend on the basis that a superseding cause cut off the defendant's liability. There is no liability for a superseding cause unless it is foreseeable. Apparently the manufacturer of Tylenol shifted to caplets in order to cut off the foreseeability argument in subsequent cases.

Phillips v. Kimwood Machine Company

One defense is for the pharmacist to argue for the adoption of a strict liability rule that is the equivalent of negligence. An example of that is the case of *Phillips v. Kimwood Machine Company*,[14] an Oregon case decided in 1974. There the court adopted a test for strict liability that sounded like negligence.[15] Although the court suggested that this is a strict liability test, close examination manifests that it is merely a test for negligence. Clearly the essential question is whether "the seller would be negligent if he sold the article knowing of the risk involved."

Misuse

Using a rotary lawn mower to trim a hedge would be an example of misuse. Misuse is available as a defense to the pharmacist when the drug is used in a way that is not foreseeable to the pharmacist. An example of misuse might be where a customer used "the pill" as a mouthwash or ingested it to cure her stomach cramps. In such a case the pharmacist could argue that the customer's use of the drug was not foreseeable and, therefore, constituted a misuse.

The Texas Court of Appeals has stated: "A product is not misused merely because the manufacturer intended that it be used in a different manner: the manufacturer must show that the use which caused the injury was not reasonably foreseeable."[16] Because most uses of a product are foreseeable, it is not common for the courts to apply the defense of misuse.

Service

In suits against a hospital[17] and a dentist,[18] courts have held that their activities are primarily the provision of a service, not the sale of a product. Therefore, strict liability is not yet available against the professional, and the plaintiff must prove negligence.[19] However, in 1986 a trial court in Washington permitted the jury to apply strict liability against a pharmacist in a DES case.[20]

In a strict liability suit the pharmacist could argue that his primary activity is rendering a service, and his secondary activity is selling a product, the pharmaceutical. This was rejected in a New Jersey case involving a suit against a beautician.[21] The defendant applied a hair wave that caused dermatitis. The court held that the beautician was involved in a sales-service hybrid activity and was therefore subject to strict liability. It should be noted that a recent survey suggests that the work of a pharmacist is primarily ministerial, with little discretion involved in most sales.[22]

Murphy v. Squibb,[23] a recent California case, has adopted the service rationale in a strict liability suit against a pharmacy. In *Murphy* a twenty-three-year-old woman developed vaginal cancer because her mother had used DES. The jury found that the defendant pharmacy, Exclusive, had sold DES to the plaintiff's mother. The California Supreme Court rejected the plaintiff's argument that a pharmacist merely "sells" products:

> [T]he pharmacist is engaged in a hybrid enterprise, combining the performance of service and the sale of prescription drugs. . . . A key factor is that the pharmacist who fills a prescription is in a different position from the ordinary retailer because he cannot offer a prescription for sale except by order of the doctor. In this respect, he is providing a service to the doctor and acting as an extension of the doctor. . . .[24]

However, the court felt bound by the legislature: "The Legislature has provided in Section 4046 that the practice of pharmacy is . . . a . . . service."[25] The court believed that strict liability would be too heavy a burden to place on the pharmacy:

> The Legislature might have decided . . . that since the doctor who ordered the drug provided by the pharmacy cannot be held strictly liable for its defects and in some circumstances the manufacturer who created the defect can also escape liability, it would be unfair and burdensome to expose the pharmacy alone to

strict liability since it may provide the drug only on a doctor's prescription, which the pharmacist must strictly follow.[26]

In contrast to *Murphy*, one court has applied strict liability against a pharmacist.[27]

Comment k

Comment k to Restatement (Second) section 402A provides: There are some products which, in the present state of human knowledge, are quite incapable of being made safe for their intended and ordinary use. These are especially common in the field of drugs. . . . Such a product, properly prepared and accompanied by proper . . . warning, is not defective nor is it *unreasonably* dangerous.[28]

A pharmacist might argue that comment k protects him from strict liability for the sale of a defective drug. Comment k suggests otherwise:

The seller of such products, again with the qualification that they are properly prepared and marketed, and proper warning is given . . . is not to be held strictly liable for unfortunate consequences attending their use merely because he has undertaken to supply the public with an apparently useful and desirable product, attended with a known but apparently reasonable risk.[29]

The section leaves the door open to hold the pharmacist strictly liable if the drug he or she sold was improperly prepared or lacked an appropriate warning. A recent California case against a DES manufacturer has stated that negligence (under comment k) and not strict liability must be shown against the manufacturer of a defective drug, however.[30]

PLAINTIFF'S COUNTERARGUMENTS

The purpose of this section is to respond to the major policy arguments that the pharmacist will put forward to refute strict liability. Some of the arguments stem from the nature of the pharmacist's work.

Service

The pharmacist will argue that his or her work is a "service" and therefore immune from strict liability. The argument will be that the sale is trivial. The problem with the sales-service approach is that it forces the court to "hunch" on the question of liability. In sales-service cases the court usually concludes without careful analysis that the act is a sale or a service. When a court implements the sales-service test, it fails to examine important social policies. The court does not ask who is best able to bear the loss, who can best spread the loss or who can best obtain insurance. The court in *Murphy v. Squibb*,[31] for example, failed to ask whether the defendant could join with other pharmacists to engage in research on how to avoid DES types of cases. The court also failed to explain why it is better for the plaintiff to rely on welfare (funded by taxpayers) to cover her medical bills, rather than to place the loss on the pharmacist.

One judge has reasoned in favor of strict liability that marketing a pharmaceutical is essentially a sale.[32] Little judgment is involved in the sale of most prescriptions:

> Only 22 percent of patients who purchase prescription drugs are counseled by the retail druggist, who spends an average of only one and one-half hours a day performing this service. . . . [I] n the vast majority of prescription drug sale transactions, the customer receives only a product and no service from the retail druggist.
>
> The predominance of the sale is also reflected by the fixed prices the retail druggist charges. . . .[33]

The defendant pharmacist will also argue that he or she is completely bound by the doctor's prescription. It has never been decisive whether the seller had the power to select what he sold, however. Strict liability has been applied to a wholesale-retail tire dealer who "supplied whatever tires the manufacturer specified."[34] Car dealers, for example, are subject to strict liability although they are unable to select which models they sell.

Comment k

By adopting comment k, to the effect that strict liability does not apply to the sale of prescription drugs, the court fails to balance important factors:

> [t] he gravity of the danger posed by the challenged design, the likelihood that such danger would occur, the mechanical feasibility of a safer alternative design,

the financial cost of an improved design, and the adverse consequences to the product and to the consumer that would result from an alternative design.[35]

Statutory Exclusion for Pharmacists

There may be a statute to the effect that the pharmacist provides a "service." The court must examine the statute carefully to see if the legislature intended to protect the pharmacist from strict liability. In *Murphy v. Squibb*[36] the dissent concluded that there was little evidence of a legislative intent to protect pharmacists from strict liability.

It is, of course, likely that the phrase "service" may have been inserted at the behest of a "special-interest" lobbying group and may have never received the close scrutiny of the legislature. In that situation there is no reason to presume that the statute represents the will of the people. It is the court's duty to reject the "special-interest" legislation unless the exclusion is clearly the intent of the legislature.

Increased Prices

One argument is that strict liability will lead to increased prices that will drive the pharmacist out of business. Pharmacists are engaged in a form of monpoly. If a drug is prescribed, it must be purchased at a pharmacy. There is no "cut-rate" competition to drive the pharmacist out of business. There is, indeed, "no evidence that the imposition of strict liability would cause the supply of prescription drugs to dry up."[37] After a short period of time, all pharmacists would be subject to strict liability, and none would have a price advantage.

For example, although automobile dealers have been subject to strict liability for over twenty-five years, there is no apparent shortage of cars to sell. It has been noted that "[a]s to the concern that prices might rise, this possibility has long been recognized and accepted as part of the strict liability doctrine."[38]

Finally, it will be argued by the pharmacist that strict liability will have a severe impact on "mom and pop" pharmacies. In response, it must be noted that the sole-proprietorship pharmacy is better able to obtain insurance than the injured patient.[39] Because of the uniform application of strict liability, there is no reason to think that the large chains will have an advantage over the sole-proprietorship pharmacies.

Strict liability should apply when a pharmacist sells a defective product, such as a drug, or makes a mistake in filling a prescription. The pharmacist is in a better position than the injured patient to spread the loss through increased prices and the purchase of insurance. Such a rule will encourage the pharmacist to exercise a high degree of care, and this will protect life and health. In most cases the pharmacist has superior knowledge, and the patient has relied on the expertise of the pharmacist.

A recent case dealing with the application of strict liability to pharmacists is *Murphy v. Squibb.*[40] At first blush, it appears to be a strong victory for pharmacists because it holds, in part, that the pharmacist provided a "service" rather than a sale, and therefore strict liability was inappropriate. *Murphy* is a weak victory for pharmacists because it concerns DES, however. There is no way to discover who manufactured the DES that the plaintiff's mother consumed. Causation is not provable in DES cases. To deal with this disturbing problem, the courts have turned themselves inside out to reach a compromise. The compromise is that if the daughter with cancer sues the manufacturers of a "substantial share" of DES, proof of traditional cause in fact will be waived. This radical compromise was hard fought. In *Murphy* the plaintiff attempted to disregard the battle and the compromise, to treat them as trivial. The court correctly rejected plaintiff's requested expansion. It would be erroneous for pharmacists to read *Murphy* as a bastion, however. It is merely a tenacious adherence to the rule in *Sindell*, which was a radical departure from traditional cause in fact.[41] *Murphy* is not a strong case. Indeed, a recent decision has applied strict liability to a pharmacist.[42]

NOTES

1. Thomas v. Winchester, 6 N.Y. 397 (1852).
2. RESTATEMENT (SECOND) OF TORTS § 402A (1965).
3. *See* Keeton, *Products Liability–Design Hazards and the Meaning of Defect*, 10 CUM L. REV. 293 (1979).
4. *See* Barker v. Lull Eng'g Co., 20 Cal. 3d at 413, 573 P. 2d 443, 143 Cal. Rptr. 225 (1978).
5. Phillips v. Kimwood Mach. Co., 269 Or. 485, 525 P. 2d 1033 (1974).
6. Calabresi & Hirschoff, *Toward a Test for Strict Liability in Torts*, 81 YALE L. J. 1055, 1060 (1972).
7. *See* chapter 4.

8. *See* Epstein, *Medical Malpractice: The Case for Contract*, 1976 AM. B. FOUND RESEARCH J. 87, 105.

9. *See, e.g.*, Tunkl v. Regents of Univ. of Calif., 60 Cal. 2d 92, 383 P. 2d 441, 32 Cal. Rptr. 33 (1963). *See also* Porubianski v. Emory Univ., 156 Ga. App. 602, 275 S.E. 2d 163 (1980).

10. W. PROSSER, HANDBOOK OF THE LAW OF TORTS 523 (4th ed. 1971).

11. *Id.* at 236.

12. *See* Green, *The Duty Problem in Negligence Cases* (pt. 1), 28 COLUM. L. REV. 1014 (1928).

13. *See* W. PROSSER, *supra* note 10, at 270-86.

14. Phillips v. Kimwood Mach. Co., 269 Or. 485, 525 P. 2d 1033 (1974).

15. *Id.* at 487, 525 P. 2d 1036 (footnotes omitted).

16. Proctor & Gamble Mfg. Co. v. Langley, 422 S.W. 2d 773 (Tex. 1967).

17. *See* Perlmutter v. Beth David Hosp., 308 N.Y. 100, 123 N.E. 2d 792 (1954).

18. Magrine v. Krasnica, 94 N.J. Super. 228, 227 A. 2d 539 (Hudson County Ct. 1967), *aff'd sub nom.* Magrine v. Spector, 100 N.J. Super. 223, 241 A. 2d 637 (App. Div. 1968), *aff'd*, 53 N.J. 259, 250 A. 2d 129 (1969).

19. *But see* chapter 7.

20. Martin v. Abbott, Washington Superior Court, Pierce County, No. 302,471 (June 17, 1986).

21. Newmark v. Gimbel's Inc., 102 N.J. Super. 279, 246 A. 2d 11 (1968), *aff'd*, 54 N.J. 585, 258 A. 2d 697 (1969).

22. *See* Reinsmith, *Patient-Centered Community Pharmacy: A Mirage*, NS25 AMERICAN PHARMACY 6 (Jan. 1985).

23. Murphy v. E. R. Squibb, 40 Cal. 3d 672, 710 P. 2d 247, 221 Cal. Rptr. 447 (1985). Three states agree with California in rejecting the application of strict liability to pharmacists: Florida, McLeod v. W. S. Merrell Co., 174 So. 2d 736, 739 (Fla. 1965); North Carolina, Batiste v. American Home Prods., 32 N.C. App. 1, 10, 231 S.E. 2d 269, 275 (1977); and New York, Bichler v. Willing, 58 A.D. 331, 335, 397 N.Y. 2d 57, 59-60 (N.Y. 1977).

24. Murphy v. E. R. Squibb, 40 Cal. 3d 672, 678-79, 710 P. 2d 247, 251, 221 Cal. Rptr. 447, 451 (1985).

25. *Id.* at 679, 710 P. 2d at 252, 221 Cal. Rptr. at 452.

26. *Id.* at 681, 710 P. 2d at 253, 221 Cal. Rptr. at 453 (footnote omitted).

27. *See Martin v. Abbott*, *supra* note 20.

28. RESTATEMENT (SECOND) OF TORTS § 402A comment k (1965).

29. *Id.*

30. Brown v. Superior Court, April 15, 1988, BNA Product Safety and Liability Reporter 358 (Cal. Supreme Ct. March 31, 1988).

31. Murphy v. E. R. Squibb, 40 Cal. 3d 672, 710 P. 2d 247, 221 Cal. Rptr. 447 (1985).

32. *Id.* at 689, 710 P. 2d at 258, 221 Cal. Rptr. at 458 (Bird, C. J., dissenting).

33. *Id.* at 695-96, 710 P. 2d at 263, 221 Cal. Rptr. at 463.

34. Barth v. B. F. Goodrich Tire Co., 265 Cal. App. 248, 71 Cal. Rptr. 306 (1968).

35. Barker v. Lull Eng'g Co., 20 Cal. 3d 413, 432, 573 P. 2d 443, 456, 143 Cal. Rptr. 225, 238 (1978).

36. *Murphy*, 40 Cal. 3d at 689, 710 P. 2d at 265, 221 Cal. Rptr. at 465.

37. *Id.* at 689, 710 P. 2d at 265, 221 Cal. Rptr. at 465 (Bird, C.J., dissenting).

38. *Id.*

39. Murphy, 40 Cal. 3d 672, 710 P. 2d 247, 221 Cal. Rptr. 447 (1985).

40. *Id.*

41. Sindell v. Abbott Labs., 26 Cal. 3d 588, 607 P. 2d 924, 163 Cal. Rptr. 132, *cert. denied*, 449 U.S. 912 (1980).

42. *See Martin v. Abbott supra* note 20.

BIBLIOGRAPHY

Calabresi & Hirschoff, "Toward a Test for Strict Liability in Torts." 81 *Yale L. J.* 1055 (1972).

Epstein, "Medical Malpractice: The Case for Contract." 1976 *Am. B. Found. Research J.* 87.

Green, "The Duty Problem in Negligence Cases" (pt. 1). 28 *Colum. L. Rev.* 1014 (1928).

Keeton, "Products Liability–Design Hazards and the Meaning of Defect." 10 *Cum. L. Rev.* 293 (1979).

Prosser, W., *Handbook of the Law of Torts* (4th ed. 1971).

Reinsmith, "Patient-Centered Community Pharmacy: A Mirage." NS25 *American Pharmacy* 6 (Jan. 1985).

Restatement (Second) of Torts §402A (1965).

9

The Backlash: Proposed Reforms to Strict Liability

A substantial volume of material has been written arguing that there is too much litigation and that as a result, insurance rates have increased dramatically.[1] These increased rates, it has been urged, have forced small businesses to close and, in general, priced many types of insurance beyond reach.[2] The most popular cure has been to call for far-reaching tort reform, especially in the area of strict liability.[3] This chapter suggests that there is inadequate data to support such reform and that the existing products liability system, based on strict liability, is an inexpensive solution to a far-reaching problem.

The first section, the products liability insurance problem, argues that hard facts in regard to insurance are unavailable. It suggests that since most goods and services have increased in price over the last fifteen years, it should not be surprising that the price of insurance is also increasing. The second section, an economic analysis of the "crisis," suggests that the increase in the price of insurance may help solve the insurance availability problem. The third section, strict liability and socialized medicine, explains the underlying reason for strict liability in the products area. It concludes that strict liability is cheaper than other options. The final section manifests the inadequacies of several current reform proposals dealing with products liability and strict liability.

THE ALLEGED PRODUCTS LIABILITY INSURANCE PROBLEM

Impetus for reform has reached a fever pitch in products liability.[4] Manufacturers, suppliers and insurance companies insist that the products liability insurance problem is of acute proportions.[5] Some manufacturers claim that high insurance rates may force them out of business.[6] Insurance companies claim that a products liability "crisis" exists and have requested legislative protection of manufacturers' interests.[7]

The Interagency Task Force on Products Liability, under the direction of the U.S. Department of Commerce, prepared an intensive study of products liability problems.[8] The study revealed that the problem was not of "crisis" proportions.[9] The task force attempted to define the problem and to provide insight into the possible legislative reforms. It concluded that a number of small buisnesses must choose between foregoing products liability insurance or purchasing it at very high premiums.[10] In most industries studied, products liability premiums appeared to have risen substantially during the period studied.[11] The industries most severely affected by the increased insurance costs were engaged in the manufacture of industrial chemicals and certain consumer goods, such as pharmaceuticals, automotive parts and medical devices.[12] The problem of expensive insurance for smaller firms in other industries was found to be less severe.[13]

The task force identified three causes of the recent rise in products liability insurance premiums: insurance ratemaking procedures, the tort-litigation system and unsafe manufacturing practices.[14] Several less substantial causes also were identified: inflation,[15] consumer and worker awareness, increases in the number and complexity of products and product misuse.[16] Finally, the task force stated that it was uncertain whether the total number of pending claims in the industries studied had increased during the period studied.[17]

Doubling and tripling of insurance rates should not be viewed with alarm. Many products have increased dramatically in price in the last fifteen years. In 1972, for example, the price of a basic Datsun 1200 was $2,051.[18] In 1987 the price of a basic Nissan Sentra was $6,199,[19] a 300 percent increase. Why, then, is anyone surprised that insurance rates have doubled or tripled? Also, look at the prices for health care. During the period 1967–1983, hospital room rates increased by 520 percent.[20] During the same period the Consumer Price Index for all goods increased by almost 200 percent.[21] It is clear that "[t]he tremendous growth in health care expenditures is expected to continue on into the future. By 1990, total health spending is expected to reach some $758 billion, more than double what it is today."[22] Is it any wonder, then, that damages awarded in personal injury suits have increased over the last few years? A portion of the increase is due to higher medical expenses.

On the other hand, in assessing the nature of the insurance problem, it becomes clear that few facts are available from the insurance companies.[23] No information is generally available as to how much insurance is sold, how much is paid out in claims or how much is made in profit.[24] In reflecting this, one judge has held: "The 'crisis' in medical malpractice insurance is a sham. . . . There is no empirical data to support the claim that a medical malpractice insurance crisis exists."[25]

In direct contrast to the insurance industry's claims of near bankruptcy, recent earnings by the insurance industry are impressive. Quoting figures compiled by A. M. Best Co., an independent firm that follows the insurance industry, one author has stated: "Best's Review reported that in 1985, property-casualty stock prices rose 50%, twice the rate of increase for the Dow Jones Industrial Average. In the first quarter of 1986, these stocks were up an additional 26%."[26] Other data suggests that if there ever was an insurance "crisis," it has now passed.[27]

AN ECONOMIC ANALYSIS OF THE "CRISIS"

Let us assume for the moment that products liability insurance rates are very high, some manufacturers and sellers cannot obtain insurance and a few have therefore decided to go out of business. What should be done about this? Economic analysis suggests that nothing should be done.[28]

The gasoline shortage of the mid-1970s is a good example of how the market functions.[29] The price of gasoline went up dramatically, and people altered their driving habits—driving less and taking vacations closer to home, for example. Also, automobile manufacturers—especially the Japanese—responded with smaller, more fuel-efficient cars.[30] Because of the opportunity to make a profit, many countries (such as Saudi Arabia, the United States, England and Mexico) expanded drilling for oil and production. The result has been that much more oil is available and the price of gasoline has tumbled. Small, fuel-efficient cars are now plentiful. The market has worked and crisis has been averted.

As the economists say, what we should do in this insurance price and availability "crisis" is "let the market work."[31] Permit the price of insurance to rise. That will be an indication that people are willing to spend more for insurance. This will encourage others to enter the market for the purpose of selling insurance. In fact, this is beginning to occur. Numerous states have insurance now being provided by cooperatives; medical malpractice insurance is a leading example.[32] Indeed, these co-ops are "reasonably successful."[33] Some manufacturers are self-insuring.[34] With the increased competition, insurance premiums will fall. With time, the insurance "crisis" will resolve itself through the function of the market.[35]

But what of the manufacturers and sellers who cannot obtain insurance? If these are profitable companies, in time, someone will offer them insurance at high rates. If they are not profitable companies, the next question is: Why aren't they profitable? If companies are not profitable because of high risks and large losses in products liability lawsuits, this is the market's way of saying that their products are too risky, too dangerous.

For these few companies (ultra–high-risk companies who are leaving the market), it is up to the government to decide whether to support them. For example, when pharmaceutical companies refused to produce swine flu vaccines because of fears of liability, the federal government insulated the manufacturers from liability.[36] Similarly, local governments have been forced to absorb part of the higher costs of diphtheria, pertussis and tetanus (DPT) vaccines.[37] In short, economic theory suggests that we should let the market work, and new corrective measures will automatically appear.

STRICT LIABILITY AND SOCIALIZED MEDICINE

Many products liability reform proposals have as their goal the elimination of strict liability.[38] This is unfortunate because it may be argued that strict liability is a free-market substitute for socialized medicine. In order to understand the efficiency of the strict liability system, one must examine a country with a system based upon socialized medicine. England's approach to personal injury is a substantial contrast to the litigation system in the United States. England has a "cradle-to-grave compensation" system.[39] If you break your leg while playing rugby or are seriously injured by a defective product, it makes no difference. The social insurance program pays for your medical expenses, drugs and prosthetic devices.[40] A portion of lost wages is also covered. The drawback of the British system is its great expense. This cost is paid for by an enormous tax on citizens and industry.[41] The result is that citizens have little disposable income and industry apparently has insufficient profit to make needed investments.[42] With such a high tax, the citizens have little income to spend and this results in a lower GNP.[43]

In comparison with England's welfare state, the personal injury system, including strict liability, in the United States is relatively cheap and efficient. An injured person is able to obtain an attorney even though he or she is poor.[44] This is because of the contingent fee system. The attorney will investigate the facts and study the law. What must also be remembered is that if the case has no merit, the attorney will refuse to take it.[45] Successful attorneys reject nonmeritorious suits because they know that if the case is weak, they are going to lose and this will be costly.[46]

The strict liability system in the United States is relatively inexpensive. There is no huge tax on citizens or industry to support it. Only those found liable must pay.[47] Also, unlike England and other socialized countries, there is no enormous bureaucracy. The entrepreneurial-lawyer system, based upon representation made possible by the contingent fee, means that an attorney is only brought in when an injury occurs and the attorney only takes the case if it is viable.[48] If he misevaluates a case, he recovers nothing and, in fact, may lose hundreds of thousands of dollars worth of his time.[49]

If the United States had socialized medicine (and I am not suggesting that we adopt it), as they do in Great Britain, there would be little need for trials and little need for strict liability. The verdicts would be small. Why would anyone want to sue when most of his or her damages were going to be compensated, as well as a substantial portion of lost wages?

The purposes of strict liability, then, are to provide a focused method for examination of fact patterns, to tilt the scales in favor of the consumer because of the seller bias of negligence and to pay damages to consumers who have been injured by manufacturers or sellers.[50] In some cases this will work a burden on the manufacturer or seller,[51] but it is better for the manufacturer or seller to obtain insurance, or raise the price of the product and so spread the loss, than it is to visit the entire loss on an innocent consumer.[52] It is also much cheaper to have a products liability system that is founded on strict liability than to have a compensation system that is part of an expensive welfare state, as in the United Kingdom.[53] In summary, some aspects of the strict liability system in the United States work as a free-market substitute for socialized medicine, avoiding the need for wholesale governmental intervention in the compensation process.

A CRITIQUE OF REFORM GOALS AND PROPOSALS

The goal of those who seek product liability reform is to shield manufacturers and sellers from liability.[54] The theory is that product liability suits cause the price of products to increase, and this is supposedly undesirable. However, when product liability litigation results in higher prices, one of the most valuable components of product liability law is functioning appropriately. Such price increases act as a deterrent,[55] as a warning to consumers that a given product is dangerous or defective. Aware of a higher price, consumers discontinue purchasing these dangerous products.[56] Fewer consumers are injured; fewer suits are filed. Manufacturers and sellers seek to abrogate this valuable function when they advocate reform legislation.

Legislatively protecting manufacturers from the impact of risk taking is economically unwise. A natural component of business activity involves the evaluation and acceptance of risks. Increases in the prices of products also act as signals to manufacturers that something may be wrong with their products. These signals should not be blunted.[57]

Understanding the goals of those who advocate product liability reform reform helps to provide insight into the issue. To more fully comprehend the impact of reform, however, one must examine some of the proposals advocated.

Eliminating Strict Liability: The Priest Proposal

The most thorough recent comment on tort and insurance reform is "The Current Insurance Crisis and Modern Tort Law,"[58] an article by Professor George Priest. After examining tort law and first- and third-party insurance, Professor Priest concludes that the insurance crisis has been caused by an unraveling of the insurance market. By unraveling he means that for some products, insurance is either priced so high that it becomes unaffordable or is not available at any price.[59] Before reaching this conclusion, he examines the factors that he believes have caused the unraveling.

Professor Priest contends that the chief cause of the insurance market unraveling is the growth of strict liability since 1960.[60] He argues that strict liability has caused the insurance purchasers who manufacture low-risk products to drop out of the insurance market.[61] This has forced the price of insurance to increase and led large numbers of low-risk purchasers to adopt self-insurance programs.[62] Finally, the insurance market has unraveled because these factors have led to an undifferentiation of risk within the market. That is, the only risks left seeking insurance were ones that were very likely to occur.[63] This has precipitated high prices for insurance and the discontinuation of insurance at any price for some goods and services.[64] Professor Priest argues that the impact of the unraveling of the insurance market has been widespread. He suggests that it has led to a dramatic increase in the cost of third-party insurance[65] and a decrease in the variety of available products. For example, pharmaceuticals and certain automobiles (four-wheel-drive) have increased in price or been withdrawn from the market.[66] Midwives can no longer obtain insurance, and for a period of time day-care centers were not able to obtain insurance.[67]

Professor Priest suggests that one of the foundational reasons for the development of strict liability was to provide insurance for the poor.[68] He suggests, however, that the poor have been most damaged by the unraveling of the insurance markets.[69] This has occurred because of the increased prices in products as well as the discontinuance of products. Priest argues that the manufacturers who have not been able to obtain insurance, in many situations, have been the manufacturers of products at the lower end of the price scale.[70]

In regard to Priest's argument that the insurance market unraveling has most harmed the poor, several points should be noted. First, the steady trend in the prices of most products and services since 1960 has been upward.[71] In addition, products drop out of the market for reasons unrelated to the price of insurance. For example, we do not have a large number of cars that are manufactured in France and England because they fail to meet our emission requirements.[72] Sometimes old products are discontinued because they do not work as well as new ones. Manual typewriters and belt-drive dentists' drills are examples. Some pharmaceuticals have dropped out of the American market because their risks far exceed their benefits. DES,[73] Mer 29[74] and Oraflex[75] are examples. More pointedly, however, under strict liability the poor at least have a basis for recovery if they are injured by a defective product. If the increase in prices now tends to make some products and services unavailable to the poor, it may be necessary for government to assist them. Examples where government assistance may be necessary are obstetrics and day care. Also, as the prices of automobiles increase, for example, it may be necessary for employers to provide transportation for their employees. They may have to provide bus tokens, bus service or, in some cases, automobiles.

Finally, it must be noted that providing insurance for the poor has never been a stated goal of products liability theory.[76] This is Priest's original and creative interpretation of the reasons for the growth of strict liability. I have suggested in another chapter, in contrast, that strict liability began at least as early as the 1400s and has continued to expand since the 1850s in the United States. The reason for the growth of strict liability has been, in large part, the absence of socialized medicine. Indeed, for some injuries even the nonpoor may lack sufficient funds to obtain health care.[77]

Professor Priest provides a thoughtful evaluation of first-party and third-party insurance.[78] He concludes that first-party insurance (automobile and home insurance, for example) is less expensive, more precise and not as likely to unravel as third-party insurance.[79] First-party insurance is cheaper, he suggests, because there is no recovery for pain and suffering.[80] At another point in his paper, Priest indicates that recoveries at trial for pain and suffering can be 25 to 50 percent of the total.[81] In addition, he suggests that there is much less tendency to have a moral hazard (excessive expenditures) with first-party insurance as compared with third-party insurance.[82] An individual who suffers injury, such as a broken leg at a softball game, is faced with recovering from his Blue Cross–Blue Shield carrier, for example. Such a first-party insurance claimant is not likely to visit a large number of doctors, stay in a private room or extend his stay in the hospital.[83] Priest suggests that there is a substantial moral hazard problem with third-party insurance, however. He argues that people who suffer injury from defective products are likely to stay in the hospital an excess number of days, to have multiple unnecessary services by doctors and other medical personnel and to drag out the rehabilitation process.[84] This flies in the face of reality, however. An individual who has suffered an injury from a defective product has no idea whether he or she is going to be compensated until he or she receives a check from the defendant seller. This may involve litigation and can take from three to twelve years or longer. Instead of overspending, an individual who suffers injury from a defective product is likely to assume that his or her only certain recovery is from his or her first-party carrier. Therefore, the argued distinction between someone claiming under first-party insurance and someone claiming under third-party insurance is invalid. They are both the same in outlook and expectation. This only changes when the injured consumer receives a check from the seller. Only the most foolhardy consumer-patient would extend his or her extremely expensive stay in a hospital or expand medical services on the mere chance that he or she is going to recover in a settlement or a lawsuit against the manufacturer. It is much more likely that the injured consumer is going to be conservative in medical treatment just as if he or she only had first-party insurance. Indeed, the injured consumer may not realize that he or she has a suit until months after treatment has ended. Finally, staying in a hospital or obtaining medical treatment (of almost any type) is not fun. Hospitals seem to be designed to encourage patients to leave, not stay.

Professor Priest's analysis of the tort-insurance crisis is superficial and unrealistic in many respects. First, he implies that under a negligence regime industry is paying for all fault-based injuries. This is clearly unrealistic. Industry does not pay for all fault-based injuries because most injuries, in fact, are small and no case is brought. In addition, a large number of cases are lost because of proof problems. Many cases are not brought because fault cannot be shown, or cause in fact is not clear, or the statute of limitations has run. It may be simply too much of a hassle for the plaintiff to bring a suit. The point is that industry is not paying for all injuries that it negligently causes.

Second, his analysis is superficial in that it fails to examine what might happen if all product-related injuries were handled under first-party insurance, as he suggests.[85] Are there pressures that would develop causing first-party insurance to unravel as third-party insurance has allegedly unraveled? First, Professor Priest completely fails to give any consideration to whether the strict liability system is performing a valuable social service in pinpointing high-risk activities. For example, because of recent suits we are now aware that the use of midwives is a high-risk activity, off-road vehicles, such as Jeeps, are extremely dangerous and three-wheel all-terrain vehicles (ATVs) are so hazardous that they have been banned from sale in the United States.[86] Certain pharmaceuticals such as Oraflex, Mer 29 and DES, as well as contraceptives such as the Dalkon Shield, have been labeled, through litigation, as enormously risky. Recent price increases have made it clear that small airplanes are much more hazardous than commercial airplanes.[87] Professor Priest completely ignores the red-flag function provided by the tort-litigation system, including strict liability. Fourth, he fails to suggest where the funds will come from to compensate attorneys who are handling personal injury suits. He vigorously attacks the awarding of pain and suffering in lawsuits and implicitly acknowledges that recoveries for pain and suffering may well be used to compensate attorneys,[88] but fails to indicate how, under his new regime, individuals bringing personal injury suits will pay attorney's fees.

Finally, Professor Priest's most unrealistic thesis is that sellers can avoid paying for injuries they have caused through defective products by shifting the responsibility to the consumer, who must then purchase first-party insurance.[89] Most of the free world has socialized medicine in order to provide for injured citizens.[90] In contrast, the United States provides compensation for injured consumers through the courts. The American torts system has expanded, in part by means of strict liability, in order to make certain that the injured consumers have sufficient funds to purchase expensive medical care.[91] But Priest suggests that sellers can completely avoid paying. He implies that sellers can skirt the expense of socialized medicine and also avoid the costs of strict liability by requiring the consumer to purchase first-party insurance.[92] This is false. The choice is not between no liability for the seller and strict liability, as Priest suggests. The choice, instead, is between strict liability and socialized medicine. As I have suggested in another chapter, the fault-based system, including strict liability, is both cheaper and more precise than socialized medicine.[93]

In order to prevent the alleged unraveling of the insurance market, Professor Priest has proposed a solution. His cure is not a reform of insurance process and procedures, but rather a wholesale reform of tort law. His solution boils down to asking at trial one question:

Is it possible to identify any specific cost-effective action that either the injurer or victim could have taken which would have prevented the accident? If so, then liability should be placed on the party that could have prevented the accident most effectively in order to create incentives to take such actions in the future.[94]

This language is novel and vague. What does it mean? Is it strict liability, negligence or something else? For his test, Professor Priest refers generally to Dean Calabresi's book, *The Cost of Accidents.* But this is not Calabresi's strict liability test. The actual language of Calabresi's test is as follows:

> The strict liability test we suggest does not require that a government institution make such a cost-benefit analysis. It requires of such an institution only a decision as to which of the parties to the accident *is in the best position to make the cost-benefit analysis between accident costs and accident avoidance costs and to act on that decision once it is made.* The question for the court reduces to a search for the cheapest cost avoider.[95]

There are several important differences between Priest's test and Calabresi's strict liability test. First, Calabresi does not require the decision to be made at a trial. Priest, however, suggests that a trial is necessary.[96] Second, Calabresi asks which party is in the best position to make the cost-benefit analysis. Priest, on the other hand, is not talking about a cost-benefit analysis but rather a specific cost-effective action. To Priest, "cost-effective" means "sensible."[97] Is this a helpful change or merely substitution of one lexicon for another? Third, Calabresi does not suggest that the decision must be a cost-effective one or a practical one.[98] Fourth, in almost all product liability cases the Calabresi cheapest cost avoider test will result in holding the manufacturer liable because he has the expertise in regard to the product.[99] In contrast, under Priest's test the victim will often be found able to take a "cost-effective" act and, therefore, be unable to recover.

Another possibility is that Priest is suggesting a negligence test. In regard to that claim, Priest states specifically, "I deny this assertion."[100] Regardless of his disclaimer, the test looks like negligence because it uses the phrase "cost-effective," which sounds a lot like "cost-benefit,"[101] a negligence test.

However, if Priest's test for liability is related to negligence, it is a very old cousin of negligence dating back to 1850 in the *Brown v. Kendall*[102] case. The Priest standard, whether it is negligence or something else, is not the modern concept of negligence as it has developed over the last 139 years. Rather, it is the nub concept of negligence stripped bare of any of the recent advancements. That is, Priest has excised the evolutionary additions. For example, he is opposed to any of the liberalizing changes in the area of cause in fact[103] as well as any of the recent modifications in regard to warnings.[104] Priest's apparent goal is to develop a theory where, in case of doubt, the seller wins.

It is still unclear what is meant by Priest's test, and rather than applying his test to a number of everyday products liability cases, he devotes a substantial portion of his article to challenging Professor Wade's test for strict liability.[105] The result is that Priest has given us a test without meaning. Because of the ambiguity, the Priest test is unlikely to be adopted by the courts and, further, if adopted, will take years of litigation to clarify. Priest accepts this vagueness as part of the cost inherent in protecting sellers from suits based on strict liability.

As part of his explanation for the proposed solution, Priest argues that strict liability can only be justified on the basis of insurance.[106] He fails to accept the point that holding a manufacturer strictly liable may have very important long-run implications. For example, holding a manufacturer strictly liable will encourage the manufacturer to engage in safety research. It may also encourage better product testing on the part of the manufacturer. The manufacturer being sued may decide to keep records of the various suits and at some point will decide to modify or drop the product or perhaps select safer methods for manufacturing the product. That is, strict liability affects the conduct of a manufacturer and does not have merely an insurance function.

At another point, Priest seems to be opening a debate with economists on the question of efficiency.[107] This theory has been severely criticized elsewhere,[108] and Priest apparently wishes to be counted with those who are opposed to the efficiency theory of tort law. Priest rejects the efficiency debate because it is largely academic:

> Engineers, designers and business executives do not seek to implement the efficiency standard. They try to make sensible decisions given the range of available alternatives open to them. The litigation process could be informed by attempting to place the court or jury in a similar position: to recreate for them the alternatives the defendants considered (or failed to consider).[109]

He fails to tell us how the word "sensible," on the part of engineers and designers, is different from the word "efficiency" as used by economists.[110] Because of his unqualified embrace of first-party insurance, rejection of strict liability and failure to define the terms in his test, Priest's reform proposals, "while interesting and thought-provoking, are unpersuasive and unworkable."[111]

Statutes of Repose

In order to reduce seller liability, numerous states have adopted statutes of repose. Statutes of repose are sometimes confused with statutes of limitations. The impact of a repose statute is different from a statute of limitations, however.[112] Statutes of repose provide a fixed period of time from the date of the original sale, usually five to twelve years, in which a product liability suit must be brought.[113] A statute of limitations begins to run at the time of injury. As a result, a product liability suit may be barred by a statute of repose before the injury even occurs.

Statutes of repose will prevent some victims of injury from an old defective product from suing for damages.[114] However, the majority of plaintiffs involved in products liability litigation have not been injured by old products. Ninety-seven percent of bodily injuries occur within five years of purchase.[115] Therefore, a statute of repose will have little effect on most claims.[116] There are several types of victims on whom a statute of repose will have a devastating impact, however. First are those whose injuries are revealed years after the initial exposure, such as victims of DES[117] or asbestos.[118] Second are persons who are injured by long-lasting workplace machinery.

The constitutionality of product liability statutes of repose has been tested. Ten states have held that the statutes violate the "open courts" provisions of their constitutions,[119] while four states have held that they violate "equal protection."[120] In contrast, four states have held that their statutes of repose were constitutional under their "open courts" provisions.[121]

Statutory Compliance

A popular reform proposal calls for holding a product nondefective where the manufacturer has complied with the requirements of an existing statute.[122] For example, an automobile manufacturer might defend on the basis of compliance with bumper requirements. Compliance with governmental standards is one factor considered at common law in determining whether a manufacturer has acted with due care.[123] However, to provide that compliance with a governmental standards statute would create a presumption that a product was not defective or unreasonably unsafe would be an unfair defense to a products liability claim. The result will be that manufacturers will prevail when they otherwise would have lost in certain cases.

The defense of statutory compliance will discourage manufacturers from developing safer products. The proposal provides financial incentives for manufacturers to lobby for weaker regulations rather than develop safer products.[124] Opponents of the statutory compliance defense argue that the current products liability system is one in which decisions are made by institutions that are relatively immune from political pressure, such as courts and juries.[125] Administrative agencies, however, are not immune. It is well known, for example, that manufacturers frequently influence administrative agencies to adopt less rigid safety standards.[126] Because of this influence, manufacturers prefer to have agencies rather than courts set applicable standards.[127] We will see weaker guidelines resulting in more dangerous products if the statutory compliance proposal is adopted.

The Double-Burden Requirement

Under section 104 of the Model Uniform Product Liability Act[128] the plaintiff must prove that the product is "unreasonably unsafe."[129] Clearly the plaintiff would have two burdens under this proposal: to prove that the product is "unreasonable" and that it is "unsafe." The result is that the plaintiff must prove negligence twice. This will confuse the jury and perhaps lead to unintended verdicts. Because of the confusion, this type of reform should be avoided.

A host of other reforms have been adopted, such as caps on punitive damages,[130] limiting joint and several liability[131] and retrenchment on comparative fault.[132] These are merely "Band-Aid" solutions to the alleged insurance crisis, however.

Before any reform is adopted, the relevant facts must be carefully examined. The search for the crisis that would support products liability reform is a snipe hunt, however. We are told that insurance rates must increase or the insurers will be forced out of business, but we see that in terms of profit, the insurance industry has recently had gold-banner years. To be sure, few critical facts are available from the insurance industry in regard to the amount of insurance sold, the number of claims made and the amount of claims paid. How can legislatures intelligently pass reform measures when such crucial information is lacking? The answer appears to be that most products liability reform proposals are the result of the lobbying pressures brought by sellers, the defense bar and insurance companies.[133] The present reality is that products liability reform is based on political pressure, not facts.

The goal of those who would "reform" our products liability system is clear: to shift the cost of injuries back onto the shoulders of consumers and victims. In a country with socialized medicine, like England, this would make sense because consumers would be compensated for medical expenses and a portion of lost wages. In the United States, however, it means that manufacturers and insurers would profit at the expense of injured consumers. Injured parties will no longer be fairly compensated if the "reformers" are successful. This deviation would represent a reversal of over one hundred years of reasoned development in products liability theory.

NOTES

1. *See* Molotsky, *Drive to Limit Product Liability Grows As Consumer Groups Object*, New York Times, March 1, 1986, at 32, col. 1; Mayer, *Change Urged in Product Liability Law; Product Liability Laws Overhaul Being Sought*, Washington Post, March 10, 1982, at D7; Ross, *Reforms, Profits Swallow Up Insurance Crisis*, Los Angeles Times, January 5, 1987, at 2, col. 3; J. C. Rose and A. F. Abbott, *Federal Liability Law Would Lessen Uncertainty*, Legal Times, July 9, 1984, at 15.

2. *See* S. 2760, 99th Cong., 2d Sess., Report 99-422, at 2 (Aug. 15, 1986) [hereinafter cited as Report].

3. *See supra* note 1.

4. *Supra* note 1.

5. The American Insurance Association suggests:

> [P]roduct liability rates have increased sharply during the last two years. They reflect the risks associated with the production and distribution of products. The number of federal product liability suits has increased 75% since 1974. During the same period of time, the average jury verdict has increased from under $400,000 to over $1.8 million in product liability cases.

Hearings on S. 2760 Before the Committee on the Judiciary of the United States Senate, 99th Cong., 2d Sess. 666 (Sept. 9, 10, 1986) [hereinafter cited as *Hearings*].

These arguments have been around since 1978:

> In recent years, manufacturers have been charged dramatically increased fees for product liability insurance. Some manufacturers have testified during the eighteen months that they may have to go out of business because of their high insurance rates. Insurance companies have claimed that there is a product liability "crisis" and that it is caused by the products liability legal system. They have demanded immediate legislative protection for manufacturers' interests in lawsuits. They have claimed that pro-consumer products liability legal doctrines result in unfair harassment of business by injured persons and that opportunistic consumers and money-hungry lawyers are gaining windfall wealth from responsible manufacturers. They have followed these claims with nationwide advertising campaigns for products liability "reform."

Johnson, *Products Liability "Reform": A Hazard to Consumers*, 56 N.C.L. REV. 677, 678 (1978) (footnotes omitted). *See* Bell, *Averting a Crisis in Products Liability: An Evolutionary Process of Socioeconomic Justice*, 65 ILL. B.J. 640 (1977).

6. The Introduction to S. 2760 stated:

> The inefficiency and unpredictability of the product liability system have been linked to the increasing cost and unavailability of liability insurance. An increasing number of companies, whether they make such products are [*sic*] sporting goods, textile manufacturing equipment, machine tools, medical devices or vaccines, cannot buy adequate insurance coverage. Some have had their insurance cancelled or have experienced reduced coverage with increased deductibles at higher prices. Others cannot obtain coverage at any price.
>
> Thus, the present system has an adverse impact on plaintiffs and defendants, manufacturers, product sellers and consumers. The individual states cannot fully address the problems of the product liability system.

Report, *supra* note 2, at 2. It should be noted, however: "After withering on the legislative vine since June, product liability legislation has died on the 99th Congress." Starobin, *Senate Product Liability Bill Killed After Brief Filibuster*, CONGRESSIONAL QUARTERLY 2316 (Sept. 27, 1986).

7. The American Insurance Association endorses the federal reform proposal S. 2760 and has placed substantial blame on the legal system. *See Hearings*, *supra* note 5, at 666.

8. *See Hearings*, *supra* note 5, and Report, *supra* note 2. *See also* U.S. Dept. of Commerce, Interagency Task Force on Product Liability, Final Report (I, at

26) (1977) [hereinafter cited as Task Force Final Report]. The task force also published a seven-volume legal study that was prepared by independent contractors as part of its study of products liability problems. U.S. Dept of Commerce, Interagency Task Force on Products Liability, Final Report of the Legal Study (1977) [hereinafter cited as Task Force Legal Study].

9.

> [T]he data that has become publicly-available belies the claims of the insurance industry. For example, earlier this year the industry stated losses of over $5 billion in 1985. When challenged by the National Insurance Consumer Organization, the industry acknowledged a profit of at least $1.7 billion, even though the data gathered by NICO show a profit level even higher. The General Accounting Office found in an April 1986 study that the property/casualty industry has made between $50 and $75 billion in net gains over the period 1976–1985.

Hearings, *supra* note 5, at 305.

10.

> [T]he inefficiency, and unpredictability of the product liability system is cited as a cause of the insurance availability and affordability crisis facing many companies today, whether they produce vaccines, medical devices, textile manufacturing equipment, sporting goods, machine tools, et cetera.

Hearings, *supra* note 5, at 1.

11. Professor Joseph Page, of Georgetown University School of Law, stated in March, 1985:

> There is no reason to believe that the tort system contributed at all to the decrease of product-liability insurance premiums at the end of the last decade, or to the increases which may currently be taking place. No correlation in the slightest exists between expansions or contractions of tort doctrine during those periods and the level of premiums. The same may be said with respect to the size of jury awards and settlements.

Hearings, *supra* note 5, at 307.

12. *See* Report, *supra* note 2, at 2.

13. Schwartz, *Proposed Remedies for the American Problem: U.S. Governmental Activity*, 29 MERCER L. REV. 437, 439 (1978).

14. Task Force Final Report, *supra* note 8, at I–20.

15. From 1967 to 1983 the Consumer Price Index for all goods increased by 198 percent. *Hearings Before the Joint Economic Committee, Congress of the United States*, 98th Cong., 2d Sess. 93 (Apr. 12 and Aug. 29, 1984).

16. Task Force Final Report, *supra* note 8, at I–31.

17. *Id.* at I–26. *But see* Schwartz, *supra* note 13, at 442 (claims "increased substantially").

18. Datsun 2-door. CONSUMER REPORTS, April, 1972, at 226.

19. Nissan (Datsun) Sentra 2-door. CONSUMER REPORTS, April, 1987, at 213.

20. *Hearings Before the Joint Economic Committee, Congress of the United States*, 98th Cong., 2d Sess. 93 (Apr. 12 and Aug. 29, 1984).

21. *Id.*

22. *Id.*

23. Hearings, *supra* note 5, at 305.

24. *Id.*

25. 5 LAWYERS ALERT 10 (1986), quoting from Bernier v. Burris, No. 85 CH6627 (Cook County Circuit Court, Chicago, Ill., Dec. 19, 1985).

26. Scherffius, *The Insurance Crisis: Causes and Cures from a Plaintiff's Lawyer's Perspective*, Atlanta Lawyer 15 at 17 (Fall, 1986).

27.

> The emergency, it seems, has dissolved in a flood of insurance company profits.
>
> According to the Insurance Service office, which advises carriers on rate setting, operating profits tripled during the first nine months of 1986, compared to the same period of 1985. Earnings rose to $3.6 billion from $1.2 billion in 1985.

Ross, *Reforms, Profits Swallow Up Insurance Crisis*, Los Angeles Times, January 5, 1987, at 2, col. 3.

28. *See* M. FRIEDMAN, FREE TO CHOOSE 13-18 (1980); A. POLINSKY, AN INTRODUCTION TO LAW AND ECONOMICS 11 (1983); R. POSNER, ECONOMIC ANALYSIS OF LAW 208, 485 (2d ed. 1977); P. SAMUELSON, ECONOMICS 368-70 (11th ed. 1980). *See also* Landes & Posner, *Tort Law as a Regulatory Regime for Catastrophic Personal Injuries*, 13 J. LEGAL STUD. 417 (1984); Epstein, *The Legal and Insurance Dynamics of Mass Tort Litigation*, 13 J. LEGAL STUD. 475 (1984); Danzon, *Tort Reform and the Role of Government in Private Insurance Markets*, 13 J. LEGAL STUD. (1984).

29. *See*, for examples, TIME, December 31, 1973, at 18; TIME, January 14, 1974, at 15; NEWSWEEK, May 28, 1979, at 67; NEWSWEEK, June 18, 1979, at 22; NEWSWEEK, June 7, 1982, at 55.

30. Every major manufacturer now has at least one small, fuel-efficient model.

31. *See* M. FRIEDMAN, *supra* note 28.

32. *See* Browning, *Doctors and Lawyers Face Off*, 72 A. B. A. J. 38 (1986); Lynch, *The Insurance Panic for Lawyers*, 72 A. B. A. J. 42 (1986); Blodgett, *Premium Hikes Stun Municipalities*, 72 A. B. A. J. 48 (1986); Goldberg, *Manufacturers Take Cover*, 72 A. B. A. J. 52 (1986).

33. James R. Posner, an insurance expert, reports:

> Nearly forty malpractice insurance companies were formed between 1975 and 1982 with the sponsorship of state medical societies and other physician groups. Eleven state hospital associations also formed insurance companies, either in the United States or "offshore." In part, these companies were formed to replace lost coverage in states where commercial companies had withdrawn entirely from the market. . . . These companies have made primary insurance available to doctors and hospitals in nearly all parts of the country.

Posner, *Trends in Medical Malpractice Insurance, 1970-1985*, 49 LAW AND CONTEMPORARY PROBLEMS 37, 39 (1986).

Doctor Harold L. Hirsch argues: "On the surface it appears that physician-owned companies have been reasonably successful so far, but . . . they are facing a crisis of affordability." Hirsch, *Malpractice Crisis of the '80s*, 14 LEGAL ASPECTS OF MEDICAL PRACTICE 4, 5 (March, 1986).

34. *See* Posner, Hirsch, *supra* note 33.

35. *See* M. FRIEDMAN, *supra* note 28.

36.

> Congress, to insure that the swine flu program would proceed, enacted legislation in 1976 to resolve the problem. *See* 42 U.S.C.A. § 247b(j)-(l). The legislation provides that the United States would be liable for all injuries caused by the vaccine, not the manufacturers or other participants in the program. The federal government was made subject to liability according to the laws of the state where the claim arose under the same legal principles as would have applied against the manufacturer or other participant–including negligence, breach of warranty, and strict liability in tort. Sovereign immunity and limitations on liability under the Federal Tort Claims Act were thus waived to this extent. In turn, the United States retained the right to obtain indemnification against any manufacturer or other participant whose negligence resulted in the claim. In effect, then, drug manufacturers were made ultimately liable only for negligence, while the burden of strict liability awards fell only on the government. In addition, the United States funded $230 million of liability insurance to protect the drug manufacturers against indemnity claims.

W. KEETON, D. OWEN, & J. MONTGOMERY, PRODUCTS LIABILITY AND SAFETY 356 (1980).

37. "Lederle Laboratories announced in May that to combat rising liability insurance costs, it would nearly triple the price of its DPT vaccine to private physicians from $4.29 to $11.40 per dose." Washington Post, July 16, 1986, at 17.

38. The "Kasten" Bill, S. 2760, 99th Cong., 2d Sess. (1986) provides:

> Sec. 301. A person seeking to recovery [*sic*] for harm caused by a product may bring a civil action against the product's manufacturer or product seller pursuant to applicable State or Federal law, except such law is superseded by this Act.
>
> UNIFORM STANDARDS OF PRODUCT SELLER LIABILITY
>
> Sec. 302 (a) Notwithstanding the provisions of section 301 of this title, in any civil action for harm caused by a product, a product seller other than a manufacturer is liable to a claimant, only if the claimant establishes by a preponderance of the evidence that—
>
> (I) (A) the individual product unit which allegedly caused the harm complained of was sold by the defendant; (B) the product seller failed to exercise reasonable care with respect to the product; and (C) such failure to exercise reasonable care was a proximate cause of the claimant's harm; or
>
> (2) (A) the product seller made an express warranty, independent of any express warranty made by a manufacturer as to the same product; (B) the product failed to conform to the warranty; and (C) the failure of the product to conform to the warranty caused the claimant's harm.

The present House bill (H.R. 5471) provides:

> LIABILITY FOR IMPROPER DESIGN OR FORMULATION—A manufacturer is liable to a claimant in a product liability action on the basis of negligence if the claimant establishes that—
>
> (1) the manufacturer manufactured the product involved in such action,
>
> (2) the manufacturer was negligent—
>
> (A) in designing or formulating such product, or
>
> (B) in providing warnings or instructions to the appropriate person about a danger connected with such product, or about the proper use of such product, and
>
> (3) such negligence was a proximate cause of the harm complained of by the claimant.

H.R. 5471, 99th Cong., 2d Sess., § 4 (1986).

39. *See* Gibson, *Products Liability in the United States and England: The Difference and Why*, 3 ANGLO-AM. L. REV. 493 (1974). Plummer, *Products Liability in Britain*, 9 ANGLO-AM. L. REV. 65 (1980). *See also* P. SAMUELSON, *supra* note 28, at 816–17.

40. Interview with Professor A. L. Diamond, Director of the Institute for Advanced Legal Studies, London, England (March 17, 1984). 1 Royal Commission on Civil Liability and Compensation for Personal Injury 48 (1978).

Neither Gibson nor Plummer attach much weight to the impact of socialized medicine on the nondevelopment of British products liability law. Gibson states:

"For some reason, English courts have not been as reluctant to create new criminal offenses as they have been to expand civil remedies." Gibson, *supra* note 39, at 518.

Plummer entirely overlooks the role of "free" medical care:

> Unless a person injured by a defective product can invoke the terms of the 1978 Consumer Safety Act, or is fortunate enough to be able to convince a court he should have a civil cause of action for breach of a duty imposed by a statute which does not specifically provide for such an action, he must rely on the contractual remedies provided by the Sale of Goods Act of 1893 or be able to prove negligence.

Plummer, *supra* note 39, at 68.

41. *See* P. SAMUELSON, *supra* note 28, at 816-17.

42. *Id.*

43. *Id.*

44. Schmidt, *Contingent Fee: Key to the Courthouse*, 92 CASE & COM. 2-10 (1987).

45. *Id.* at 5-6.

46. *Id.*

47. However, others would argue that the cost for liability is borne by our entire society through distribution of losses through insurance companies and in the increased cost of products.

48. *See* Schmidt, *supra* note 44.

49. *Id.*

50. *Id.* Cowan notes:

> The . . . policy operating in this change of law is a clear recognition of the effects upon consumers of mass production and distribution of goods and services aided by the mass media of advertising. The policy which the decisions exemplify can be stated as an attempt to tilt the balance more favorably toward the single or individual consumer injured by a vast impersonal merchandising juggernaut.

Cowan, *Some Policy Bases of Products Liability*, 17 STAN. L. REV. 1077, 1086 (1965).

51. *See* S. 2760, 99th Cong., 2d Sess., Report 99-422, at 2 (Aug. 15, 1986).

52. "The purpose of [strict] liability is to insure that the costs of injuries resulting from defective products are borne by the manufacturers . . . rather than by the injured persons who are powerless to protect themselves." Greenman v. Yuba Power Products, Inc., 59 Cal. 2d 57 at 63, 377 P.2d 897 at 901, 27 Cal. Rptr. 697 (S. Ct. 1963).

53. *See* P. SAMUELSON, *supra* note 28, at 816-17.

54. *See Hearings*, *supra* note 5, at 2. Reforms, such as caps on damages, elimination of strict liability, presumption of due care and statutes of repose, were

developed to protect the manufacturer from suit, provide the manufacturer with a strong defense and limit or cut off the manufacturer's liability. The intent is to reduce the amount the seller spends on damages.

55. Deterrence is a major function of tort law. W. P. KEETON, D. B. DOBBS, R. E. KEETON & D. G. OWEN, PROSSER AND KEETON ON THE LAW OF TORTS, 25-26 (5th ed. 1984).

56. A. M. Polinsky & W. Rogerson, Products Liability, Consumer Misperceptions, and Market Power (May 1982) (working paper available from Frank J. Vandall).

57. Calabresi, *Product Liability: Curse or Bulwark of Free Enterprise*, 27 CLEV. ST. L. REV. 313, 322-23 (1978). *But see* Comment, *Solving the Products Liability Insurance Crisis: A Study of the Role of Economic Theory in the Legislative Reform Process*, 31 MERCER L. REV. 755 (1980) (advocates adoption of statute limiting manufacturers' risk to solve product liability insurance crisis).

58. G. L. Priest, *The Current Insurance Crisis and Modern Tort Law*, 96 YALE L. J. 1521 (1987).

59. *Id.* at 1524, 1525, 1526, 1527.

60. *Id.* at 1523.

61. *Id.* at 1525, 1534-35, 1542, 1550.

62. *Id.* at 1526, 1546, 1560.

63. *Id.* at 1560-64.

64. *Id.* at 1564.

65. *Id.* at 1524, 1525, 1560.

66. *Id.* at 1564, 1565.

67. *Id.* at 1572.

68. *Id.* at 1585.

69. *Id.*

70. *Id.* at 1525, 1534-35, 1542, 1550.

71. *See supra* notes 18-22.

72. The old French Citroen and the English Morris-Mini are two noteworthy examples.

73. *See* Sindell v. Abbott Labs., 26 Cal. 3d 588, 607 P. 2d 924, 163 Cal. Rptr. 132 (S. Ct. 1980).

74. *See* Toole v. Richardson-Merrell, 251 Cal. App. 689, 60 Cal. Rptr. 398 (1967).

75. *See* Atlanta Journal-Constitution, December 5, 1982, at 1A.

76. *See* Greenman v. Yuba Power Products, Inc., *supra* note 52.

77. This may be true for very long stays in the hospital, for an injury that is serious and exceeds policy limits or for an injury that requires psychiatric care.

78. *See* Priest, *supra* note 58.

79. *See id.* at 1553-60.

80. *Id.*

81. *Id.* at 1554.

82. *Id.* at 1553.

83. *Id.*

84. *Id.*

85. *See id.* at 1550–63.

86. United States v. American Honda Motor Co., No. 87-3525 (D.D.C. Dec. 30, 1987); United States v. Polaris Inds., No. 87-3525 (D.D.C. Dec. 30, 1987); 134 CONG. REC. S288 (daily ed., Jan. 28, 1988).

87. *See* Priest, *supra* note 58, at 1566–67.

88. *Id.* at 1556.

89. *Id.* at 1588–89.

90. In Britain it is possible to obtain treatment from a doctor who is not part of the state-supported system.

91. Charges for hospital rooms increased over 500 percent from 1967 to 1983. *See Hearings Before the Joint Economic Committee*, *supra* note 15, at 93.

92. *See* Priest, *supra* note 58, at 1588–89.

93. *See* chapter 3.

94. Priest, *Modern Tort Law and Its Reform*, 22 VAL. L. R. 21 (1987).

95. Calabresi, *Toward a Test for Strict Liability in Torts*, 81 YALE L.J. 1060 (1970).

96. *See* Priest, *supra* note 94, at 21. However, Priest also states: "I am unsure that it is possible to continue to endorse the system of trial by jury in the context of a serious effort to reduce the accident rate." *Id.* at 36.

97. Priest, *supra* note 94, at 23.

98. Calabresi, *supra* note 95.

99. *See* chapter 4.

100. Priest, *supra* note 94, at 21.

101. W. P. KEETON, D. B. DOBBS, R. E. KEETON & D. G. OWEN, PROSSER AND KEETON ON THE LAW OF TORTS (5th ed. 1984).

102. 60 Mass. (6 Cush.) 292 (1850).

103. Priest, *supra* note 94, at 35.

104. *Id.* at 31.

105. *Id.* at 26–29.

106. *Id.* at 21–22.

107. *Id.* at 23.

108. *See* chapter 5.

109. Priest, *supra* note 94, at 23.

110. *Id.*

111. Bloomquist, *Goals, Means, and Problems for Modern Tort Law: A Reply to Professor Priest*, 22 VAL. L. R. 642 (1988).

112. *See* Comment, *Limiting Liability: Products Liability and a Statute of Repose*, 32 BAYLOR L. REV. 137, 143 (1980) (statutes of repose will bring uniformity to the limitations area of product liability, reduce uncertainty by placing a limit on manufacturers' liability and lower insurance costs for manu-

facturers). As of February, 1986, at least eighteen states had passed statutes of repose: Alabama, Arizona, Florida, Hawaii, Illinois, Indiana, Kentucky, New Hampshire, North Carolina, Oklahoma, Oregon, Rhode Island, South Carolina, South Dakota, Texas, Utah, Wisconsin and Wyoming. 5 LAW ALERT 7 (1986).

113. *See, Limiting Liability: Products Liability and a Statute of Repose, supra* note 112, at 137.

114. Gingerich, *The Interagency Task Force "Blueprint" for Reforming Product Liability Tort Law in the United States*, 8 GA. J. INT'L & COMP. L. 279, 288 (1978).

115. Task Force Final Report, *supra* note 8, at VII-16.

116. Johnson, *supra* note 5, at 690.

117. Diethylstilbestrol–commonly known as DES–is a drug formerly used for the prevention of miscarriages. In 1971 the U.S. Food and Drug Administration banned the drug for such use because of evidence that the drug was ineffective in preventing miscarriages and was dangerous to unborn children. THE SLOANE-DORLAND ANNOTATED MEDICAL-LEGAL DICTIONARY 202-03 (1987).

118. Product liability claims arising from workers who were exposed to asbestos decades ago have only been filed in recent years as asbestos victims have become ill. *See* Preger, *Asbestos-Related Disease* (Book Review), 6 AM. J. L. & MED. 390, 391 (1980); Richard & Meier, *Lawyers Lead Hunt for New Groups of Asbestos Victims*, CHICAGO DAILY LAW BULLETIN, Feb. 19, 1987, at 1, col. 1.

119. The ten states are Alabama, Arizona, Florida, Kentucky, New Hampshire, Rhode Island, South Dakota, Texas, Utah and Wyoming. 5 LAWYERS ALERT 6 (1986).

120. The four states are Hawaii, Oklahoma, South Carolina and Wisconsin. *Id.* at 7.

121. The four states are Illinois, Indiana, North Carolina and Oregon. *Id.*

122. For example, the Model Uniform Product Liability Act provided: "When the injury-causing aspect of the product was, at the time of manufacture, in compliance with legislative regulatory standards or administrative regulatory safety standards relating to design or performance, the product shall be deemed not defective. . . ." Model Uniform Product Liability Act § 108(a), 44 Fed. Reg. 62,714, 62,730 (proposed Oct. 31, 1979).

123. Johnson, *supra* note 5, at 687; PROSSER AND KEETON ON THE LAW OF TORTS, *supra* note 101, at 233.

124. Manufacturers have the power to influence the formation of government standards. Agencies often adopt regulations that are "rubber-stamped" versions of voluntary standards already practiced by the industry. There will be no incentive to improve products since the existing practice is acceptable. Johnson, *supra* note 5, at 687-88.

125. *Id.* at 689.

126.

> According to the so-called interest group or economic theory of legislation, market forces provide strong incentives for politicians to enact laws that serve private rather than public interests, and hence statutes are supplied by law makers to the political groups or coalitions that outbid competing groups. The widespread acceptance of interest group theory has led to suspicion about much of what Congress does, creating, in turn, a climate hospitable to judicial interference with legislative outcomes.

Macey, *Promoting Public-Regarding Legislation Through Statutory Interpretation: An Interest Group Model*, 86 COLUM. L. REV. 223, 224 (1986); *see also* R. POSNER, THE FEDERAL COURTS 271 (1985); Green & Nader, *Economic Regulation vs. Competition: Uncle Sam the Monopoly Man, 82 Summary*, 4 ANTITRUST L. & ECON. REV. 1 (1970).

127. Johnson, *supra* note 5, at 689.

128. 44 Fed. Reg. 62,714 (proposed Oct. 31, 1979).

129. Model Uniform Prod. Liab. Act § 104 (1979).

130. Sec. 51-12-5.1 Ga. Code (1987).

131. *See* CCH Products Liability Reporter ¶11,533 (1987).

132. Sec. 51-11-7 Ga. Code (1987).

133. See Page & Stephens, *The Product Liability Insurance "Crisis:" Causes, Nostrums and Cures*, 13 CAP. U. L. REV. 387 (1984) (the tort system is one of the forces pushing product liability insurance rates skyward).

BIBLIOGRAPHY

Bell, "Averting a Crisis in Products Liability: An Evolutionary Process of Socioeconomic Justice." 65 *Ill. B. J.* 640 (1977).

Blodgett, "Premium Hikes Stun Municipalities." 72 *A. B. A. J.* 48 (1986).

Bloomquist, "Goals, Means, and Problems for Modern Tort Law: A Reply to Professor Priest." 22 *Val. L. R.* 642 (1988).

Browning, "Doctors and Lawyers Face Off." 72 *A. B. A. J.* 38 (1986).

Calabresi, "Product Liability: Curse or Bulwark of Free Enterprise?" 27 *Clev. St. L. Rev.* 313 (1978).

Calabresi, "Toward a Test for Strict Liability in Torts." 81 *Yale L. J.* 1060 (1970).

Cowan, "Some Policy Bases of Products Liability." 17 *Stan. L. Rev.* 1077 (1965).

Danzon, "Tort Reform and the Role of Government in Private Insurance Markets." 13 *J. Legal Stud.* 517 (1984).

Epstein, "The Legal and Insurance Dynamics of Mass Tort Litigation." 13 *J. Legal Stud.* 475 (1984).

Friedman, M., *Free to Choose* (1980).

Gibson, "Products Liability in the United States and England: The Difference and Why." 3 *Anglo-Am. L. Rev.* 493 (1974).

Gingerich, "The Interagency Task Force 'Blueprint' for Reforming Product Liability Tort Law in the United States." 8 *Ga. J. Int'l & Comp. L.* 279 (1978).

Goldberg, "Manufacturers Take Cover." 72 *A. B. A. J.* 52 (1986).

Green & Nader, "Economic Regulation vs. Competition: Uncle Sam the Monopoly Man, 82 Summary." 4 *Antitrust L. & Econ. Rev.* 1 (1970).

Hirsch, "Malpractice Crisis of the '80s." 14 *Legal Aspects of Medical Practice* 4 (March, 1986).

Johnson, "Products Liability 'Reform': A Hazard to Consumers." 56 *N. C. L. Rev.* 677 (1978).

Keeton, W. P., D. B. Dobbs, R. E. Keeton & D. G. Owen, *Prosser and Keeton on the Law of Torts* (5th ed. 1984).

Keeton, W., D. Owen & J. Montgomery, *Products Liability and Safety* (1980).

Landes & Posner, "Tort Law as a Regulatory Regime for Catastrophic Personal Injuries." 13 *J. Legal Stud.* 417 (1984).

"Limiting Liability: Products Liability and a Statute of Repose." 32 *Baylor L. Rev.* 137 (1980).

Lynch, "The Insurance Panic for Lawyers." 72 *A. B. A. J.* 42 (1986).

Macey, "Promoting Public-Regarding Legislation Through Statutory Interpretation: An Interest Group Model." 86 *Colum. L. Rev.* 223 (1986).

Page & Stephens, "The Product Liability Insurance 'Crisis:' Causes, Nostrums and Cures." 13 *Cap. U.L. Rev.* 387 (1984).

Plummer, "Products Liability in Britain." 9 *Anglo-Am. L. Rev.* 65 (1980).

Polinsky, A. *An Introduction to Law and Economics* (1983).

Polinsky, A., & W. Rogerson, "Products Liability, Consumer Misperceptions, and Market Power" (May 1982) (working paper available from Frank J. Vandall.)

Posner, R. *Economic Analysis of Law* (2d ed. 1977).

Posner, R. *The Federal Courts* (1985).

Posner, "Trends in Medical Malpractice Insurance, 1970-1985." 49 *Law and Contemporary Problems* 37 (1986).

Priest, "The Current Insurance Crisis and Modern Tort Law." 96 *Yale L. J.* 1521 (1987).

Priest, "Modern Tort Law and Its Reform." 22 *Val. L. R.* 21 (1987).

Samuelson, P., *Economics* (11th ed. 1980).

Scherffius, "The Insurance Crisis: Causes and Cures from a Plaintiff's Lawyer's Perspective." *Atlanta Lawyer* 15 (Fall, 1986).

Schmidt, "Contingent Fee: Key to the Courthouse." 92 *Case & Com.* 2 (1987).

Schwartz, "Proposed Remedies for the American Problem: U.S. Governmental Activity." 29 *Mercer L. Rev.* 437 (1978).

"Solving the Products Liability Insurance Crisis: A Study of the Role of Economic Theory in the Legislative Reform Process." 31 *Mercer L. Rev.* 755 (1980).

Starobin, "Senate Product Ad Bill Killed After Brief Filibuster." *Congressional Quarterly* 2316 (Sept. 27, 1986).

U.S. Dept. of Commerce, Interagency Task Force on Product Liability, *Final Report of the Legal Study* (1977).

U.S. Dept. of Commerce, Interagency Task Force on Product Liability, *Final Report* (1977).

Index

ABOUT THE AUTHOR

FRANK J. VANDALL is Professor of Law at Emory University, Atlanta, Georgia. He wrote *Police Training for Tough Calls* and numerous articles appearing in the *Denver Law Review*, *International Legal Practitioner*, *Toledo Law Review*, *Emory Law Review*, *Wisconsin Law Review*, and the *Indiana Law Journal*, among others.